SCIENCE IN COURT

Issues in Law and Society
General Editor: Michael Freeman

Titles in the Series:

Children's Rights: A Comparative Perspective
Edited by Michael Freeman

Divorce: Where Next?
Edited by Michael Freeman

Exploring the Boundaries of Contract
Edited by Roger Halson

Law as Communication
Edited by David Nelken

Iraqgate: The Constitutional Implications of the Matrix-Churchill Affairs
Edited by Rodney Austin

Positivism Today
Edited by Stephen Guest

Governing Childhood
Edited by Anne McGillivray

Legislation and the Courts
Edited by Michael Freeman

Child Abuse
Michael Freeman

Law and Religion
Edited by Rex Ahdar

Law, Culture, Tradition and Children's Rights in Eastern and Southern Africa
Welshman Ncube

Locality and Identity: Environmental Issues in Law and Society
Edited by Jane Holder and Donald McGillivray

Science in Court

Edited by
MICHAEL FREEMAN and HELEN REECE
University College London

Routledge
Taylor & Francis Group
LONDON AND NEW YORK

First published 1998 by Dartmouth and Ashgate Publishing

Reissued 2018 by Routledge
2 Park Square, Milton Park, Abingdon, Oxon, OX14 4RN
711 Third Avenue, New York, NY 10017, USA

Routledge is an imprint of the Taylor & Francis Group, an informa business

A Library of Congress record exists under LC control number: 98024499

Typeset in Times by Express Typesetters Ltd, Farnham, Surrey

ISBN 13: 978-1-138-34810-3 (hbk)
ISBN 13: 978-1-138-34814-1 (pbk)
ISBN 13: 978-0-429-43677-2 (ebk)

Contents

Preface

Science in Court is one of two volumes to result from a very successful colloquium on 'Law and Science' held in the Faculty of Laws at University College London on 30 June and 1 July 1997. The other volume, *Law and Science* is being published by Oxford University Press as part of UCL Law School's Current Legal Issues programme. The volumes can be read separately: we hope that they will be read together. 'Law and science' is a growth area, as witness the interest shown in the interpretation of the evidence in the Louise Woodward trial in Cambridge, Massachusetts, which was held some months after the colloquium. The subject warrants continuing interdisciplinary involvement. We hope that the publication of two volumes will help to stimulate interest, thinking, collaboration and further research.

This volume could not have been produced without not just the assistance of its authors but also the direction and insight of Helen Reece and Andrew Lewis. It requires administrative and secretarial skills also to bring a project like this to fruition. Jo Johnstone was a tower of strength and Helen Louise and Ruth Redfern also gave invaluable assistance. All those involved in the project are indebted to all of them.

MICHAEL FREEMAN
February 1998

Contributors

Shirley A. Dobbin is in the Inter-disciplinary Programme in Social Psychology at the University of Nevada, Reno. She has published work in the areas of social and behavioural science and the law.

Michael Freeman is Professor of English Law at University College London. He is the general editor of this series.

Sophia I. Gatowski is in the Inter-disciplinary Programme in Social Psychology at the University of Nevada, Reno. She has published work in the areas of social and behavioural science and the law.

Sheila Jasanoff is Professor of Science Policy and Law and the founding chair of the Department of Science and Technology Studies at Cornell University. Her research interests include environmental regulation and risk management, comparative policy and science and law. In all these areas her work combines perspectives from law, political science and social studies of science and technology. She is the author of *Fifth Branch: Science Advisers as Policymakers* (1990) and *Science at the Bar* (1995).

Margaret Llewelyn is the Common Law Institute of Intellectual Property Law Lecturer in Intellectual Property Law at the University of Sheffield. Her main research work focuses on the relationship between patents and plant variety rights. She is currently advising both the European Commission and Parliament on the European Directive on the Legal Protection of Biotechnical Inventions.

David Nelken is Distinguished Professor of Sociology and Sociology of Law at the University of Macerata, Italy, where he is Head of the Department of Social Change, Legal Institutions and Communications. Since 1990 he has been Honorary Visiting Professor of Law at University College London, where he was previously Reader in Law, and since 1995 Distinguished Research Professor of Law at Cardiff Law School, University of Wales. Recent publications include *The Futures of Criminology* (1994); (with Alberto Febbrajo) *The European Yearbook of Sociology of Law* (1994); *White-Collar Crime* (1994); *Globalization, Legal Culture and Diversity* (1995); *Law as Communication* (1996); (with Mike Levi) *The Corruption of Politics and the Politics of Corruption* (1996); *Comparing Legal Cultures* (1997); (with Piers Beirne) *Issues in Comparative Criminology* (1997); and (with Roberto D'alimonte) *The Centre-Left in Power: Italian Politics A Review* (1997).

Patricia Park is Principal Lecturer at Southampton Institute and chair of The Law Research Centre. She is a member of the Regional Environmental Protection Advisory Committee to the Environmental Agency for the Southern Region. She has recently completed research into the use of tradeable emission credits in California.

Mike Redmayne is Lecturer in Law at Brunel University. His research interests include the use of scientific evidence in criminal litigation and the use of probability theory to model legal fact finding.

Helen Reece is Lecturer in Law at University College London. She is the editor of *Law and Science*, the companion volume to this one. Her article, 'Losses of Chances in the Law', was awarded the Wedderburn Prize by the *Modern Law Review.*

Jason Schklar is a social psychology doctoral student at the University of Illinois at Chicago and a research assistant at the American Bar Foundation (adviser: Dr Shari S. Diamond). His current areas of research include juror reactions to DNA and other probabilistic evidence and the experiences of scientific experts with the legal system.

Lynda M. Warren is Professor of Environmental Law at the University of Wales, Aberystwyth. Her research is mainly on nature conservation law and policy and marine environmental protection. She is a marine biologist by original training. She is a member of the Countryside Council for Wales and the Joint Nature Conservation Committee.

Christine Willmore is Lecturer in Law, University of Bristol, and a barrister. She lectures in evidence and environmental law. With Paul Roberts of the University of Nottingham (a contributor to *Law and Science*) she carried out research for the Royal Commission on Criminal Justice into the use of forensic science in the criminal courts.

1 Law and Science: Science and Law

Michael Freeman

What do other disciplines think of law? Since it dropped its pretence to discreteness,[1] like a mendicant it has wandered round the corridors of academe seeking first succour here and there. It was nearly a century ago that it tried sociology,[2] and since then it has sought support in a variety of disciplines including anthropology[3] (this taught lawyers something about dispute resolution[4] and may have helped to spawn the ADR (Alternative Dispute Resolution) movement[5]), political science,[6] philosophy,[7] literature,[8] history,[9] geography[10] and economics.[11] Economics embraced law with open arms but, like a Victorian marriage, it was not a partnership of equals. The 'law and economics' movement is much the most successful of the 'law and' movements - at least if success is to be judged by influence (how many common law courses ignore its most famous theorems?)[12] and research output.[13]

Law has always sought the assistance of scientists, though never more so than today.[14] But it is only in the last decade[15] that we have begun to talk of law and science as previously we may have talked of law and sociology or law and economics. As scholarships, in terms of methodologies, law is quite distinct from science. What is meant by 'law' here is the standard legal scholarship to be found in law review articles. This may trace origins or explain contexts but essentially it is a critique of a statute or a series of cases and a prescription to those with the authority to do so to redesign the law, to develop a different concept or establish a better process.[16]

There is some irony in the fact that, long before the interrelationship between law and science was explored, legal scholarship purported to model itself on the model of natural science. It was against this Langdellian orthodoxy[17] that the early so-called 'American Realists' rebelled.[18] Hence Holmes's famous aphorism that 'the life of the law has not been logic; it has been experience'.[19] There are still those who, as Frances Mootz puts it, are 'desperately seeking science'.[20]

There are several differences in methodology and in discourse between legal scholarship and that of the natural sciences.[21] Natural scientists start from the premise that there is a real world which can be described. When legal scholars – the formalists – aspired to think of law as natural science they also believed (or at least adopted a metaphor) that law was 'out there' and as such was a phenomenon immune from values, prejudices or conscious decision making. Legal scholarship today adopts, as has been indicated, a prescriptive stance. 'True' legal scholarship today has severed its links with formalist traditions: it recognizes the human element in legal decision making.[22] Unlike scientific truth,[23] law is created, not discovered.

Legal scholarship also differs from scientific enterprise in the resources it uses. Natural scientists use data. Data are generated, defined and given significance by the academic discipline that studies them. Initially data are a passive subject of research that must be generated by the discipline itself. Discovery is the product of scholarship, but this is consistent with the vision of external reality as a passive subject for research. Legal scholarship, by contrast, works with events, judicial decisions, legislative enactments and administrative regulations. These are not 'discovered' in law libraries, nor can they be observed. Rather they were generated by judges, legislators and the like, by people, non-academic actors, with the capacity to generate the events that provide the source for legal scholarship.

Data are different from events in at least three ways. Edward Rubin has summarized these differences.[24] First, 'the nature of the discovered phenomenon in science is defined by the discipline, whether this definition consists of determining the discovery itself ... the boundaries of the discovery ... or the mere fact that it is new'. But events are already 'prepackaged, either by their human originators or by a pattern of human observations that is much broader than the one that the discipline establishes'.[25]

Secondly, the significance of data is determined by scholars. 'It is the scientist who tells us if the newly-discovered dinosaur bone is just a piece of Cretaceous garbage that some local museum can display to visiting Boy Scout troops, or whether it changes our basic understanding of what dinosaurs were like.'[26] This will sometimes happen in the case of legal events as well, and more often than Rubin acknowledges. But most decisions do identify their own importance and establish their importance by means of that identification. Decisions are, however, sometimes plucked from obscurity and recognized as a 'jurisprudential Armageddon whose implications had escaped the justices at the time when it was handed down'.[27]

The third distinction lies in the 'noncumulative quality of legal scholarship'.[28] As Rubin notes: 'It has always been a source of envy to other academic disciplines that science actually progresses, that existing controversies are resolved, and that new insights can be based on those resolutions.'[29] Kuhn,[30] of course, challenged this analysis and his theory of successive scientific revolutions, engendered by changes in the underlying paradigm of scientific understanding, almost became for a time the new orthodoxy. But Kuhn overstated his case: paradigm shifts represent major revisions, not wholesale transformations.[31] Kuhn does 'not refute the basic fact that over long periods of time, the area of scientific agreement increases, and the new problems addressed are increasingly sophisticated and complex'.[32]

It is a unified theory of causality that is at the root of the cumulation of scientific knowledge. Scientists agree that their enterprise involves a sustained effort to explain the causes of observed phenomena. And they are in agreement as to the sort of statements that will count as explanations. Scientists from different branches work with different data but they share a similar basic methodology. Legal scholars, by contrast, are 'not trying to describe the causes of observed phenomena'.[33] Rather they are involved in evaluation, and to this end they express values and prescribe alternatives. As Rubin observes, 'this does not lend itself to the notions of causality that lie at the base of natural science and its cumulative method. It does not, moreover, involve the sort of statements about external reality that can be verified or falsified by data, the process through which the cumulation of scientific knowledge is effected'.[34]

For law, both the academic discipline and the practice, science has proved an invaluable resource. From the discovery of X-rays[35] to the formulation of DNA profiling,[36] scientific evidence has underpinned trials, whether prosecutions or claims for damages or proceedings involving issues of child welfare. Not all scientific discovery has been for the good[37] (and there is much 'junk science'[38]) but law has on the whole profited from the fruits of scientific research. Law and science also interact as law is used to regulate scientific advances in areas such as medically assisted reproduction[39] and genetic therapy and engineering.[40] Litigation may also encourage research and stimulate funding institutions to support projects in the wake, or even in anticipation, of projected legal action. But it is the use of scientific evidence in courts which currently provokes most interest.

The *Daubert* decision[41] in the United States has proved a stimulus to thinking about the uses and limitations of such evidence. By affirming that trial judges must screen scientific evidence before admitting it, the Supreme Court has rekindled the question as to how a court should determine scientific validity. Previously, with the *Frye* test,[42] courts deferred to extrajudicial scientific authority.[43] Imwinkelried saw the *Frye* rule as having the effect of 'delegating' the decision about admissibility to scientists.[44] A greater role for the courts raises many questions. The law and science have, as Nelken points out,[45] different concepts of the 'truth'. The law may not be seeking the truth as science understands it. The law may have other concerns beyond scientific truth: it may have particular policies to uphold (is this why legislation in California mandated courts to admit 'unscientific' evidence on battered wife syndrome?)[46] or, speaking especially through juries,[47] it may wish to endorse community sentiment rather than uphold 'professional' expertise.[48] The law also tends to exclude, for reasons of policy, matters which scientists might regard as the best evidence: evidence of an accused person's previous convictions is one example of this. Law and science also operate according to different timescales: legal trials must reach conclusions; scientists can delay the determination of findings until they are convinced that the evidence supports them.

Daubert does not offer a definitive checklist for evaluating scientific validity. However, a number of observations made by the Supreme Court are instructive. First, the Court recognized that a theory or technique constitutes valid scientific knowledge only if it is testable and has in fact been tested: 'Scientific methodology today is based on generating hypotheses and testing them to see if they can be falsified; indeed, this methodology is what distinguishes science from other fields of human inquiry.'[49] Secondly, the Court acknowledged the important role of peer review and publication in the development of theories and techniques on which testimony or evidence is based.[50] Thirdly, the Court set out special considerations applicable to scientific techniques, including the known or potential error rates and the standards controlling a technique's operation.[51] Finally, the Court emphasized that general acceptance could still have a bearing on the inquiry into the validity of scientific evidence. And, just as 'widespread acceptance can be an important factor in ruling particular evidence admissible',[52] so the converse was also true and a well-known but not widely recognized technique 'may properly be viewed with scepticism'.[53]

This checklist is a useful starting point but it needs to be developed further.[54] Courts ought to be made aware that science offers more than observational data. Black *et al.* point out the way science can explain and clarify relationships and provide a plausible mechanism which, in the absence of discoveries that may be years away, is interesting rather than scientifically useful. Thus continental displacement, though supported by evidence, was rejected until the theory of plate tectonics provided a plausible mechanism for it.[55] Black *et al.* point to another aspect of the explanatory power of valid science, namely, that it is 'predictive as well as descriptive. ... A simple and direct predictive explanation is usually more likely to be correct than complex adumbrations concocted to keep a hypothesis alive'.[56]

Explanatory power was omitted by the Supreme Court in its list. It is important to emphasize also that a valid hypothesis cannot be self-contradictory or logically ill-formed. Though this may be self-evident, the fault may not always be easy to detect. This may be the case particularly in mathematical equations and mathematical language.[57]

Courts ought also to be made aware of the way scientific knowledge develops: that it is cumulative and progressive. This is a good reason to be sceptical of a hypothesis which is not consistent with accepted theories. Of course, Thomas Kuhn's insight,[58] even if exaggerated, cannot be overlooked: orthodox science may be resistant to change. But are courts equipped to join in such debates? That a hypothesis may ultimately turn out to be true cannot legitimate a court accepting it when the scientific community does not. To this extent, the *Frye* test retains force, a fact which the Supreme Court in *Daubert* acknowledged (it listed 'acceptance' as one of the factors to be considered in evaluating science).[59] The recognition and acceptance of a scientific claim by the scientific community must be regarded as an important indicator of its validity. That others are joining a bandwagon and putting their efforts into research based on new findings may confirm that scientists will commit themselves to a theory once it is likely to be correct.[60] 'Science,' as Black *et al.* note, 'does not move from one uncertain explanation to another, but from less certain to more certain knowledge'.[61] On the way it produces a range of opinions, some more widely shared than others.

Scientific evidence will play a greater and greater part in criminal trials and civil litigation. Effort must be concentrated on the practicalities of ensuring that it is used with understanding, and effectively. In civil litigation in Britain there will rarely be any question of a jury having to evaluate a scientific claim. In criminal trials this will happen with continuing frequency. Juries are capable of deciding disputes about scientific evidence[62] and, as Schklar shows,[63] are more complex decision makers than many of those who are sceptical of jury abilities are prepared to accept. The way juries deal with science may in part reflect their attitude to the legal system and to the criminal justice process. The Supreme Court in *Daubert* favoured a preliminary judicial screening of scientific evidence.[64] This is understandable – and it is a view with support – but it is premised on a view that juries are unable to deal with complex scientific evidence. Arguments about the use of juries in fraud trials[65] and their supposed inability to grasp complex accounting issues[66] are similar. Yet we expect juries to grapple with complicated, often psychological, questions of intention, foresight, recklessness and the like because we are able to categorize these as legal (they relate to *mens rea*). Doubts about cognitive competence – and not just of juries – led in the 1970s for calls, in the United States in particular, for a 'science court',[67] composed of experts who would resolve scientific disputes referred to them by the courts. Since then there have been other proposals: for example, for boards to assist courts with scientific issues,[68] for the appointment of panels of specially qualified judges,[69] for the creation of an adjunct judicial office staffed by technical specialists.[70]

But is there any reason to doubt the capacity of courts, as presently constituted, to assess and evaluate scientific evidence as part of the adversary process? If a similar ruling to *Daubert* were developed in England, it would require a more searching inquiry into the merits of scientific evidence than most courts currently undertake. We need to find ways of improving the scientific information available to courts. We must address ways of enabling courts to obtain the scientific knowledge they require. We must equip them with the knowledge and confidence to be able to subject scientific experts to close scrutiny. The expectation that this will happen may have the effect of improving the quality of science that finds its way into court. The pressures of litigation can distort science and flaws that result will not always be exposed. But, once admitted into evidence, science is accorded a legitimacy which it may be difficult to undermine.

With civil justice in a process of change, the time is ripe for a rethinking of the relationship between the legal process and science. If, as predicted, there is an upsurge in environmental and medical litigation – though changes to the legal aid system may frustrate this – there will be many opportunities to test the value of scientific testimony. Serious thought needs to be given to techniques and processes, the ways such evidence is tested and admitted, and to its probative value.

Notes

1 See Judith Shklar, *Legalism* (Cambridge, Mass., 1964). But contrast Ernest J. Weinrib, *The Idea of Private Law* (Cambridge, Mass., 1995) and see Hamish Stewart, 'Contingency and Coherence: The Interdependence of Realism and Formalism in Legal Theory' (1995) 30 *Valparaiso University Law Review* 1.

2 In the writings of the sociological jurist, Roscoe Pound. See, for example, his programme dating from 1911 in Lloyd's *Introduction to Jurisprudence* (6th edn, London, 1994), pp.572–3.

3 For example, Karl Llewellyn and E.A. Hoebel, *The Cheyenne Way* (Norman, Okla., 1941) and K. Llewellyn, 'The Normative, The Legal and the Law-Jobs: The Problem of Juristic Method' (1940) 49 *Yale Law Journal*, 1355. See also Lloyd, *Introduction*, pp.790–97.

4 For example, June Starr, *Dispute and Settlement in Rural Turkey: An Ethnography of Law* (New York, 1978); Barbara Yngvesson (1976) 3 *Amer. Ethnologist* 353; Brenda Danet, 'Language in the Legal Process' (1980) 14 *Law and Society Review* 445. See also Michael Freeman, *Alternative Dispute Resolution* (Aldershot, 1995).

5 Note the influence on the Woolf report, *Access to Justice* (London, 1996) or the Family

Law Act 1996. See further Hazel Genn, 'Understanding Civil Justice' (1997) 50 *C.L.P.* 155.

6 Note, for example, the writings of Harold D. Lasswell and Myres S. McDougal: (1943) 52 *Yale Law Journal* 203; (1952) 61 *Yale Law Journal* 915; (1967) 21 *Rutgers Law Review* 645.

7 An encyclopaedic survey is Dennis Patterson (ed.), *A Companion to Philosophy of Law and Legal Theory* (Oxford, 1996).

8 James Boyd White, *When Words Lose Their Meaning* (Chicago, 1984); James Boyd White, *Justice As Translation* (Chicago, 1990); Ian Ward, *Law and Literature* (London, 1995).

9 Though this can be traced back to Sir Henry Maine, whose *Ancient Law* was published in 1861.

10 On one level, germs of this can be detected as long ago as Montesquieu's *The Spirit of the Laws* in 1748.

11 Richard Posner, *Economic Analysis of Law* (Boston, 2nd edn, 1992); A.M. Polinsky, *An Introduction to Law and Economics* (Boston, 2nd edn, 1989). But see C.A.E. Goodhart, 'Economics and the Law: Too Much One-Way Traffic?' (1997) 60 *Modern Law Review* 1.

12 For example, R. Coase, 'The Problem of Social Costs' (1960) 3 *Journal of Law and Economics* 1.

13 And see George Priest's comment in 'The Inevitability of Tort Reform' (1992) 26 *Valparaiso Law Review* 701, 704. A recent assessment is the special issue of the *New York University Law Review* (64(4), 1997).

14 See Sheila Jasanoff, *Science at the Bar: Law, Science and Technology in America* (Cambridge, Mass., 1995).

15 One of the first English accounts is Carol A.E. Jones, *Expert Witnesses* (Oxford, 1994).

16 See Edward L. Rubin, 'Legal Scholarship', in Patterson, *A Companion*, p.562.

17 See Thomas Grey, 'Langdell's Orthodoxy' (1983) 45 *University of Pittsburgh Law Review* 1 and Dennis Patterson, 'Langdell's Legacy' (1995) 90 *Northwestern University Law Review* 196 (which criticizes Langdell's claims to have used the methodology of natural science).

18 On the revolt against formalism more generally, see Morton G. White, *Social Thought in America: The Revolt Against Formalism* (New York, 1959).

19 *The Common Law* (Boston, 1881), p.1. For a discussion of what Holmes meant by 'experience', see M. Wiener, *Evolution and the Founders of Pragmatism* (New York, 1949).

20 (1995) 73 *Washington University Law Quarterly* 1009.

21 On scientific methodology, see Alan F. Chambers, *What Is This Thing Called Science?* (New York, 2nd edn, 1982).

22 Ronald Dworkin, *Law's Empire* (London, 1986).

23 But see B. Latour and S. Woolgar, *Laboratory Life: The Social Construction of Scientific Facts* (Beverley Hills, 1979).

24 'Law and the Methodology of Law' (1997) *Wisconsin Law Review* 521, 524–8.

25 Ibid, p.526.

26 Ibid.

27 Ibid.

28 Ibid.

29 Ibid.

30 *The Structure of Scientific Revolutions* (Chicago, 2nd edn, 1970).

31 See Imre Lakatos and Alan Musgrave, *Criticism and the Growth of Knowledge* (London,

1970).

32 'Law and the Methodology of Law', 527.

33 Ibid.

34 Ibid., pp.527–8.

35 The X-ray was discovered in 1895; for its influence on the problem of child abuse, see S. Pfohl, 'The Discovery of Child Abuse' (1977) 24 *Social Problems*, 310

36 See the discussion by William C. Thompson and Simon Ford, 'DNA Typing: Acceptance and Weight of the New Genetic Identification Tests' (1989) 75 *Virginia Law Review* 45. See also Francisco J. Ayala and Bert Black, 'Science and the Courts' (1993) 81 *Am. Scientist* 230 (the process is explained at pp.232–3). In relation to paternity, see Ira M. Ellman and David Kaye, 'Probabilities and Proof: Can HLA and Blood Group Testing Prove Paternity?' (1979) 54 *New York University Law Review* 1131.

37 See Freeman Dyson, 'Can Science Be Ethical?' XLIV (6) *The New York Review of Books*, 46 (10 April 1997) (also in his *Imagined Worlds*, Cambridge, Mass., 1997).

38 Peter W. Huber, *Galileo's Revenge: Junk Science in the Courtroom* (New York, 1991) criticizes this. A famous example is *Berry* v. *Chaplin* 169 P.2d 442 (Cal. Dist. CE. App. 1946) (finding Charles Chaplin to have fathered a child, even though the child's blood type made paternity impossible). Huber has in turn been criticized (for example, Robert Blanquist, 'Science, Toxic Tort Law, and Expert Evidence: A Reaction to Peter Huber' (1991) 44 *Arkansas Law Review* 629 and Jeff L. Lewin, 'Calabresi's Revenge? Junk Science in the Work of Peter Huber' (1992) 21 *Hofstra Law Review* 183, the latter asserting that Huber's methodology would not pass his own test of scientific legitimacy).

39 See Robert Blank, *Regulating Reproduction* (London, 1993).

40 See LeRoy Williams and Julie Gage Palmer, *The Ethics of Human Gene Therapy* (New York, 1997).

41 113 S.Ct 2786 (1993). There is an extensive literature on this case, including Bert Black, Francisco J. Ayala and Carol Saffran-Brinks, 'Science and the Law in the Wake of *Daubert*: A New Search for Scientific Knowledge' (1994) 72 *Texas Law Review* 715; Joseph Sanders, 'Scientific Validity, Admissibility and Mass Torts after *Daubert*' (1994) 78 *Minnesota Law Review* 1387; Margaret G. Farrell, '*Daubert* v. *Merrell Dow Pharmaceuticals, Inc*: Epistemology and Legal Process' (1994) 15 *Cardozo Law Review* 2183; Heidi Li Feldman, 'Science and Uncertainty in Mass Exposure Litigation' (1995) 74 *Texas Law Review* 1. In England, with nothing like *Daubert* as a guide, the approach to scientific evidence tends to be pragmatic.

42 See *Frye* v. *United States* 293 F. 1013 (D.C. Cir. 1923). There was considerable criticism of *Frye*, including Paul C. Giannelli, 'The Admissibility of Novel Scientific Evidence: *Frye* v. *United States*, a Half Century Later' (1980) 80 *Columbia Law Review* 1197, 1205–28; Michael D. Green, 'Expert Witnesses and Sufficiency of Evidence in Toxic Substances Litigation: The Legacy of the Agent Orange and Bendectin Litigation' (1992) 86 *Northwestern University Law Review* 643.

43 In *United States* v. *Addison* 498 F. 2d at 744, the D.C. Circuit noted that 'General acceptance ... assures that those most qualified to assess the general validity of a scientific method will have the determinative voice.'

44 'The Evolution of the American Test for the Admissibility of Scientific Evidence' (1990) 30 *Medical Science and Law* 60, 61.

45 'The Truth About Law's Truth', in A. Febbrajo and D. Nelken (eds), *The European Yearbook for the Sociology of Law* (Milan, 1993), p.87; see also Chapter 2 of the present volume.

46 And see D.A. Downs, *More Than Victims: Battered Women, the Syndrome Society and the Law* (Chicago, 1996). See also Mary Ann Dutton, 'Understanding Women's

Responses to Domestic Violence: A Redefinition of Battered Woman Syndrome' (1993) 21 *Hofstra Law Review* 1191.

47 J. Sanders, 'From Science to Evidence: The Testimony on Causation in the Bendectin Cases' (1993) 46 *Stanford Law Review* 79.

48 As in the Peter Sutcliffe ('Yorkshire Ripper') trial.

49 'Science and the Law in the Wake of *Daubert*' p.796, quoting Green, 'Expert Witnesses' 645.

50 Ibid., p.797.

51 Ibid.

52 Ibid.

53 Ibid.

54 Two developments are Nancy Levit, 'Listening to Tribal Legends: An Essay on Law and the Scientific Method' (1990) 58 *Fordham Law Review* 263, 266–72, and Black *et al.*, 'Science and the Law in the Wake of *Daubert*', 782–5.

55 Black, *et al.* 'Science and the Law in the Wake of *Daubert*', 782, 783.

56 Ibid., 783.

57 Ibid., 758–9.

58 *The Structure of Scientific Revolutions.*

59 'Epistemology and Legal Process', at p.2797.

60 As with DNA findings or the development of cloning techniques (on the latter, see Gina Kolata, *Clone: The Road to Dolly and the Path Ahead*, London, 1997).

61 'Science and the Law in the Wake of *Daubert*', 784.

62 See, in support, Kenneth R. Kreiling, 'Scientific Evidence: Toward Providing the Lay Trier with the Compulsive and Reliable Evidence Necessary to Meet the Goals of the Rules of Evidence' (1990) 32 *Arizona Law Review* 915, 930–35.

63 See Chapter 6 of the present volume.

64 'Science and the Law in the Wake of *Daubert*', p.796.

65 As in the Roskill Committee Report on *Fraud Trials* (London, 1986), paras 8.21–8.40. See also Michael Levi, *The Investigation, Prosecution and Trial of Serious Fraud* (London, 1993), p.190.

66 See *Ross* v. *Bernhard* 396 U.S. 531, 538 n. 10 (1970).

67 James A. Martin, 'The Proposed "Science Court"' (1977) 75 *Michigan Law Review* 1058.

68 Troyen A. Brennan, 'Helping Courts With Toxic Torts' (1989) 51 *University of Pittsburgh Law Review* 1, 5.

69 John W. Osborne, 'Judicial/Technical Assessment of Novel Scientific Evidence' (1990) *University of Illinois Law Review* 497, 540–46.

70 Edward V. DiLello, 'Fighting Fire with Firefighters: A Proposal for Expert Judges at the Trial Level' (1993) 93 *Columbia Law Review* 473.

2 A Just Measure of Science

David Nelken

It is not necessary to accept everything as true, one must only accept it as necessary. (Franz Kafka)

This chapter, like others in this volume, will be discussing the practical problems of divergences between law and science which can arise while trying to do justice. Its main aim, however, is not so much to recommend a method for resolving such disagreements but rather to compare and contrast some of the different ways of theoretically formulating or reformulating the problem itself. After outlining the background to the current debate over 'junk science' in the United States, it will be suggested that it is reductivist simply to criticize legal proceedings for their failure to ensure that their findings correspond to scientific truth. The chapter goes on to describe three more nuanced approaches to understanding the relationship between law and science, and attempts to link these to corresponding aspects of what we may call 'law's truth'.[1] The chapter ends with some tentative conclusions showing how different ways of 'posing the problem' each have relevant implications for the arduous challenge of finding a just measure of science.

Law and the Politics of Expertise

Although concern about the role of expert evidence in common law jurisdictions is long-standing, there are now few trials regarding personal injury and products liability, in the United States at least, which do not involve several expert witnesses;[2] the same is true elsewhere for prosecutions for some serious crimes or proceedings involving issues of child welfare. The latest arguments over the role of science in law, as with previous rounds, are intrinsically connected to larger social developments.[3] Critics argue that the greedy 1980s gave rise not only to 'junk bonds' but also to so-called 'junk science' (and 'junk law'), all methods of making a lot of money using something which will pass, at least briefly, as long as others accept its worth. In the realm of tort litigation, the misuse of expert witnesses is condemned as having increased the costs of American business in an increasingly globalized and competitive economic environment.[4] In the realm of criminal law, on the other hand, the introduction of new excuses based on evidence of psychological syndromes has been criticized as (yet again) menacing the value of personal responsibility.[5]

Debates over expert evidence vary by culture and jurisdiction. The Supreme Court decision in *Daubert*[6] instructed judges to play a larger role as gatekeepers over the admission of expert evidence. But there have been no dramatic decisions comparable to *Daubert* in England and Wales. Even after the controversy occasioned by the role played by forensic scientists in the famous cases of miscarriages of justice which led to a Royal Commission report, the higher courts continue to deal with expert evidence in an altogether pragmatic fashion.[7] Many American commentators blame the growth of 'junk science' on their contingent fee system and the relatively easy resort to legal proceedings.[8] By contrast, the recent Woolf recommendations on the reform of civil justice in England and Wales suggest that the increasing expense of resorting to expert evidence is limiting access to litigation for those who cannot afford such fees but this argument is then used to support the introduction of 'no win no fee' schemes! On the European continent the use of court-appointed experts seems to raise less public debate, even if few are convinced by saving formulas such as the Italian saying that 'the judge checks the expertise of the expert'. But differences between law and science do lead to highly contested decisions,[9] and there is recurrent concern over the appropriate role of law in the regulation of technological breakthroughs connected to the biogenetic revolution.

The politics of these controversies is not one-sided. Huber and others with a right-libertarian political agenda have certainly made the running in the tort debate, claiming that courts have given awards on the basis of scientifically fanciful theories in support of propositions that cancer can be caused by impact, that power lines represent risks to health, or that it is plausible to sue for loss of psychic powers.[10] But others, with different political views, have also offered critical case studies of recent mass toxic torts litigation concerning silicon breast implants or the drug Bendectin (involved in the *Daubert* case).[11] Worries have also been expressed about the way expert evidence is used by prosecutors in criminal law,[12] and there has been considerable unease over the increasing importance of DNA evidence.

Whilst the empirical status of many of these accounts of the use of science in the law is highly contested, there is certainly some evidence behind them. Government support has been required to provide childhood vaccines because of the high insurance costs resulting from costly litigation, and there have been notorious criminal trials, for example those of O.J. Simpson or the Menendez brothers. But what this debate too often takes for granted is the idea that legal proceedings can and should reach the same result as that which would be produced in other fora. Thus when Huber or others criticize judicial decisions they do so relying on what the Food and Drug Administration (FDA) or other administrative agencies have established as scientific truth regarding the matter being litigated. As Huber puts it, 'the rule of law is not half so grand as the rule of fact' and 'there can be no appeal from the (higher) laws of nature'; it follows that good science must be the only way of doing justice.[13] The solution to the problem of junk science is therefore for judges to find some better way of curbing the use of dubious experts, for example by limiting those scientists who can be called upon to give testimony to those who have already published relevant work in reputable scientific journals. More generally, increasing the scientific knowledge of decision makers in their recourse to expertise is seen as the only and obvious answer to those instances where law seems hospitable to scientific error.

Yet this begs almost all the important questions which need to be faced here. How much will it help to exclude junk science when courts' proceedings often seem to distort or transform the evidence of even reputable experts? Where the law arrives at different conclusions from those which scientists would have reached, could this not be an unavoidable and even desirable result of having correctly working legal institutions? Huber insists proudly that 'good science is unburdened by concerns about what is fair, just, reasonable or socially acceptable'. But is that not precisely why law brings other criteria to bear (for example, when the judge protects the jury from expert evidence which would be too definitive of the case)? Why else not leave everything to experts or at least model law on their methods of inquiry? Is the question of how much law should correspond to science one which should be left for scientists to answer?

Decisions about what expertise to include or exclude struggle to find an overall rationale. Take a currently popular justification which is recommended as representing a more respectful method of introducing science into law so as not to undermine but rather assist the jury in its role. This is to allow expert witnesses to testify at least as to the falsity of the 'myths' on which juries may be relying as they assess the evidence - for example, to counteract the belief that battered women on murder charges could, and therefore should, have left the family home rather than have retaliated with deadly force.[14] But where and how should the line between 'facts' and 'myths' (in relation both to judges and to juries) be drawn? The task of science here would be unending, given that its mandate is precisely to show that 'lay' understanding and reasoning rests on corrigible misconception and error. And what if it is law's task actually to defend some 'myths' which a community chooses to live by – not least the notion of individual responsibility?[15] Put another way, if law is to unfold a community's 'nomos',[16] might this not require it also to act as a bulwark against the spread of 'technical rationality'? Attempting to get a purchase on these questions, it has been rightly claimed, 'covers the totality of contemporary society's attempts to understand and control threats to its stability and identity'.[17]

Three Approaches to Disagreements between Law and Science

Attempts to understand breakdowns in collaboration between law and science often take refuge in metaphors, even (unconvincingly) comparing these to the difficulties of human relationships. In an attempt to take matters further, the following outlines and compares three styles of work or general approaches, each well represented in different bodies of academic literature yet rarely brought together, which try to explore where, why and how law draws the line between itself and science. The points made by these approaches are not necessarily incompatible. Indeed it will be suggested that they may, at least in part, be offering answers to different questions. But for heuristic purposes it will be best to begin by setting out the salient differences in the ways they each conceptualize and explain the problem of reconciling law and science.

The first of these approaches, which could be called the *trial pathology* approach, is concerned with the alleged malfunctioning of the institutions and processes of adversarial systems. It is typical of the numerous, sometimes repetitive, discussions in the law reviews, especially in the United States, of the rules of evidence regarding admissibility of expertise, the challenge of novel forms of evidence, the gatekeeping role of judges and the aftermath of the Supreme Court ruling in the *Daubert* case.[18] At its simplest level, trial pathologies are attributed to foolish juries, lazy judges or greedy lawyers tempted by contingency fees, but in more sophisticated versions they are seen as a result of more intractable structural features of adversarial systems. At issue here is not the status of scientific truth in general but the particular difficulties of 'science in law' conceived as one form of expert witnessing. Commentators note how experts are made to authorize conclusions they would not endorse outside the courtroom; that the wrong people come to be seen as experts; that judges and juries have difficulty in making sense of scientific information; and that it is unreasonable to expect laymen to be able to resolve 'the battle of the experts'. Illustrations of suspicious expertise range from the dangers of 'junk science' in the area of mass toxic torts to the complications of using so-called 'suppositional' social science evidence, for example that concerning psychological traumas.[19] But most articles in legal journals take the role of expertise as such for granted and many favour enlarging it, for example by extending the ambit of new criminal defences.[20]

The second, *competing institutions* approach, focuses on law and science as powerful and often rival institutions, or 'expert spaces', which coexist or collaborate under conditions of unstable compromise.[21] Drawing both on the sociology of science and on the sociology of knowledge,[22] it offers both social conflict and social constructionist accounts of the interaction between legal and scientific institutions. As is well illustrated by the sophisticated work of Jasanoff,[23] controversies over law and technology are investigated by identifying the political and economic interests at stake in these battles - and their wider public policy ramifications - and careful attention is given to the negotiation of truth claims and boundaries between different forms of authority.

This approach has a rather different take on the 'problem' of legal and scientific expertise. Rather than limit itself to the mechanisms and aberrations of the trial process, it ranges much more widely into exchanges with science in other legally-related administrative and regulatory decisions.[24] What happens in the trial is also put into context in relation to what happens before or around it. Various studies of the rise and fall of different sorts of expert prestige show that science obtains its crucial victories not so much in the courtroom as by producing socially respected problem solvers.[25] Trials are of interest mainly because they show how each of these institutions can turn their methods on each other in the course of constructing or deconstructing each other's credibility. Unlike the first and third approaches which, in very different ways, tend to take the distinctiveness of law and science as their starting point, this second approach insists on the many similarities as well as differences in the way law and science produce their determinations.[26] It therefore gives attention, in Jasanoff's words, to the way the institutions of law and science are 'articulated to look as if separate'.

The third way of formulating the relationship between law and science can be termed the *incompatible discourses* approach. It is currently particularly associated with the autopoietic theories of Luhmann and Teubner,[27] though it can be formulated in a variety of other ways drawing on different strands of contemporary social and legal theory. The aim of the Luhmann/Teubner theory is to observe law and science as discourses each of which reproduces itself according to its own specific discursive or communicative codes. Seeking to integrate neofunctionalist, systems theory and cybernetic concepts, those who follow this approach move from an analysis of the characteristics of law, of social systems and of knowledge production in (post)modernity to an examination of legal reflexivity and the way this does or should be used to mediate the 'collision of discourses' and limit the damage of consequent 'fall-out'.[28]

The third approach is even less interested than the second in examining the details of the adversarial system as the source of the communication difficulties which afflict the relationship of law and science. Indeed, it is often developed by theorists at home with continental European legal systems which rely more on inquisitorial methods and court-appointed experts. The problem for this approach, as Teubner puts it, is rather that law finds itself caught in an 'epistemic trap'.[29] On the one hand, its concepts and practices need the stamp of scientific credibility in a world where science has the legitimated monopoly of truth claims; on the other hand, its efforts to align its ideas with those of science are destined to fail as it reproduces itself according to its own code so that it only succeeds in generating 'hybrid artefacts', terms with ambiguous epistemic status and unknown sociological consequences.[30] For this approach the significance of the trial is the way it shows how law 'has enslaved science in its contexts of law offices and courts',[31] whereas outside the courts, by contrast, law is more likely to have to give way because scientific methods of fact finding have superior credibility.

In general, it is the radicality of its social epistemology which distinguishes the third approach from the previous, *competing institutions*, approach.[32] The second approach works with 'open systems' theorizing about the relationship between law and science, each of which is treated as a semi-autonomous institution subject to reciprocal influence. For Jasanoff, 'ideas of truth and ideas of justice are co-constructed in the context of legal proceedings',[33] as in the mediating role of experts such as forensic psychiatrists, or in the way litigation stimulates developments in science, and vice versa. Jasanoff's aim is indeed to encourage what she calls a more 'reflective alliance' between these two institutions in pursuit of overall public policy objectives. The *incompatible discourses* approach, on the other hand, calls for a shift from theorizing in terms of the actions of human agents and institutions to that capable of understanding the reproduction of discourses and codes. The systems theory adopted by Luhmann and Teubner rejects the idea of law as a semi-autonomous institution[34] and offers instead a perspective in which law is both more and less open to influence than in the 'open systems' approach. According to these theorists, law, like other social sub-systems, is simultaneously both open and closed. And it is open just because it is closed, coding the world normatively in terms of the distinction legal/illegal as it processes other communications.[35] For this approach it makes little sense to ask discourses to be more reflective unless this takes into account the way they already constitute themselves through their own reflexivity. Discourses do not and cannot help constitute each other; each discourse only uses the inputs received from its environment by applying its own code so as to reproduce its own elements. Law and science cannot really engage in fighting over boundaries or in processes of co-construction – and any project to improve their collaboration, including Jasanoff's, which overlook their incommensurability,[36] must be doomed. Strategies of intervention begin rather by exploring the possibility of influencing existing processes of self-organization, in relation to what Teubner[37] calls the 'interference' and 'structural coupling' which results from the fact that specific discourses are also part of the overall cycle of societal communication.

The systems theories of Luhmann and Teubner have in common with otherwise quite different postmodern work such as Lyotard's writing about the 'differend'[38] that they all assume a differentiation of discourses linked to the conditions of (post)modern social complexity.[39] For autopoietic theory any cognition, be it scientific or legal, is a purely internal construction of the outside world[40] (the production of 'legal order from social noise'). Certainly Teubner in particular would like to use law also to improve communication among social sub-systems and discourses. But ultimately law can only regulate other sub-systems by regulating itself. Thus, as with other post-modern writing, rather than improving its contribution to society's search for effective technical solutions to social problems, law's (new) task must be to do justice to the 'heterogeneity of discourses' aiming at least to check their various imperialisms so as to limit the damage of fall-out from 'the clash of discourses'.[41]

As would be expected, rather different conceptions of law and science lie behind these formulations of the problem. The first approach tends to view science as a normally reliable institution which provides true or false answers. It is represented in trials by hired experts who may turn out to be unreliable or even dishonest in single instances. It is thus the task of the law to ferret out these cases if science is to make its proper contribution to law. But, though it has its uses, expertise can also be both irrelevant or improperly influential in the legal process. Moreover there are important borderline cases where the issue faced by law is the scientific status of the expertise as such. Law reaches out to science for certainty but also has to adjudicate on the boundaries of science. The second approach sees science more as a collective communal enterprise and stresses the point that it is the tactics which are used for reaching agreement amongst practitioners which then produce its aura of reliability. These, often implicit, techniques of 'closure' which undergird all good science can, with uncertain results, be exposed by lawyers in forensic contests or political struggles. The range of potential divergence between legal and scientific solutions to individual cases of harm or injustice goes well beyond the issue of 'junk science'. Competition between legal and scientific truth claims can be an index of differing practical interests or visions of the good life and such controversy - and uncertainty itself - can often be fruitful. And different forms or factions of expertise fight their own turf battles, sometimes even through the courts. The third approach assumes that the codes of law and science have different relationships to the social function of distinguishing truth and falsehood and that little is to be gained by encouraging their direct confrontation. Law's increasing attempt to provide certainty by engaging experts to tell it how to reduce social risks is only likely to exacerbate uncertainty.[42] It is not sufficient to condemn 'junk science' if law's attempt to integrate science is bound to produce it. The way forward lies in using legal oversight to proceduralize the question of which discourse is to be given responsibility for which aspects of social regulation.

Aspects of Law's Truth

Whatever their other underlying theoretical differences, the strengths and weaknesses of the three approaches considered so far can also be related to their different standpoints. Addressed respectively to the judge, the legislator and the observer of systems, the first approach focuses mainly on law as adjudication, the second concentrates on law as public policy, while the third treats law as a form of communicative discourse. In keeping with these standpoints, the first approach tends towards adopting an 'internal' legal point of view, so as to identify pathologies for which it offers prescriptions, the second seeks to examine controversial features of interaction between law and science from an external point of view, whereas the third approach tries to model the relationship between 'the two internal points of view' of legal and scientific discourses.[43] The first approach, by its very mimicking of the normative legal viewpoint, is truer to the detail and contingencies of legal processes, but its blind spots are often the same. The second approach offers all the advantages of exposing what internal accounts of law and science do not themselves see.[44] Only the last approach claims, but perhaps with exaggerated confidence,[45] to reveal the paradoxical functioning of the blind spots themselves.

All three approaches agree that there is something about law which can lead it to conclusions at variance with those reached by science. But their standpoints lead them to highlight somewhat different aspects of law's 'truth'. To clarify this point, it is suggested below that the contribution of each of these approaches can best be brought out by considering, in turn, law's procedures, law's goals and law's reasons. Again, it is not intended to suggest that a hard-and-fast line can be drawn amongst these keys to law's distinctive way of producing and handling truth claims. Indeed an attempt will be made to show that each of these features of law can also be seen as aspects of a larger whole.

Law's Procedures

For science or other technical evidence to influence legal outcomes it has to be turned into proof in ways compatible with the many specialized rules of procedure and evidence which govern legal processes. Thus, as rightly emphasized by the *trial pathology* approach, one way of explaining why law's truth differs from that which would be produced by a more specifically scientific enquiry depends on appreciating the procedures and fact-finding methods which characterize legal institutions. Although these points can be seen particularly clearly in relation to adversarial legal proceedings, above all, in the common law adversarial trial, they are also of wider significance.

Relying on the parties to bring forward their evidence sets severe limits to the nature of legal enquiries. Through the institution of the trial, legal truth must be made to emerge by means of publicly examined witnesses. Involving laymen, whether it be to force lawyers to clarify their arguments, to provide a check on life-tenured judges or to involve the public, provides an alternative to technical, routinized and distant decision making by experts. Juries are allowed and expected to give unpredictable verdicts for unknowable motives. The need for lay participation can also be linked to legally specific methods of truth finding such as cross-examination. Even the continued, if increasingly questioned, reliançe on eyewitness testimony within law reflects modes of procedure which are quite different from those which would shape an enquiry conducted by experts. But the filters which are imposed on what can be used as a basis for adjudication reflect wider procedural concerns. From the outset law seeks to avoid basing liability on facts which can only be discovered by the use of improper methods. At the stage of determining responsibility, the need for evidence to be both reliable and not prejudiced, admissibility standards, and rules about what must be kept from the jury exclude much that scientific enquiry would think at least potentially worthy of inclusion. As compared to expert inquiries, timing is all-important; issues of fairness determine when parties are allowed to introduce or to challenge certain claims or when juries are allowed to reflect on the level of probability of guilt.

Procedure and evidence rules can be highly technical in ways that often have little or no bearing on their scientific accuracy. Hundreds of pages in legal textbooks are devoted to hearsay rule exceptions or the meaning of 'similar facts' in judicial processes. Rules about proof, liability and responsibility can be quite different in the various branches of law, as in the difference between the burden of proof in criminal and civil trials. In criminal trials the contrast with scientific enquiry is shown by the exclusion of evidence of previous convictions, or the way the prejudicial effects of evidence gathered unfairly are weighed against the advantages of including it. Likewise, it has been argued, were the American civil process to take the form of an unbridled search for truth, the rules about the 'discovery' of evidence would be looser, there would be no statutes of limitation and there would no justification for many doctrines such as privity for lawyer–client communications, protection orders, gag orders, exclusionary rules or sealed settlements.[46] How evidence is supposed to be employed can vary even within the same branch of law; thus the use of expert evidence in criminal trials can depend on whether and when it is being used to convict or defend (as with the case of rape trauma syndrome).[47] Again, unlike the supposedly universal practices of scientific method, rules of evidence and procedure are deliberately varied by court level and between different jurisdictions.

The pragmatics of all this are something else again. The way evidence rules are actually applied, or avoided by judges, will in practice often depend on the results sought in each case (just as the actual burden of proof required will reflect what is at stake in a particular case). Common law fact finding articulates a complicated interplay between legal expertise and scientific and technical inputs, on the one hand, and judicial and lay 'common sense' on the other. If the parties are to convince judge and jury, they must do so bearing in mind the expectations of these decision makers rather than the requirements of a scientific exercise. What actually convinces decision makers has as much to do with its shape as a narrative as its correspondence with what can be discovered in other ways.

Expertise is called for where legal competence or lay common sense is not deemed sufficient. But it must not be so persuasive as to displace the role of the jury – yet the actual interpretation of the 'ultimate issue' rule is far from consistent. While psychologists question the claims of common sense to understand the secret roots of action of normal people, in law trials experts must be limited to interpreting the abnormal. Some forms of psychological insight are deemed to be necessarily within the competence of the jury, while other problems are seen to be beyond the reach of any known science. The division of responsibilities between judge and jury likewise depends less on scientific than on normative considerations (and does not correspond to the in any event slippery distinction between questions of 'law' and of 'fact').[48]

Of special importance for our purposes are the criticisms that have been made of the effects of the adversarial process on the role of expert witnesses.[49] The way parties shop around in choosing experts often favours extreme and unrepresentative opinions. The contribution which experts can make to truth finding may also be hampered by their responsibility or allegiance to the side which employs them. In the trial itself, methods which have some efficacy when used to test the reliability and credibility of ordinary witnesses are often applied improperly also to experts. Questions are put to confuse rather than to clarify, scientifically irrelevant small doubts are picked on and magnified, and qualifications and demeanour are made to stand in as substitutes for the hard task of checking scientific reliability or validity. Experts are not told the full facts, not allowed to confer before trial so as to narrow differences with each other and are not allowed to bring out in court all that they would deem to be relevant. They are forced to be more definite than they would wish to be and obliged to choose between clarity and accuracy in giving testimony for lay decision makers which exposes them to risks of misunderstanding in either case. Because of the way they are selected and the difficulty they face in getting over their opinions, many of the scientific leaders in their field will be reluctant to testify and court experts are likely to become a specialized breed of those willing to become experts in testifying.

Given these arguments, it is not surprising that the claim is often made that jurors, and to some extent also judges, are led to wrong conclusions because they make judgments about the credibility of experts rather than the substance of evidence. In his excellent study of the Bendectin litigation, Sanders sets out to explain why in mass toxic tort litigation 'trial verdicts and damage awards can bear little relation to the weight of science'.[50] His study starts from the puzzle that there was overwhelming scientific opinion based on epidemiological analysis that Bendectin is not a cause of damage to new-born children, yet the success rate for plaintiffs in these cases was not out of line with other mass toxic tort litigation. Sanders explains this by arguing that juries erred because the evidence was not presented to them properly. Trial procedures made it possible for each side to appear to have the support of an equal number of reputable experts. Plaintiffs were able to provide the jury with a persuasive narrative, whereas the defendants were unable or unwilling to construct a complete alternative story; importantly plaintiffs were able to bolster the very weak scientific evidence on causation with stronger proof of breach of duty and of damages.

There are many scholars who consider current attacks on the adversarial system biased and exaggerated. They argue that there are relatively few cases which are as complicated as the asbestos or Bendectin litigation and that, even in cases as difficult as ones alleging medical malpractice, juries are at least as generally competent as judges.[51] There have also been important interventions arguing that lay reasoning may even be particularly suitable to the task of assessing guilt and that it is self-defeating to try and show otherwise.[52] But a focus on law's procedures does show that the question whether law should even be trying to arrive at the same results as a scientific enquiry is far from hypothetical. Should we allow law to produce the 'wrong' findings for the right institutional reasons (or, in other words, how do we know when we are faced with a trial pathology)?

In an early but still topical discussion of expertise in the common law trial,[53] Tribe warns that, whatever its other utility, expert evidence should not be admitted to induce juries to attach mathematical values to probabilities arising from non-scientific evidence adduced at the trial.[54] He argues that any advantages in greater precision would be more than outweighed by the risk of juries being led to make mistakes, for example by giving undue attention to quantifiable variables as compared to such 'fuzzy factors' as evaluating a person's intentions. He strongly opposes methods of decision which require assuming an initial level of probability of guilt because the normative presumption of innocence depends on not forcing jurors to focus on the meaning of 'beyond reasonable doubt' before the trial is over.[55] Mathematics distorts or destroys important values which society means to express or to pursue through the conduct of legal trials – principles too subtle to be translated into anything less complex than the intricate symbolism of the trial process:

> Far from being either barren or obsolete, much of what goes on in a lawsuit – particularly in a criminal case – is partly ceremonial or ritualistic in a deeply positive sense, and partly educational as well; procedure can serve a vital role as conventionalised communication among a trial's participants, and as something like a reminder to the community of these principles.[56]

The normal reply to this argument is to insist that nothing is gained by obscuring rather than clarifying the mathematical and scientific basis of the operations of legal institutions. This is also the only way to work out how they can be redesigned in the face of mounting criticisms. Why is Bayes's theorem outlawed but other types of expertise admissible? Why do courts allow so-called 'handwriting experts' to testify?[57] Can we justify an adversarial system for processing tort claims in which almost 40 per cent goes in running costs rather than being spent on victims? Tribe insists that, even when considering what sort of decision-making procedures we want to create, we must avoid openly addressing such questions as what proportion of innocent persons we can risk convicting.[58] But this type of argument becomes less convincing the more we think about how to redesign legal institutions[59] so as to achieve specific goals of public policy.

Law's Goals

Another way of putting the points about legal proceedings illustrated so far is to say that scientific truth finding is not and cannot be the only goal of law.

Modern law and modern science both have an interest in truth finding,[60] each have influenced each other's conceptions of truth finding and have much in common in comparison to less rational methods.[61] This said, law also has different or at least collateral concerns: it usually aims at more than truth and sometimes settles for less. From a functionalist perspective, law's tasks include, at a minimum, dispute channelling, processing and adjudication; maintaining social order; legitimating power; expressing and unfolding community and traditional identities and values; and regulating - or purporting to regulate - social, political and economic behaviour. The way legal goals are defined will also depend on the level of abstraction we adopt: functional accounts can be offered at the level of single institutions, procedures or rules. Different branches of law, such as for example the law of torts or criminal law, will also be found to be pursuing different goals. The priority given to reaching or employing 'scientific' truth will vary across legal fields, at different stages of the legal process and so on.

Explaining law's operations in terms of its various goals can allow us to account for much that is puzzling about law's divergence from science. The different way law classifies events in the world, such as its insistence on artificial dichotomies and apparently arbitrary cut-off points, responds to the goals of adjudication. Its different definitions of life and death show its concern with the wider social implications of these, and other, fundamental categories. 'Presumptions' or 'findings' which seem to fly in the face of science usually indicate the intrusion of 'policy' considerations aimed at reinforcing family values, deterring crime, protecting the integrity of legal processes and so on. Legislatures sometimes define what will count as truth for legal purposes, as in the way California legislation mandated courts to admit testimony on battered wife syndrome. Explicitly, or implicitly, judges rely on 'policy' in holding that the taking of drink or drugs does not negate the *mens rea* of criminal behaviour. American courts applying the death penalty routinely give credit to psychiatrists who make 'unscientific' claims to be able to predict dangerousness, but they are reluctant to allow psychologists with more valid arguments to inform juries of the fallibility of witness memories, eyewitness testimony and so on.

When they contrast law with science, judges themselves are particularly apt to stress law's role in the authoritative resolution of disputes. As the US Supreme Court in *Daubert* put it recently, law must be prepared to miss out on learning about some scientific innovations because its truth-finding methods are intended 'not for the exhaustive search for cosmic understanding but the particularised realities of legal disputes'.[62] In practice this goal often interacts with others. As compared to science, law usually cannot wait before making an authoritative determination and will thus often be in a hurry to reach a verdict before 'all the scientific evidence is in'. On other occasions, however, for example in criminal trials, law seems to demand the reaching of verdicts whose certainty lies beyond the margin of error which would be used in other undertakings. And, as part of its role in unfolding community values and maintaining stable expectations, it can be right for law deliberately to lag behind scientific discoveries. In any event, it would be inconsistent with its other roles if law were to have to change regularly in the light of every new scientific finding.

Because doing justice to the individual case matters more than the establishing of scientific regularities, legal investigations can be both more and less expeditious than scientific ones. The criminal law may insist that the accused be subjected to only the one trial, thus cutting off, in most cases, the possibility of later reconsideration. By contrast, in tort cases in the United States, even when expert opinion is relatively settled about a particular controversial issue of scientific causation, the plaintiff is allowed to rely on whatever experts can be found so as to raise the same claim in state court after state court, in the not unfounded hope that sooner or later a jury might award lucrative damages.

A central goal of law is that of creating a framework of *governance*; rules prescribing legal conduct must be actually capable of being followed. Such rules include both 'decision rules' for use by courts and other decision makers in judging behaviour, as well as 'conduct rules' which are directed at individuals generally.[63] Decision rules and conduct rules are, however, intertwined. The task of creating a uniform system of 'conduct rules' involves taking care to see that rule determinations do not need to become too individualized and concerned with the subjective experience of those subject to law. If law's truth-finding concerns were to go too far in this direction it might find itself forced to become too intrusive, with too much discretionary power being placed in the hands of decision makers. This, it is said, explains the apparently idiosyncratic mix of subjective and objective criteria for judging conduct which is adopted in the different branches of law and the use of concepts such as 'the reasonable man' and so on.[64] Considerable complications arise in trying to match the goals of law and the goals of science, for example in clarifying the role of experts in psychiatry and psychology because we are sometimes unclear whether what we want to know is what an accused person actually felt at the time she acted or rather what she should have felt.

A focus on law's goals can also help us understand why law both collaborates and competes with science. Law seeks to transform naked power into legitimate authority so that decisions (including its own) be considered credible and authoritative. The pursuit of this role, however, requires law to gain legitimacy both by passing difficult decisions to experts (and so incorporate scientific credibility) and by keeping science and expertise within proper bounds. On the one hand, in embracing science law attributes to it more certainty than it would claim for itself;[65] on the other hand, legal values and lay judgment are sometimes treated as more entitled to respect than expert calculations.

The *competing institutions* approach to the relationship of law and science is best adapted to this aspect of law's truth. The problem of integrating science and law inside and outside the courtroom then becomes that of helping each to reach its respective goals by doing what each does best. An external point of view can make clearer what this involves. Thus the House of Lords may tell experts that they can only be useful to the court if they are seen to be independent of legal battles.[66] But, argues Jasanoff, in many areas of law and technology it is precisely the onset of litigation which encourages the development of relevant funded research projects. Acting as bridging institutions, the litigation process can then make transparent the values, biases and social assumptions that are embedded in experts' claims and apparently technical choices.

The unresolved issue raised by this approach, however, is how, if at all, we can come to know what are law's goals – and who, judges, scientists or others, should decide them. What status should be given to judicial pronouncements which assert, for example, that procedure in civil cases is designed to be a genuine search for truth and not merely a contest between the parties?[67] Are judicial claims about law's goals descriptive or normative, concerned with what law does or what it claims to do, limited to the case at hand or of more general application? But, if we cannot rely on judges to tell us how to reconcile legal and scientific goals, scientists themselves are not necessarily more reliable. It is only by taking law to be a mechanism for implementing specific public policy goals that scientific methods can be brought to bear on ascertaining how far these are being achieved. But there are many who argue that to talk of law as having collective goals itself misdescribes the nature of law or at least certain types of law and legal institutions. What does effectiveness mean within law's self-understanding? Seeking to tackle disagreements between law and science by identifying the goals law is trying to pursue usually entails taking sides with the types of goal-directed behaviour presupposed by the discipline (economics, psychology or whatever) which is used to undertake the analysis.

Law's Reasons

Those who object to treating law as no more than a branch of social policy insist that law has a special concern for creating and maintaining its own brand of normative coherence. It is not just that law has its reasons, but that it is in some essential way all about reasoning and justification, that practical reasoning within law is mainly about the meaning of authoritative materials and their implications for practical issues that arise in social life.[68]

Unlike scientific disciplines which are typically addressed mainly to academic peers, legal decisions are directed at other judges, lawyers, the jury and, at least indirectly, the general public. Law refuses to deal with hypotheticals, rarely spells out defeasible empirical propositions, has different ways of arguing from authority and precedent, and special techniques of analysis such as reasoning from analogy. Lawyers and judges are involved in processing already categorized data, events which have been generated by non-academic actors, judges, litigants and so on. Legal practice cannot therefore aspire to develop the sort of cumulative knowledge characteristic of certain scientific disciplines,[69] but nor does it wish to. As compared to scientific reasoning, law is more prescriptive than explanatory, concerned in the main with evaluating social behaviour in the light of rules, principles and values.

Law does not possess the tools for assessing effectiveness which are employed by applied scientists in relation to their policy interventions. But, more than this, it has been argued that, were law even to attempt to do so, it would undermine its own method of reproduction. Luhmann asserts that law maintains normative expectations by 'not learning' from the evidence of its prescriptions being sometimes flouted. Tribe, in reflecting on legal procedure, claims that, not only is it not law's aim to predict the likelihood of an accused having committed a crime, but it has a responsibility not even to let the jury think in these terms.[70]

Does law really have its own unique form of reasoning, or does it merely use an eclectic mix of other forms of reasoning (including non-legal forms of expertise)? Greenawalt, a leading mainstream philosopher of law, tells us that 'reasoning within law is not simply a sub-category of other forms of reasoning. It combines different kinds of reasoning. No particular feature of reasoning within law is distinctively and uniquely "legal" but the context of legal decision colors the force of the reasons that matter'.[71] For Greenawalt, therefore, law's autonomy 'rests on the distinctive mix of relevant reasons within the law': the unique blend of appropriate arguments, how they are combined and the weight they are assigned. The mix derives from 'the special functions of law, the richness and complexity of legal materials, the institutions that make legal decisions, and the coercive force of legal judgements'.[72] Lawyers agree on which arguments have force, even if they disagree about how much force they have in a given case. Amongst these arguments law does sometimes resort to economics and other efficiency considerations; and it cannot operate without reference to political morality or community sentiment. Thus experts can find a place in law as bearers of such reasons: 'although the legal context affects the import of much of this reasoning, critical aspects of reasoning within law can often be carried out as effectively by non lawyers as lawyers'.

Even if we settle for Greenawalt's balanced perspective we will have to expect law's use of expertise to produce something foreign to the way scientists use their concepts. Many of the recent 'hard cases' regarding so-called 'abuse excuses'[73] turn on how far legally relevant distinctions in types or levels of responsibility correspond to distinctions which would be recognized by the behavioural sciences (but much the same ambiguity surrounds more established defences, for example the distinction between 'excuse' and 'justification', or the meaning of 'duress' or 'provocation'). In tort law, too, 'causation' is a special legal construct which seeks to integrate expert judgment about the plausibility of a particular causal story with the law's normative interest in deciding which stories are best for individuals and society.

Controversies over these legal constructs in the United States demonstrate how law manipulates the meanings of cause and responsibility so that these can be either equated, combined or contrasted. In some mass toxic tort cases large companies may be held responsible for not having taken all the steps they might have to ensure the safe marketing of their products, even where there is little or no evidence that they actually caused the harm suffered by the plaintiff in the case at hand. The rise of such new criminal defences such as battered wife syndrome, on the other hand, can be seen as an attempt to deny or reduce responsibility where causation is not in question. The consequences of employing even good scientific evidence soon become unpredictable if links between cause and responsibility can be forged or prised apart at will.

Other legal theorists, however, go further than Greenawalt in restricting the type of arguments that can find a place in legal reasoning. Dworkin, for example, sees law as itself an all-embracing metatheoretical search for its own meaning. Law as an interpretative activity is concerned not only with understanding the legal significance of nature and behaviour but above all with deciding what is to count as law itself. And this can only be grasped hermeneutically from an internal legal point of view, not through an analysis carried out using external disciplines. Likewise, those who adhere to the 'law as literature' approach also argue that law should not be seen as an instrument of social control or social policy. For James Boyd White, for example, law is a conversation:

> it is concerned with who you are and why you speak as you do. As a culture (of argument) the conversation that it creates is at once its method and its point; its function is to provide a rhetorical coherence to public life by compelling those

> who disagree about one thing to express their actual or pretended agreement about everything else.[74]

In a particularly forthright rejection of law as policy, Weinreb argues that law, and above all private law, is a form of self-understanding which involves a search for immanent form and unifying structure.[75] Expounding his ideas of 'legal formalism' with reference to Aristotelian and Kantian ideas of corrective justice, Weinreb treats law as a set of concepts, a distinctive institutional setting and a characteristic mode of reasoning. Law is more than the authoritative form given to conclusions reached by non-legal thinking. Like love and friendship, law exists for itself, not as a means to something else, and does not shine in the borrowed light of extrinsic ends. He strongly criticizes those who think of law as an instrument for serving collective purposes. When such an 'external' approach is adopted, goals are assigned to law rather than derived from it and the definitions applied then tend to be either over- or underinclusive of law's juristic concerns. Such a starting point can all too easily lead to modifying or even abolishing those rules or even branches of law which do not perform well according to the imposed criteria, as bad, functionalist approaches require given branches of law to pursue and trade off competing goals and therefore risk turning them into congeries of incoherent purposes.

None of these authors denies that law may on occasion need to use the best scientific evidence available. They merely insist on the important proviso that this must be done on law's own terms. Private law, for Weinreb, regards other disciplines from its own perspective and assimilates them to its own immanently rational purpose. Scientific reasoning, on the other hand, is unable to make those relevant distinctions, including that between public and private law, which are so crucial to law's unfolding as it seeks to 'impress reality with the stamp of its regulatory form'.[76]

In line with these arguments, the *incompatible discourses* approach emphasizes the difficulties which can arise in any attempt to put together the reasons of incommensurable discourses. (In addition it offers the advantage of explaining the social developments which provide the changing background to the way law reproduces its autonomy.) Teubner, for example, has argued repeatedly that when scientific concepts are transformed into legal considerations they are made to reappear as 'legal values, legal principles, norms, purposes, interests and ambits for decision making':

> Calculations of costs and calculations of power, policy arguments and scientific constructs, they are all treated by the law in the same way. They all become strange hybrids which are now, however, the solemn responsibility of the legal discourse. Legal discourse does not all of a sudden act in an authentic manner

morally, ethically, scientifically, economically, or politically when it uses non legal arguments.

As in the case of conflict of laws, foreign concepts are radically reconstructed.[77]

Teubner's warnings are particularly applicable to some recent uses of psychological evidence in American criminal cases,[78] but they also have wider application. Consider the attempt in *Daubert* to have judges check what – for law's purposes – should be counted as science. Should this decision be seen as an advance or a retreat from *Frye*'s attempt to delegate this question to the 'general acceptance' of scientists themselves? What justifies the Supreme Court giving such importance to Popper's criteria of falsifiability from amongst the rival theories of the philosophy of science? *Daubert* does not face up to the reasons why law proves so hospitable to junk social science.[79] Nor can it do anything to stop the further interpretation and evolution of this decision from reflecting legal niceties rather than scientific reasoning.[80] On the other hand, the third approach seems to go, if anything, too far in drawing a sharp distinction between legal and non-legal communications. And it remains to be demonstrated whether autopoiesis theory can find a way of reconfiguring law so as to allow it to act as a provocation to 'justice between discourses' despite the incompatibility between it and other discourses which the approach itself presupposes.

Inconclusions

Looking for a way to 'fix', or otherwise respond to, difficulties in the relationship of law and science makes us participants in the process of formulating and reformulating the meaning and significance of their boundaries. It may well be that the 'problem' of their disagreement can only be handled in different practical contexts rather than settled in the abstract.[81] But, even if there may be something quixotic about the theoretical search for 'a set of legal principles for using science's truth in the interests of justice',[82] the three approaches discussed in this chapter may still offer interesting insights into the possible meanings of a just measure of science and the place in law of lay understanding and technological rationality.

Each approach canvasses those solutions which best meet its diagnosis of the problem. Is the question how collaboration between law and science should best be organized in the course of well adjusted legal proceedings? Is the issue how and when periods of open disagreement can serve healthy functions for the body politic? Or does the challenge have to do with the clashing of discourses? The first approach helps us in thinking about what uses of science are compatible with the integrity of the trial process, the second in deciding what considerations are relevant to assessing whether legal oversight is helping to improve the standards of science (and vice versa); the third stimulates us to reflect on the overall role of law and legal regulation in relation to other self-referential discourses in the complex interchanges of modern society.

For the first approach the way to tackle difficulties created by the adversarial process - and by legal procedure in general - is to change the rules about expert testimony, or move towards court-appointed experts, bifurcated trials, special masters or blue ribbon (well-informed) juries. Beyond this lies the elimination of jury trials for all or certain cases, the creation of science courts and the reduction of litigation by encouraging alternatives to adjudication or shifting to administrative regulation. But those who propose more limited reforms fear that these will be easily nullified by lawyers' resistance in or out of court, while more radical changes can involve even more politically unpalatable reductions in the role of legal institutions. The second approach, by contrast, is ready to embrace much which the first finds problematic. Whether and when a plaintiff in a tort claim should get compensation is a question which goes beyond guaranteeing experts the best opportunities to present their opinions. Disagreement between law and science, including battles of experts through the courts, can serve to reveal value biases and social assumptions and play a vital role in forming an educated public. The second approach argues that the solutions proposed by the first approach will have as their main result merely the production of a new 'matrix of contingencies': increasing the relative power of the judge in relation to the jury, helping some litigants compared to others, favouring or penalizing different interests or forms of professional expertise. This approach asks that we monitor the effectiveness of legal processes and where necessary redesign them in terms of the public policy purposes we wish them to serve. But this approach has some trouble in moving from description to prescription and explanation to policy making. It could be argued that here, too, any proposals made will only have the effect of changing the 'matrix of contingencies' in the power relationships of those involved in particular controversies. There is a real risk of infinite regress if we apply to the approach itself the lessons taken from the sociology of science concerning the way truth claims and recommendations are constructed and applied. How do such sociologists themselves construct their claims and persuade us of the appropriateness of their policy recommendations?

The third approach, on the other hand, takes these and other paradoxes of self-reference as the key to how far discourses can be made responsive to their social environment. But, as some different emphases between Luhmann and Teubner indicate, this approach has to decide how far it can go in recommending interventions to deal with the 'fall-out' from discursive clashes. Is it really the case that 'discursive collisions can only be decided decentrally, only within each discourse and in each case afresh and differently'?[83] Can and should law and science be treated as epistemologically equal discourses? Is it possible to arrive at a metatheory capable of guiding competing discourse?[84]

The advantage of drawing on more than one of these approaches is that it can also allow us to make critical progress in relation to some of the most interesting current work on the relationship between legal proceedings and scientific expertise. It has been rightly noted, for example, that evidence scholars do not always face up to the choice between asking lay decision makers to defer to experts or instead to be educated by them.[85] Our review would suggest that this dilemma persists also because education is required even to know when to defer. And all the approaches we have considered have relevant points to make about the deeper issue whether to seek to merge law and science or to acknowledge their need to be separated in some form of division of labour.

For those who wish to make law and science somehow compatible, the admissibility of scientific evidence in conditions of uncertainty is said to turn as much on the question of its 'necessity' as it is of its trustworthiness.[86] Counterintuitively it has been suggested that expert opinion should be particularly admissible to educate the court when research is still at an early and inconclusive stage.[87] But, as we have seen, this search for commensurability takes too much for granted. It is doubtful that this or any other solution could ever mean that 'law and science be integrated into a seamless harmony'.[88] It may be queried whether it is the case that 'judges confront the same possibilities of error as scientists'[89] and lawyers would certainly try to double-guess when it suits them to resort to such alleged scientific evidence.

Take, finally, the vexed issue of syndrome evidence. The first of the approaches considered here helps explain why law's concern with formal criteria of science made it easy for psychologists and psychiatrists to bring opinion on these matters before the court. The second approach directs our attention to the politics of interests and professions which shape these developments both in and out of the courtroom – and also the potential educational value of law helping to promote debate concerning syndrome evidence. The third approach offers a provocative analysis of why law keeps producing such hybrid concepts. In his recent thorough account of the remarkable fortunes of battered wife syndrome, Downs argues strongly that courts must now abandon 'the woozle of learned helplessness' and learn to work with the much sounder alternative 'killing for survival' theory.[90] Yet his own data show why the law finds it easier to accept explanations which deny or reduce responsibility, and he shows how activists deliberately used one description of battered women in their political campaigning but a quite different one at court. Differences between the legal and political codes may undo this attempt to recast the courts as havens of political responsibility. If lawyers are unwilling to risk their clients' interests by abandoning the apparent scienticity of syndrome evidence, could they still be behaving properly?

Notes

1 D. Nelken, 'The Truth about Law's Truth', in A. Febbrajo and D. Nelken (eds), *The European Yearbook for the Sociology of Law* (Milan, 1993), pp.87–163; also D. Nelken, 'The Loneliness of Law's Meta-Theory', in R. de Lange and K. Raes (eds), *Plural Legalities: Critical Legal Studies in Europe* (The Hague, 1991), p.172; D. Nelken, 'Are Disputes Between Law and Science Resolvable?', in J.F. Nijbour, C.R. Callen and N. Kwak (eds), *Forensic Expertise and the Law of Evidence* (Amsterdam, 1993).

2 S.R. Gross, 'Expert Evidence' (1991) *Wisconsin Law Review* 1113; J. Sanders, 'From Science to Evidence: The Testimony on Causation in the Bendectin Cases' (1993) 46 *Stanford Law Review* 79.

3 L. Friedman, *Total Justice* (Boston, 1985).

4 P.W. Huber, *Galileo's Revenge: Junk Science in the Courtroom* (New York, 1991); see also P.W. Huber, 'Junk Science in the Courtroom' (1992) 26 *Valparaiso Law Review* 723.

5 A.M. Dershowitz, *The Abuse Excuse* (Boston, 1994); G.R. Fletcher, *With Justice for Some* (Reading, Mass., 1995); D.A. Downs, *More than Victims: Battered Women, the Syndrome Society and the Law* (Chicago, 1996).

6 *Daubert* v. *Merrell Dow Pharmaceuticals Inc* 509 US 579 (1993).

7 P. Roberts, 'The Admissibility of Expert Evidence: Lessons from America' (1993) 4 *Expert Evidence* 3.

8 D.E. Bernstein, 'Junk science in the United States and the Commonwealth' (1996) 21 *Yale Journal of International Law* 123.

9 At the end of 1997 the Italian press highlighted the ruling by a magistrate in Lecce obliging the local health authorities to pay for a child to have the benefits of a largely untested treatment for cancer offered by Professor Di Bella of Modena, even though the scientific community through the relevant governmental commission had approved the use of the relevant drugs for the cure of an entirely different kind of disease. The medical profession then threatened to take legal proceedings against doctors prescribing Di Bella's unapproved treatment.

10 This last example in particular is based on a misreading of the case concerned; in general Huber, as well as others in the anti-mass torts lobby, have been accused of selective use of evidence; see, for example, K. Chesebro, 'Galileo's Retort: Peter Huber's Junk Scholarship' (1993) 42 *American University Law Review* 1637, and M. Rustad, T. Koenig *et al.*, 'The Supreme Court and Junk Social Science: Selective Distortion in Amicus Briefs' (1993) 72 *North Carolina Law Review* 91.

11 Angell, *Science on Trial* (New York, 1995); Sanders, 'From Science to Evidence'.

12 The *Frye* decision (293 F 1013 DC Cir 1923) finally overruled by *Daubert* had determined that the threshold for admissibility of expertise should be based on the criterion of scientific consensus. *Frye* involved an attempt by defence counsel to introduce polygraph evidence. But strong arguments have also been made criticizing the

way the prosecution has succeeded too often in introducing suspect science, for example 'bite mark evidence': see especially P. Giannelli, 'Junk Science: The Criminal Cases' (1993) 84 *Journal of Criminal Law and Criminology* 105.

13 Huber, *Galileo*, pp.225ff.

14 Downs, *More than Victims*.

15 'Note: feasibility and admissibility of Mob Mentality Defenses' (1993) 108 *Harvard Law Review* 1111.

16 See M. Minow, M. Ryan and A. Sarat (eds), *Narrative Violence and the Law: Essays of Robert Cover* (Ann Arbor, 1995).

17 S. Jasanoff, *Science at the Bar: Law, Science and Technology in America* (Cambridge, Mass., 1995), p.205; see also B. de Sousa Santos, *Toward a New Common Sense: Law, Science and Politics in the Paradigmatic Transition* (London, 1995).

18 The extensive US law review material on which I draw here was gathered when I taught as visiting Professor of Law at the University of California in Berkeley in 1996. I would like to thank both Professor Malcolm Feeley and the librarians of the Cardozo Library for their invaluable help.

19 D. Faigman, 'To Have and Have Not: Assessing the Value of Social Science to Law as Science and Policy' (1989) 38 *Emory Law Journal* 1005.

20 See, for example, 'Fatal Defence: Analysis of Battered Woman's Syndrome Expert Testimony for Gay Men and Lesbians Who Kill Abusive Partners' (1993) 58 *Brooklyn Law Review* 1379.

21 For example, T. Ward, in 'Law, Common Sense and the Authority of Science' (1997) 6 *Social and Legal Studies* 343, suggests that the 'last issue' rule of evidence law could be seen as part of law's effort to contain the inroads of triumphalist 19th-century science.

22 S. Shapin, 'Here and Everywhere: The Sociology of Scientific Knowledge' (1995) *Annual Review of Sociology* 289.

23 See, for example, Jasanoff, *Science at the Bar*.

24 See, for example, W.E. Wagner, 'The Science Charade in Toxic Risk Regulation' (1995) *Columbia Law Review*, 1613.

25 See, for example, J. Donzelot, *The Policing of Families* (London, 1979); R. Smith, *Trial by Medicine* (Edinburgh, 1981); Ward, 'Law, Common Sense and the Authority of Science'.

26 R. Smith and B. Wynne, *Expert Evidence: Interpreting Science in the Law* (London, 1989); S. Fuchs and S. Ward, 'What is Deconstruction and where and when does it take place? Making Facts in Science, Building Cases in Law' (1994) 59 *American Sociological Review* 481–500.

27 For N. Luhmann, see his 'The Unity of the Legal System' and 'Closure and Openness: On Reality in the World of Law', both in G. Teubner (ed.), *Autopoietic Law: A New Approach to Law and Society* (Berlin, 1988), pp.12–36, 335–48. For G. Teubner, see his 'How the Law Thinks: Toward a constructivist epistemology of law' (1989) 23 *Law and Society Review* 727–57; *Law as an Autopoietic System* (Oxford, 1993) and 'Altera Pars Audiatur: Law in the collision of Discourses', in R. Rawlings (ed.), *Law, Society and Economy* (Oxford, 1997).

28 Teubner, 'Altera Pars Audiatur'.

29 Teubner, 'How the Law Thinks', 742–6.

30 Ibid., 747; this process starts with the very notions of science or expertise used by law.

31 Ibid., 745.

32 The contrast so sharply marked here is blurred in the writings of some of those adopting the second or third approaches. Jasanoff uses social constructionism also so as to show how law and science 'constitute' truth and justice, whilst Teubner also talks in terms of

(radical) social constructivism. My summary tries to capture the sense of Teubner's claim to have gone beyond social constructionism.

33 Jasanoff, *Science at the Bar*, p.xiv.

34 D. Nelken, 'Changing Paradigms in the Sociology of Law', in G. Teubner (ed.), *Autopoietic Law*, pp.191–217.

35 'Luhmann, Closure and Openness'; Teubner, How the Law Thinks', 749, citing D. Nelken, 'Beyond the Study of Law and Society' (1986) *American Bar Foundation Journal* 323.

36 But see C. Sunstein, 'Incommensurability and Valuation in Law' (1994) 92 *Michigan Law Review* 779.

37 Teubner, *Law as an Autopoietic System*.

38 J.F. Lyotard, *The Differend: Phrases in Dispute* (Manchester, 1988).

39 There are of course important disagreements among postmodernist writers about how far to emphasize or pursue the differentiation or the fragmentation of discourses. For one recent effort to reconstruct an 'ethics of alterality' for law, see C. Douzinas and R. Warrington, *Justice Miscarried* (Hemel Hempstead, 1994).

40 Teubner, 'How the Law Thinks', 737.

41 Teubner, 'Altera Pars Audiatur'.

42 As M. King and F. Kaganas argue in H. Reece (ed.), *Law and Science* (Oxford, 1998), by certifying the existence of social risks law helps create them.

43 See Nelken, 'The Truth about Law's Truth'.

44 D. Nelken, 'Can there be a sociology of legal meaning?', in D. Nelken (ed.), *Law as Communication* (Aldershot, 1996), 107.

45 See Nelken, 'Loneliness'.

46 Chesebro, 'Galileo's Retort', at 1652 (note 74).

47 T.M. Massaro, 'Experts, Psychology, Credibility and Rape' (1985) 69 *Minnesota Law Review* 359; S. Stefan, 'The Protection Racket: Rape Trauma Syndrome Psychiatric Labeling and Law' (1994) 88 *Northwestern University Law Review* 1271.

48 J.D. Jackson, 'Questions of Fact and Questions of Law', in W. Twining (ed.), *Facts in Law* (Weisbaden, 1984), p.85.

49 Gross, 'Expert Evidence'.

50 Sanders, 'From Science to Evidence'.

51 M.S. Jacobs, 'Testing the Assumptions Underlying the Debate about Scientific Evidence: A Closer Look at Juror "Incompetence" and Scientific "Objectivity"' (1993) 25 *Connecticut Law Review* 1083; N. Vidmar, 'Are Juries Competent to Decide Liability in Tort Cases Involving Scientific/Medical Issues? Some Data from Medical Malpractice' (1994) 43 *Emory Law Journal* 855.

52 L.J. Cohen, *The Probable and the Provable* (Oxford, 1977); L.J. Cohen, 'Freedom of Proof', in Twining, *Facts in Law*, p.1. What Twining calls the 'optimistic rationalism' of modern evidence scholarship aims to maximize what it considers the already fairly high probability of accurate trial determinations. But see M.L. Seigel, 'A Pragmatic Critique of Modern Evidence Scholarship' (1994) 89 *Northwestern University Law Review* 995; and E. Scallen, 'Classical Rhetoric, Practical Reasoning and the Law of Evidence' (1995) 44 *American University Law Review* 1717.

53 The recent decision in *Regina* v. *Adams no. 2* (*The Times*, 3 November 1997) held that it was acceptable to present DNA evidence based on statistical data but that reliance on 'the Bayes theorem in relation to non-scientific evidence was a recipe for confusion, misunderstanding and misjudgement'.

54 L. Tribe, 'Trial by Mathematics: Precision and Ritual in the Legal Process' (1971) 84 *Harvard Law Review* 1329.

55 Ibid., 1370.
56 Ibid., 1391; see also P.A. Winn, 'Legal Ritual' (1991) 2 *Law and Critique* 207, who notes how legal rituals, like other rituals, need to have vague, ambiguous and contradictory features.
57 D.M. Risinger, M.P. Denbeaux and M. Saks, 'Exorcism of Ignorance as a Proxy for Rational Knowledge: The Lessons of Handwriting Identification "Expertise"' (1989) 137 *University of Pennsylvania Law Review* 731.
58 Tribe, 'Trial by Mathematics'. His argument is that here too the risk is that we will give more attention to that which we can model better.
59 See N.K. Komesar, *Imperfect Alternatives* (Chicago, 1994); Jasanoff, *Science at the Bar*.
60 This does not presuppose that either or both law and science operate with a correspondence theory of truth. Fuchs and Ward, in 'What is Deconstruction?', indeed offer an interesting social constructionist account of the similar ways each sustains its 'truth-claims'.
61 But, in contrast to historical accounts of the (somewhat different) drives to rationalization of 'the science of law' in the European continental and common law systems, there are those who claim that law's methodology seems to have more in common with those of failed than with those of successful sciences; see P. Schlag, 'Commentary: Law and Phrenology' (1997) 110 *Harvard Law Review* 877.
62 *Daubert* 173 S. Ct at 2798.
63 M. Dan-Cohen, 'Decision Rules and Conduct Rules: On Acoustic Separation in Criminal Law' (1984) 97 *Harvard Law Review* 625.
64 K. Greenawalt, *Law and Objectivity* (Oxford, 1992), pp.93–120.
65 C. Jones, *Expert Witnesses* (Oxford, 1994); Smith and Wynne, *Expert Evidence*.
66 Jones, *Expert Witnesses*, p.81.
67 *Davies* v. *Eli Lily and Co.* [1987] 1 WLR 128 at 131–2.
68 Greenawalt, *Law and Objectivity*.
69 E. Rubin, 'Law and the Methodology of Law' (1997) *Wisconsin Law Review* 521.
70 Tribe, 'Trial by Mathematics'.
71 Greenawalt, *Law and Objectivity*, 193.
72 Ibid., 202.
73 Dershowitz, *The Abuse Excuse*.
74 J.B. White, *When Words Lose their Meaning* (Chicago, 1984), p.268.
75 E.J. Weinreb, *The Idea of Private Law* (Cambridge, Mass., 1995).
76 Ibid., pp.214–15.
77 Teubner, 'Altera Pars Audiatur', 166ff.
78 Downs, *More than Victims*.
79 J.T. Richardson, G. Ginsburg, S. Gatowski and S. Dobbin, 'The Problems of Applying *Daubert* to Psychological Syndrome Evidence' (1995) 17 *Judicature* 10.
80 'Note: Developments in the Law: Confronting the New Challenges of Scientific Evidence' (1995) 108 *Harvard Law Review* 1482; J. Sanders, 'Scientific Validity, Admissibility and Mass Torts after *Daubert*' (1994) 78 *Minnesota Law Review* 1387; A. Tamarelli, '*Daubert* v. *Merrell Dow Pharmaceuticals*: The questionable wisdom of abandoning the peer review standard for admitting expert testimony' (1994) 47 *Vanderbilt Law Review* 1175; and in general the special issues (1994) 15 *Cardozo Law Review* and (1994) 43 (3) *Emory Law Journal*.
81 Smith and Wynne, *Expert Evidence*; S. Fish, *Doing What Comes Naturally* (Oxford, 1989); S. Fish, 'The Law Wishes to Have a Formal Existence', in A. Sarat and T. Kearns (eds), *The Fate of Law* (Ann Arbor, 1991), p.159.
82 M.G. Farrell, '*Daubert* v. *Merrell Dow*: Epistemology and Legal Process' (1994) 15

Cardozo Law Review 2183 at 2217.

83 Teubner, 'Altera Pars Audiatur', 161.

84 Nelken, 'The Truth about Law's Truth'.

85 R.J. Allen and J.S. Miller, 'The Common Law Theory of Experts: Deference or Education?' (1993) 87 *Northwestern University Law Review* 1131.

86 D. Faigman, 'Mapping the Labyrinth of Scientific Evidence' (1995) 46 *Hastings Law Journal*, 555; H.L. Feldman, 'Science and Uncertainty in Mass Exposure Litigation' (1995) 74 *Texas Law Review* 1.

87 Faigman, 'Mapping the Labyrinth'.

88 Ibid., 566.

89 Ibid., 568.

90 Downs, *More than Victims*.

3 Codes of Practice: Communicating between Science and Law

Christine Willmore

Introduction

The current debate about expert evidence in Britain has stressed case-specific solutions to the problems of law and science, with an emphasis upon procedural tools, in terms of pretrial processes, court-appointed experts or specialist courts. Where the debate has moved beyond the case-specific, it has been a debate about whether there should be a Forensic Science Advisory Council or similar body.[1] This chapter argues that there is a third debate, which is not dependent upon one's views on the first two. This third debate explores the extent to which wider use of codes of practice could facilitate the evolution of law–expertise relationships,[2] whether through enhancing the case-specific approach or through external processes. The code of practice approach is not in conflict with a continued emphasis upon case-specific determination; rather it offers a tool which has shown its utility in managing uncertainties which may be of wider use.

Lord Woolf's civil justice review[3] expressed the paradox in which the legal system finds itself. It is at once dependent upon expertise to a growing extent and at the same time pressurized by it. Expertise can assist a court in processing the complexity of the external world. For example, faced with uncertainty about the identity of an offender, DNA evidence may offer some reductions in that uncertainty. But at the same time it threatens to undermine the legal process by importing fresh complexities and uncertainties: is this a reliable technique? How reliable? How should disputes between experts be evaluated? Unless properly managed, the expert evidence can produce a net increase rather than reduction in complexity.

Luhmann[4] argues that successful systems are those which simplify external complexities to a level which retains a validity and utility to the external world, but which is also useable for the purposes of the system. A failure to produce sufficient simplicity leaves the system wallowing in the chaos of external complexity. Reductionism leads to a system which fails to reflect externalities with sufficient sensitivity, becomes isolated from the rest of the social complexity around it, loses credibility and is in danger of marginalization. Within the system, reductionism will 'confuse legal thinking and produce more uncertainty'.[5]

Unless one concludes that the only way out of an escalating cycle of complexity is a withdrawal of law from certain areas, new methods are needed to balance the benefits of expertise in reducing complexity against the increased complexity which may result from importing the expertise.

The case-specific approach is so central to common law systems that it will remain the key tool by which the common law system interprets the external world. This makes it all the more important to explore the weaknesses of the approach and seek solutions to those weaknesses. This chapter examines some of these weaknesses and then explores the extent to which codes of practice could tackle some of these limitations. A code of practice for this purpose must be distinguished from the growing body of privately constructed codes.[6] Privately constructed, albeit publicly available. Even where external bodies such as NAMAS[7] provide accreditation, such manuals are a product of internal debate within a particular expert discourse. They are not socially validated by a wider debate involving a range of societal values. The chapter argues that codes produced after public debate provide an opportunity to agree complexity rules for courts, of a kind which has operated successfully in some fields, such as confession and identification evidence. This can produce a socially validated approach which limits the range of options it is necessary to consider in a particular case.

The Particular Difficulties of Expert Evidence

The legal system constructs a set of processes valid only for its own system which seek to handle the multiple complexities of the external environment. It does not exclude the external environment but does seek to react and interact with it through a process which remains essentially a tool of the legal system.

Legal systems do not admit all possible evidence. Whether using admissibility or relevance tests, the common law seeks to delimit the evidence presented to a court. In essence this is about structuring social complexity into a form the courts can manage. A long list of justifications are given for such limitations, including pragmatism in terms such as cost or trial length; complexity, as in collateral issue rules; risks of prejudice, as in the similar fact rules; policy criteria such as regulation of the police or presumptions in favour of the defence. These are perfectly standard techniques. However the common law seems to experience particular difficulty when faced with expert evidence. Why?

In general legal systems are faced with imposing organization upon the 'white noise' of social complexity. However, when legal systems seek to tackle areas labelled as expert discourses, in particular science expertise, the legal system is faced with a system which is itself a more or less powerful social system which has its own internal rationality rules for handling the complexity of science. The law in that context is not faced with creating a structure out of the chaos of white noise, but rather interacting with an alternative set of rationality rules. This can produce mutual failures of understanding or complex clashes between powerful epistemologies.

Later, this chapter considers the particular problems of handling this process within the case-specific approach, but two preliminary issues need consideration which affect the legal–expert interface at all levels, not just in the case-specific context: the difficulty legal systems face in tackling uncertainty and the problems of pursuing 'truth'. Legal systems need to produce decisions. Unlike academic research, it is not possible for a court to come to no firm conclusion. Uncertainties must therefore be resolved. Where legal systems cannot resolve uncertainties in their own terms, there seems to be a particular attraction in looking to experts to resolve those uncertainties. Such an approach both misunderstands the nature of expert systems and fails to distinguish between causes of uncertainty.

Some uncertainty arises because the answer is unknowable. No amount of research will tell a court with certainty how a coin, as yet untossed, will fall on a future occasion. It is unknowable. A practical example of this is the question of how many reefers a given quantity of cannabis will produce. The reefers have not yet been rolled, so the answer is unknowable. *Shonubi*[8] exemplifies this problem. For policy reasons, US legislation on drug trafficking required sentencing to extend beyond the quantity of drugs seized in relation to the particular charge. The judge also had to calculate the total haul of drugs carried in previous journeys by Shonubi. That is a valid policy goal, but one which introduces additional complexity and scope for dispute: how can a court assess the quantity of drugs previously carried, as by definition no seizures occurred on those occasions? Even if the court knows how many previous trips occurred, what assumptions should the court make about the quantities carried on previous occasions? A rough justice solution can be reached on an impressionistic basis. But the minute the legal system looks for an accurate answer, it introduces impossible levels of complexity.[9]

The problem here is not with gaps in evidential techniques but with the question being asked. At least in *Shonubi* the legal system knows the question it wants to ask. The problems for expert evidence are greater when the legal system is not even clear what it wants to achieve, as in the definition of dogs which can be destroyed under the Dangerous Dogs Act 1991.[10] In common parlance, and newspaper headlines, everyone had a general idea of what was a 'pit bull terrier', but it lacks the precision required by the legal system when distressed owners sought to challenge destruction orders on the basis that their dog was not technically a 'pit bull terrier'.[11] Unsuccessful appeal was made to veterinary or biological communities for a definition. Here the *Shonubi* problem of asking an unanswerable question[12] is compounded by the legislation not being clear about its aims. Was the aim to tackle a particular breed, or was the choice of name designed to help delimit types of dog the public consider dangerous? What about mongrels? The problems in both *Shonubi* and the Dangerous Dogs Act derive from failures to phrase the initial question in terms which are answerable at reasonable cost (or indeed at all). No subsequent evidential tool can resolve that problem of substantive law.[13]

The uncertain, as opposed to the unknowable, presents a different problem. Most human conduct occurs in uncertainty: indeed choice theorists would argue it is essential for markets to work. However legal systems demonstrate discomfort with uncertainty. Wells argued that, if two people were ever identified as having the same fingerprints, the effects upon the legal system would be dramatic.[14] Yet such an occurrence would not surprise experts. Fear of this sort of reaction can lead to the suppression of uncertainty.[15] Forensic scientists are often asked to match glass found on the suspect's clothes with glass found at the scene of a crime. All sorts of uncertainties arise in that process, such as the selection of which samples to test or the interpretation of whether the refractive indices of the glass provide a match within the limits of experimental uncertainty.[16] The scientist assesses the likelihood of a coincidental match by comparing the glass to the frequency with which glass of a similar kind has been present in previous FSS samples, which may not reflect local variables. None of these uncertainties features in their reports. The expert communities, both prosecution and defence, understand these uncertainties but lack a means of communicating them to juries without risking misunderstanding, with the result that such limitations can be suppressed. False certainty is perceived by the expert witnesses as better than a false uncertainty. Lacking a way of communicating the socially constructed nature of science, they opt for silence. The nub of the problem is that the legal system has so few special tools to evaluate uncertainty within other disciplines.

However in some parts of the legal process tools have been developed to deal with unanswerables: is the spouse missing for more than seven years dead or alive? Is the person therefore a widow who can remarry? Presumptions have been constructed to answer this,[17] in recognition that the question is probably unanswerable or at the very least the cost of seeking to answer it would be prohibitive. Such presumptions are largely arbitrary. In the absence of evidence as to what really happened, the law needs *an* answer, any answer, as long as it is consistent and seen as neutrally applied to particular facts. In the case of the presumption of death, after a relatively limited amount of evidence the court will apply the presumption. Yet, where science is involved, there is a pressure to render matters certain by finding an answer: rather than accepting that the question is unanswerable or that the answer be imposed artificially.[18] Questions of efficiency and the need for finality will ultimately impinge, but the line seems to be drawn at a different point for expert as opposed to lay inquiry. The fourth section of this chapter considers the future role of presumptions and codes of practice in reducing uncertainty.

An important task for any system of fact finding is to have tools which help the fact finder determine that which can be rendered certain within the limits of resources available and that which cannot, and to find a way to handle the inherent and inevitable uncertainty of the world.[19] Otherwise the legal system increases complexity with no net gain. Whereas common law and statutory presumptions have served to tackle complexity in relation to lay evidence, they have not been used in the same way in expert contexts. The statutory presumption is closely linked to the concept of the code of practice, offering a tool for managing uncertainty, unknowability or complexity.

This links to the second particular difficulty legal systems face in tackling expert systems: the fallacy of pursuing truth. This is the common belief that, whilst law does not have the tools to produce an answer from the complexity of the world, there is another expert system which can be harnessed to produce truth. Sometimes there will be an answer, but often the expert discipline will produce a contingent and uncertain answer, phrased in terms of probabilities or reflecting the uncertain state of understanding in other disciplines. If law starts with a belief that other epistemologies offer certainties, it can easily fall into the trap of pursuing questions within the alternative discipline with increasing desperation, believing there must be *an* answer, if only they could find the right questions to ask, or the right codes of communication to understand the answers. This sort of approach reflects three fallacies: (a) that there is a truth in the expert discourse waiting to be revealed, (b) that it will be revealed to the court if only the right communication tool can be found, and (c) that this information will be relevant to the question the court wishes to answer.

These problems stem from a lack of mutual understanding between expert disciplines and go to the root of social understanding of expertise. For the purposes of this chapter, they are 'given' parameters within which the review of the legal framework must operate.

The Case-specific Management of External Complexity

Choice theories would suggest that the optimum way for the distinguishing features of a science law system to emerge would be as a product of the thousands of individual decisions reached as to admissibility and weight in individual cases. How, then, has the common law set about managing the interaction with external complexities which are the subject matter of expert discourses? One option is for the law system to adopt the rationality rules of the other societal system and relabel them as its own. Another is for the law to create its own rationality rules for handling it. A third is to refuse to accept this facet of the external world. All three options can be seen in the way common law systems interact with expert systems, but all present problems. Exclusion reduces the ability of courts to reflect the world in which they operate. Absorbing and relabelling presents the risk of failing to examine whether its objectives are the same as the objectives of the system from which it is taking data and rationality. A failure to filter and rerationalize complex externalities weakens the system itself and effectively imports the external confusion into the internal system. To some extent this reflects what we are seeing in the difficulties the courts have in dealing with expert evidence. A brief review of the current common law principles for case-specific rerationalization indicates their limited efforts to filter and restructure.

Because of the way the common law rules of evidence operate it is necessary to distinguish between whether evidence is deemed appropriate to be placed before a tribunal of fact and the use made of evidence at trial. The first stage could offer an opportunity for rerationalization of expert evidence to fit the purposes of the legal system. In practice it operates only as a rudimentary gatekeeping, with such rerationalization as may exist occurring at the second stage. Luhmann's[20] approach would suggest that a system is stronger if it carries out its own rerationalizing of science at the point of entry in terms of how it is presented within the system rather than at the later stage of what the tribunal of fact makes of it. The legal system, instead, has adopted an open door policy with minimalist admissibility criteria which allow wide areas of material to be placed before the tribunal of fact, leaving them to rerationalize in a fact-specific context.

Before a technique is used by a tribunal of fact, preliminary questions need to be asked: are there social policy reasons why this technique should be accepted for the purposes of the criminal/civil trial? Even if the technique produces reliable evidence, there may be other social policy reasons for wishing to exclude it from trial.[21] Even if it passes the social policy tests, a second question arises: will the technique, in general, assist the fact finder? Will it help the fact finder reduce complexity and reach a decision, or will it add to the complexity? This is not to say that one only wants evidence which assists in case closing. Evidence which increases uncertainty can be equally important. However, in a system of bounded rationality in which the court has to reach a decision within finite resources, rational choices have to be made about which forms of uncertainty are acceptable.

Such success as common law systems have achieved in rerationalizing any body of relevant knowledge as 'expertise' has come through a simplification of external expertise, relying upon the same threshold criteria for relevance/admissibility and procedural rules for all expert evidence.[22] Whilst it can be argued that this is a useful reduction in complexity, there is a risk of oversimplification, failing to recognize the true complexity of the external environment.

The English system exerts very little control by way of admissibility tests, looking broadly at helpfulness in terms of relevance and of the balance between prejudicial effect and probative value.[23] An expert is defined as someone who knows more than the jury[24] and can give evidence on matters 'beyond ordinary human experience',[25] providing they do not impinge upon the ultimate issue,[26] which remains the exclusive domain of the tribunal of fact. Instead the tendency in England has been for expertise to be managed by way of procedural rules which require notice, exchange of expert evidence and, particularly in civil proceedings, the use of agreed experts.[27] Such procedural solutions offer a process whereby the legal system can negotiate a relationship with the complex external world, without prescribing the nature of the accommodation to be reached.

Historically the United States had gone further in using the relevance/admissibility test to control the type of expert evidence which can be used. The *Frye* test[28] regulated admissibility of a technique by reference to whether it was 'sufficiently established to have gained general acceptance in the particular field in which it belongs'. Such an approach transferred control over the acceptability of evidence from the court to the expert community and led to the spawning of specialist societies, established for the purpose of defining a field of expertise.[29] *Frye* sought a more explicit statement of the relationship between the legal system and complex externalities. Thus, whereas the English and Australian courts admitted cusum analysis,[30] it would not have been admissible in the US courts.[31]

However the federal and some state courts have moved away from this approach.[32] The Supreme Court indicated that the new statement of the US threshold for admissibility, the *Daubert* test,[33] was designed to admit a wider range of expertise. Some criticize *Daubert* as setting the wrong test,[34] or for uncritically adopting the validation tools of expert disciplines, but more fundamentally it fails to provide any effective basis for law to handle external complexity: This is typical also of the UK approach: 'Daubert's fine disregard for a philosophically coherent decision rule on admissibility may exemplify the common law's genius for muddling through on the basis of experience not logic.'[35] Canadian courts[36] look at relevance and helpfulness, but explicitly consider the clarity with which the technique can be explained in court, the extent to which the data can be verified by the court (as opposed to verification within the discipline itself) and the availability of other experts to evaluate it. Perhaps of all the common law jurisdictions the Canadian cases have gone furthest in making explicit the need for a technique to be capable of being evaluated by the court, using traditional legal techniques.

In general, therefore, common law admissibility tests offer little assistance in defining the limits of acceptable external complexity. Nor do they assist in the management of such complexity as is admitted as evidence. Admissibility tests could be defined which offer a principled approach to the relationship between law and other disciplines, but they cannot determine the case-specific questions of how well the techniques have been applied in a particular case. Once expert evidence passes the admissibility threshold, the tribunal of fact is left alone to evaluate the evidence, with little external guidance. This leaves the tribunal of fact to evaluate the limits of the technique, the credibility of individual experts, the quality of the way the technique was used in the particular case and the effect of the evidence upon the case as a whole.[37] Some of these are rightly case-specific, but others, such as the limitations of the technique itself, should not depend on the way issues are explained in particular cases but merit more consistent answers.

By leaving the tribunal of fact to its own devices the legal system runs the risk of decisions which either adopt the rationality rules of the expert system without any reference to whether they are appropriate to the legal system context or which eschew reference to the expert system's values and analyses them from traditional legal classifications. Worse still, practical evidence suggests that neither happens.[38] Where efforts are made between experts to assess the relative merits of their evidence according to their professional systems, the fact that they must do this through the mediums of communication required by the legal systems results in communication which may not comply with either the standards of data sifting of their own professional systems or be entirely within the communication and interpretation systems of the law. Wynne[39] described this as a 'social negotiation of scientific consensus'. The result is not validated by either legal or expert systems, but represents an ad hoc consensus.[40]

For example, when dealing with sentencing for water pollution offences, the judge needs to form a view of the severity of the pollution. Environmental scientists offer this in terms of numerical levels of heavy metals, suspended solids and biochemical oxygen demand. Few magistrates or judges have sufficient knowledge of water science to be able to make much sense of those figures. If prosecution and defence can agree that the pollution is 'very serious' or 'minor' then the judge can rely upon their translation. But what if the parties disagree? How can the judge determine whether it is a serious or minor incident? A common tactic for judges in such a circumstance is to look for a mode of translation which makes sense to them: hence the common question, 'How many dead fish did it produce?' This does not fully reflect the complexity of the pollution level, but offers the judge a way of reducing the complexity of reality to a form which he can handle.

Such a negotiated solution may not present a problem to either law or expert systems. Anthropological, autopoietic and power discourse analyses all interpret the process of presenting expertise in legal systems as mutually reinforcing the power of both law and expert systems. The expert attains the added authority of legal validation, and legal judgments are cloaked in a technology concealing wider social issues. Some 'high status' expert systems may reinforce legal decisions – adopting the perceived infallibility of 'science'.[41] The processes of the legal system in response structure and limit the extent to which science can be tested by external values. The debate is retained within the data-processing techniques of law or expert discipline, limiting the opportunity to open up the debate to expose wider social issues or permit participation by other discourses.

Teubner[42] would argue that this mutual relationship is inevitable in that expertise is necessary to enable law to process external events, and indeed that by processing external events law adds meaning to those external events in an evolutionary dialogue. This interaction between law and expertise develops as a dynamic relationship, in which law tries to tackle an increasingly complex environment and turns to other systems within the external environment for assistance. Once law systems admit information and processes from other systems into the environment of law systems, law systems become more complex and therefore need further external interaction in order to manage the increased internal complexity. Thus, once experts are permitted to give evidence, a complex industry of expertise, specialist courts, expert assessors and witness rules emerges.

How can one open up this mutually reinforcing relationship to show the contingency of both systems? Law depends upon the ability of experts to translate the complexity of the external environment into material which the legal system can deem to be objective fact for its purposes, thereby giving someone else the responsibility for translating the complexity of the environment into a handleable simplicity. Is it possible to provide processes which show the essential subjectivity of both legal and expert systems and provide a vehicle for real communication between law, expert systems and wider societal complexity? Are there ways to reduce the additional complexity which expert evidence brings to a case, so as to give the maximum chance for expert evidence to reduce rather than increase the net complexity of a case? This must not remove defence rights to challenge these shared prior agreements in particular cases, but must offer a common language where one is wanted.[43]

The Role of Non-case-specific Debate

Awareness of these problems sometimes produces a cri de coeur for more understanding of science by lawyers (or vice versa). This can take the form of pleas for statutes to be phrased in such a way as to make sense to scientists. This can too easily become an excuse for letting scientific epistemologies dominate, perpetuating the idea of science as a higher truth and importing other rationalities into the legal system without further scrutiny. As such it can reduce rather than enhance mutual understanding.

Seminars offer a better opportunity to enhance understanding between participants, if they can avoid becoming a training session where one epistemology dominates.[44] But there is no systematic dissemination of such enhanced mutual understanding as may emerge. However much some lawyers and judges have worked with environmentalists through such organizations as UKELA[45] to develop shared understandings, judges who have not chosen to be party to such organizations will still ask, 'Yes, but how many dead fish were there?' A process is needed which takes the lessons from such events and converts them to a format which makes them readily applicable in case-specific contexts without further training: but without ceding control to one discipline or individual.

The problem codes seek to tackle is the mechanism by which those understandings can be applied in individual cases. Codes are not new. They have a record of success at the interface between law and other disciplines. The statutory presumption is a linked idea, performing a related function. Although the remainder of this chapter talks of codes of practice, it is important to recognize that in appropriate cases the introduction of a presumption through a similar process can offer similar benefits. Before turning to examples of codes assisting in the law–expert interface, the principles of such codes must be considered.

For these purposes, a code of practice is derived neither from law systems nor from other disciplines, but is produced through a legally or politically validated system involving a wider range of sources, bringing together the rationality rules of both disciplines, and is subjected to validation by wider or lay communities. Unlike the rationality rules of particular disciplines, the resulting guidelines or codes will have been produced for a particular purpose and will have been subjected to critical comment from wider societal groups, allowing for the interplay of factors from other frameworks within society. They are able to draw on a far wider range of complexities to produce a rationality specific to the law system. The mechanisms appropriate to this can also assist in ensuring that legislation is drafted in a form which does not reflect the dominance of any one epistemology but is sensitive to a range of issues and approaches. The essential features of such a code are listed below.

1 *Ownership* The code must be the product of a wide-ranging debate between experts, lawyers and lay participants which is recognized by groups as being a jointly owned product. Codes may say the same as existing private documents,[46] but gain additional validity through being a product of public debate, not a subject of it. This inclusionary production process maximizes the social validity of the process and minimizes risks of separatism.[47]

2 *Wider debate* The case-specific approach severely limits the inclusion of wider societal factors or values from social groups not part of the particular process. A case-specific approach can evaluate the particular technique used: it cannot explore the question of whether the techniques chosen are the best – or indeed what one might mean by 'best'. As Jasanoff has argued, the case-specific approach 'exposes the cognitive and social commitments of individual expert witnesses more predictably than it identifies structurally or institutionally conditioned contingencies in scientific knowledge'.[48] The scope for debate about the role of these external questions is severely limited by tests of relevance to the particular fact in issue. Those structural and institutional questions can be explored through codes.

The way scientific evidence is allowed into the legal forum affects, not just individual outcomes, but also wider practice. Thus, in the environmental field, the Environment Act 1990 deals with liability for contaminated land, defining contaminated land as land carrying a 'significant possibility of significant harm' to specified organisms.[49] The methodology for establishing whether there is a significant risk of significant harm (and what this means) could have been left at large for individual judges to determine. It would have resulted in a free-for-all, with different judges taking different views both as to the meaning of significant and as to the degree of causal link required. Much of this might have been defined as a question of fact and therefore not amenable to appellate review.

Remediation costs are potentially large enough to have significant effects on property prices. Inconsistent judicial approaches would affect the market and may undermine the extent to which the market internalizes the objectives of the legislation.[50] To reduce those uncertainties in advance, the draft guidance note spells out in considerable detail the proposed definitions of 'significant' and the proposed process for establishing a causal link: in both cases taking a view which will minimize the number of occasions upon which it will be possible to argue successfully that land is contaminated. It could have been left to scientists to determine working rules in private, but the issue of a draft guidance note[51] has enabled a debate to occur between scientists, lay environmental and industrial organizations and lawyers, providing a mechanism for a far wider policy debate as to the appropriate extent to liability for remediation of contaminated land. The final solution will be determined by central government, but will have been subject to an express debate. This will not undermine the case-specific approach of the common law. There will remain plenty of scope for evidence and debate about the sensitivity of particular receptors, the availability of a critical path and so on. But the basic process will be defined.

3 *Normative force* Ethical codes[52] offer guidance as to ethical behaviour, but lack binding force within the trial process. As such they are useful, but limited. The process through which codes of practice are derived can lead to a more binding status. To some extent the process of deriving shared ownership itself confers additional force upon the codes. However, to be anything more than an interested sideline and yet another tool to be used to add uncertainty at trial, the code needs a higher degree of normative force, such as that produced by exclusion of evidence obtained in breach of the code. Whilst in general the common law has been reluctant to accept the exclusion of potentially reliable evidence for external reasons, experience of the use of s.78 of the Police and Criminal Evidence Act 1984 to deal with evidence obtained in breach of the PACE Codes of Practice offers some guide to the possible success of such an approach. Unlike common law exclusionary rules, it is an exclusionary process in which the rules can be context-related.

4 *Optional juridification* Codes facilitate selective juridification, as we have seen with the PACE Codes of Practice, where appellate courts have treated some aspects of the application of codes as questions of law, but do not compel appellate intervention. In the longer term this offers the common law greater opportunity to regulate itself the science–law relationship. The

problem for the common law is how to break into the cycle in which the views of other disciplines are seen as questions of fact, not law, and therefore not amenable to appellate scrutiny.[53] The law–fact divide is fragile and contingent. Questions of fact can become questions of law, depending upon how the law itself is phrased.[54] At present most external expert evidence is seen as fact, not law, because of the very loosely drawn legal tests applicable to it. Because it is a question of fact, appellate courts have little opportunity to establish wider principles.

5 *Guidance as to weight as well as admissibility* Codes are not limited to defining admissibility criteria. They can also offer guidance as to weight, by setting benchmarks and by identifying mechanisms for measuring evidence. Consequently, they offer opportunities for more subtle approaches than the all-or-nothing admissibility test.

6 *Communication* Case-specific approaches unequivocally impose the communication processes of law upon what experts have to say. Lawyers instruct experts, telling them the questions they want answered, controlling the supply of information to and from the expert and structuring how the expert is to communicate with other parties and the finder of fact.[55] Experts complain about not being allowed to talk to experts representing other parties; of being asked questions which do not make sense in their discourses and of being unable to convey what they wish to say because of the strait-jacket of examination and cross-examination. Some of these communication issues can be resolved within the existing trial processes.[56] Others will remain.

Of the core of communication problems not solvable within the trial process, there is a potential to reduce some outside the trial process. Debates outside the courts, of the kind which precede adoption of a code, offer the opportunity to develop modes of communication controlled neither by law nor by science, but is a particular application which reflects both and seeks appropriate accommodations where their demands conflict or fail to reflect other values.

Codes do not fully reflect the subtleties of the understanding of any one discipline, rather they represent a way of getting along. Like pidgin English, they are not English, but work as a means of communication in a given context. Communication is inherently context-specific,[57] yet in case-specific approaches there is little opportunity to develop a shared context. Consequently opportunity for undetected misunderstanding proliferates. In long-standing relationships or frequent transactions those shared contexts can evolve. However the nature of the law–science relationship is such that, for many of the actors, particularly from the legal system, the encounter with particular expert discourse is too rare for common contexts to evolve. Codes offer a basis for developing shared contexts outside the particular relationship.

7 *Translation of principle to particular* There is a conflict between case-specific reasoning which is individuated and reasoning concerned with probabilities. In a case the legal system is concerned with the particular facts, the application of principles of law or science to the particular evidence. Science, however, talks in terms of probabilities and principles; it is not concerned with the specific or individual. Law asks: did this gun fire the bullet which caused this injury? Science essentially answers in terms of probabilities. Courts need that reduced to certainty. This goes beyond the general problem of uncertainty considered earlier, in that it relates to individuated solutions.

Things which are unknowable will continue to create problems. But in other cases, if removed from the case-specific application, legal and expert systems both operate at levels of principle. In so far as trials present a clash between expertise wanting to talk of principles and law talking of application, moving at least part of the debate to a forum where both can talk in terms of principle may remove one obstacle to science–law discourse.

Because codes operate at a level of generality, they can be used to translate such things into a form the courts can use. With a code, there is no need to ponder the reliability of the general data. The code has determined that the empirical data are sufficiently reliable to give rise to a requirement. The finder of fact needs to decide only whether the code has been complied with and, if not, the appropriate consequence of breach. Of course, this does not preclude someone from arguing that in the particular context there are factors which merit a departure from the normal outcomes of the code. How frequently this occurs will depend upon the breadth of acceptance the code has and its responsiveness to changing external complexities. Codes accept that individual facts may not fit the normative model, but enable a wider social debate to determine the outcome in normative cases. They then take policy decisions on how to handle non-standard instances, either by reference to wider social values such as the presumption of innocence or by specific analysis of the variant warranting departure from the code.

8 *Transparency* Unlike the decisions of an expert assessor, codes can be the product of a transparent debate between science, law and popular perceptions. Increasingly courts are being used as a platform upon which to challenge the assertions of science. As Feldman has argued,[58] courts offer a platform not easily available elsewhere upon which to articulate a particular scientific or environmental agenda. By raising concerns through legal

processes groups seek to gain publicity, increase transparency and harness the power of legal discourses in their campaigns. As an example, the current UK government view of the relationship between electromagnetic fields and childhood leukaemia has been produced through a private process of scientists advising government. Opponents, denied an opportunity to participate in framing the current official English view, have turned to the legal process in search of a platform from which to voice their concerns.[59] Given the recognized difficulties courts face in arbitrating between different claimed versions of expertise, the court is not necessarily the optimum forum for such issues. Nonetheless its use for such purposes will continue and probably expand. If courts are to handle this and possibly identify more precisely when they can and cannot assist, non-case-specific tools are needed, through which some of these arguments can be articulated outside the courtroom and fed into legal decision making. The code itself does not produce this transparency, but the institutional structures and processes required to produce codes offer opportunities to make the debate more explicit.

9 *A code makes explicit the bounds of rationality being adopted* The process of deriving codes provides an explicit debate about the bounded rationality of the legal process, making explicit the distinction between bounded rationality and 'truth', thereby providing criteria under which non-certain science can establish a role. Law's use of science is explicitly seen as an institutional product not derived solely from the practices of science or law, but as an explicit reflection of wider social questions. This is not a question of what tests we need to satisfy a scientist, but rather of what tests will satisfy the need for a cost-effective solution which offers sufficient certainty and credibility to secure optimum compliance. The more views it reflects the greater its acceptance as a bounded rationality will be and the less people will seek to go behind it.

10 *A code moves the debate to the earliest stage possible* The process required to produce a code widens the pre-litigation debate. It can therefore offer reduced complexity in individual cases, without ceding authority to one discourse. There is an opportunity to reduce the range of issues which need to be canvassed in the specific case. At present, even if the parties broadly agree about a particular expert issue, it still needs to be canvassed, bringing with it a degree of unnecessary uncertainty. Codes can avoid the need to raise questions in cases, and in particular can reduce the asking of nonsense questions, such as that which asked how many dead fish there were.

11 *A code identifies uncertainty* Codes can serve to identify those areas

where answers are not knowable or where further work is required to reduce uncertainty. The process may identify the need for presumptions to resolve uncertainties or changes in substance law to avoid asking unknowables. If one accepts Lynda Warren's argument[60] that the capacity of science to measure affects what gets measured, the code process can help to determine where we need to invest effort to devise new measuring techniques or new measures. Both presumptions and codes can reduce uncertainty.[61]

12 *Formal agencies are not essential* The wider use of codes of practice as a format for translating societal debate about science law into a format usable within case-specific approaches does not depend upon the establishment of a formal body such as a Forensic Science Advisory Council or similar body.[62] The debate can come through informal networks, as long as there is a body capable of conferring formal authority at the end of that debate: most commonly this is the relevant government department involved either in primary or in secondary legislation. Environmental law is fortunate in having a well-developed network of opportunities for lawyers, scientists, industrialists, parliamentarians and the lay community to communicate. As a result, when difficulties arose with the statutory evidential requirements for proving water pollution offences,[63] these networks, including a Parliamentary Select Committee, were able to discuss the issues and recommend solutions.[64]

This can be compared with opportunities for debate about forensic science. Here no general forum or networks bring together scientists, prosecution agencies, civil liberties groups and lay communities. One aspect of this issue is the amount of detail about the case given to forensic scientists.[65] If the amount of background information is minimal, risks of prejudice to perceived objectivity are reduced and prosecution control increased. However it also restricts the ability of the scientists to comment upon the consistency with other hypotheses. As a result, the scientific work may be done in ignorance of other live hypotheses in the case, with forensic scientists only made aware of other hypotheses at the trial, possibly only in cross-examination. Thus the apparently small question of the amount of information supplied with the samples has a significant effect upon the role of the FSS within the trial. They become limited to testing one hypothesis and thereby reinforce 'case closing'.[66] At present the decision as to the amount of information supplied to the FSS is the product of the working relationship between the prosecution services and the FSS. If the issue ever arises at trial, it can only be for the purpose of exploring how the amount of information supplied in that case may have affected the evidence. It is not possible in a trial for the wider principle to be debated. Indeed there is no forum for such a debate to take place: instead it is left to private discussion between the prosecution services and the FSS. Wider societal questions about the nature of the task the FSS should be undertaking, and the whole approach to case closure, have no fora in which they can be articulated.

The Lessons of PACE

The PACE Codes of Practice illustrate how such debate can identify consensus and translate it into a format usable in case-specific situations. These were drafted by government, but involved consultation with interest groups to maximize their acceptance. The result is practical codes in which principles for the interpretation of the complex external world are established, which belong neither to law nor to a particular expert area, which reflect the full complexity of neither system, but which provide practical working rules which balance simplicity and complexity. To produce such codes carries with it dangers of reinforcing the hypercycle of complexity, but the success of the legal system in continuing to provide solutions to disputes in the real world will depend upon its ability to articulate such practical working rules which carry the authority of all affected, including external communities.

Before exploring the PACE example, it is necessary to consider how the problems it tackles compare with the issues this chapter has addressed. Code C regulates the questioning of suspects. Criminal courts have to determine the conditions in which admissions made during questioning can be considered sufficiently reliable to be placed before a tribunal of fact, and the court then needs to evaluate the weight to be placed upon such evidence. This involves disputed issues of psychology, such as the conditions in which people are suggestible, the impact of different mental states and the circumstances of false confessions. Consequently Code C is seeking to take matters of psychology and behavioural science and translate them into a form usable by courts without routine recourse to expert evidence.[67] Many were, and remain, deeply controversial.[68] Similarly, Code D takes identification evidence. Hotly contested disputes exist in expert disciplines about the reliability of identification evidence and processes which maximize the reliability of such evidence as is available.[69] Code D offers a practical manual for both police conduct and the courts which avoids the rehearsal of this expert debate in every trial. Instead, from time to time, in the light of experience, a generalized debate can lead to revisions in the code.

Prior to PACE the question of whether a confession should be placed before a jury depended upon a common law exclusionary rule phrased in terms of voluntariness[70] backed by some broad administrative rules.[71] The response to a growing body of psychological evidence, research data from behavioural and social scientists and public concern about high-profile miscarriage of justice cases had to be mediated through a case-by-case application of the voluntariness principle. The scope for defining a precise response in appellate courts was limited. At best it produced an ad hoc response, at worst it was an inconsistent shambles. The response of courts to interrogation of people with low IQs illustrates the problem. Some judges strained the voluntariness test to argue that the resulting confession was not voluntary because of the person's limited understanding.[72] Others argued that it breached the spirit of the Judges Rules and used their common law discretion to exclude it.[73] Some declined to exclude the evidence at all. Similar cases produced different answers or, at best, different rationales.[74] The effects of low IQ upon the admissibility or weight of a confession was negotiated on a case-by-case basis as a question of fact with correspondingly limited scope for appellate review. The failure to offer any concerted and consistent response to the growing body of external complexity, notably in such high-profile issues as the *Confait* case,[75] contributed to growing public cynicism about the criminal justice system.

PACE and its codes of practice set out rules for the way people are to be interviewed. Those rules do not fully reflect the thinking of psychologists and others,[76] but they offer a practical and consistent basis upon which judges can make decisions on admissibility and advise juries in individual cases. A complex externality has been reduced to a set of practical rules, which simplify the basis of evaluating the external world. The extent to which such rules will succeed depends upon the extent to which they have the support of all relevant players. If widely supported, they can serve to narrow the scope of challenges, establish 'best wisdom' and provide for increased consistency.

The process of producing the code provides space for a political and social debate as to the appropriate balance between civil liberties concerns and police desires for efficient apprehension of offenders. Instead of judges needing to revert to abstract principles to adjudicate upon police conduct in each case, possibly reaching differing views in each case, judges are offered a set of practical rules against which to measure conduct in a particular case. Rather than calling psychologists in each case to advise on whether the evidence is reliable, the code offers generalized guidance which seeks to reduce the need to call experts, without precluding their use in appropriate cases.

The rules which underlie case-specific decisions are the explicit product of public debate and compromise, not cloaked in any spurious objectivity. They are seen for what they are, working rules which express the current balance between prosecution and defence concerns, and between the views of different expert groups. The complex body of expert advice from psychologists, behavioural scientists and others has influenced the production of a practical code, but the answers do not fully reflect the complexity of the work of psychologists and behavioural scientists. They are a negotiated simplification of external complexity, in a form usable by the courts.

Conclusion

Given the experience of codes of practice in relation to interrogation or identification evidence, where work by other disciplines continues to offer increasingly complex insights into the principles at work, it is curious that this approach has not been used more widely in the context of other forms of expert evidence, notably in relation to the physical, medical and chemical sciences. Arguments against extension of the approach suggest these areas are too complex, too varied and insufficiently frequently invoked to require such an approach. Other critics appeal to a claimed 'special' nature of science to argue that codes may not be 'true' to scientific values. Such a sweeping response seems to draw more upon Tolkienesque statements of 'here be dragons' than a careful consideration of the incidence of forensic science evidence and the importance of practical solutions. A global approach would certainly not be appropriate, falling into the trap of oversimplification. But where areas of commonly tendered evidence are giving rise to problems, there may be scope for intervention.

Cannabis prosecutions offer one such opportunity. Courts often ask the likely number of reefers the quantity seized would produce, as an indication of whether it is a case of purely personal use. The answer to the question is unknowable. The reefers do not exist. They therefore cannot be enumerated. However, because the question is asked, the FSS have developed a response, based upon statistics of the cannabis content of all reefers seized by the FSS. The FSS themselves comment that this of course varies widely, between those rolled in prison, which tend to have very low cannabis content, and fairly pure ones. The FSS recognize the weakness of data which have such variability, but have been unable to secure government funding to carry out a more systematic review. Here the actual answer is unknowable, so what is needed is a working analysis. If one seeks a 'true' answer, one is met by unknowability. Studies based on any previous reefers used by the defendant run into the *Shonubi* problem.[77] All that is needed is a presumption, or starting point, expressed in a code or otherwise which does not purport to be truth, but which gives the court an answer to work with unless a more convincing one is offered.[78] This can produce increased consistency, with decisions less reliant upon whether particular defence lawyers know how to challenge the current highly contingent data.

In a world where there is not even a shared agreement about the use of the language of probabilities, the scope for increased statements of shared understanding is high.[79] Bodies such as the FSS have responded to these uncertainties by producing their own internal standards. These provide a simplification of external complexity, of the kind Luhmann[80] argues is essential for legal systems to cope effectively with an increasingly complex external world. But they are the product of a private debate within the agency. As such they lack the wider public imprint of acceptability which this chapter argues is essential to confer social validity. Legal systems have to simplify the complexity of the external world in order to be able to handle it. It is essential to the credibility of the decisions reached that those simplifications have been the product of a public debate and are reviewable in the light of changing external complexities, including public views of the appropriate response to the external world. The aim is to assert temporary limits to Teubner's hypercycle of law and expertise reinforcing each other, by defining from time to time working agreements as to how the law is to view external complexities – not as statements of truth but as working principles. Scope must always be found within an adversarial model for challenges to the established wisdom. This chapter has sought to argue that opportunities exist for making more use of codes of practice and that they can enhance rather than undermine the case-specific model of evidence evaluation.

Once created, codes do not operate in a vacuum. Their existence creates new areas of risk and uncertainty and itself interacts to alter external complexity. But if used properly they can establish interim working interpretations of the complex environment usable in legal processes, whose utility outweighs the additional risk.

This chapter has deliberately not explored particular examples of areas where codes may be useful. Any effort at unified solutions is in danger of becoming reductionist: it is for particular areas of activity to make the case for particular codes. The proliferation of private codes, such as the FSS Quality Assurance Codes, indicates the extent to which these networks have identified the need. What is now needed is for government or agencies commanding a degree of authority in particular fields to initiate the process of translating growing areas of shared understanding into formats applicable within individual trials. The process is not easy, but may offer a way to turn expert systems from external threats into internal resources, and in doing so may strengthen the ability of the common law to respond to the changing complexity of the external world.

It might be argued that this chapter takes an unduly optimistic view of the capacity of science and law to interact without science encountering a falsely under- or over-critical response. Such critiques stem from a desire to pursue solutions which are scientifically or legally valid, according to the strict processes of one or other discipline. This chapter argues that we cannot achieve such a solution. Finding a basis for mutual communication between law and science will not result in answers true to either system's internal discourses, but it is the best we can do – and considerably better than the current Babel.

Notes

1 For example, see P. Alldridge, 'Recognising Novel Scientific Techniques: DNA as a test case' (1992) *Criminal Law Review* 687.
2 While differences exist between and within civil and criminal processes, the concern here is with the common features of the case-specific approach rather than the ephemera of particular case-specific approaches. Whilst at a detailed level of application different problems are more prominent in particular contexts, there are common underlying problems.
3 Lord Woolf, *Access to Justice: final report to the Lord Chancellor on the civil justice system in England and Wales* (London, 1995).
4 N. Luhmann, *Soziologische Anfklärung*, Vol. 1 (Opladen, 1970); translated by S. Holmes and C. Larmore, *The Differentiation of Society* (New York, 1982); N. Luhmann, *Legitimation durch Verfahrer* (Frankfurt-am-Maine, 1969/1983); N. Luhmann, *Soziale Systeme, Grundißeiner allgemeinen Theorie* (Frankfurt-am-Maine, 1984).
5 S. Jasanoff, *Science at the Bar: Law, Science and Technology in America* (Cambridge, Mass., 1995), p.219.
6 Such as the Forensic Science Quality Assurance manuals.
7 National Measurement Accreditation Service, which provides external accreditation of Forensic Science Service (FSS) laboratory procedures and analytic techniques.
8 *United States* v. *Shonubi* (1995) WL 472704 (EDNY).
9 See the special issue of *Expert Evidence* devoted to *Shonubi* and its implications: (1996) 4 *Expert Evidence* 134–58.
10 Section 1 included 'pit bull terriers' in this definition – a common name for a broadly recognizable dog, but not one accepted as a recognized breed for Kennel Club or other purposes. I am grateful to Lynda Warren for this example.
11 The long title of the Act referred to 'types bred for fighting' and 'other types of dog which present a serious danger to the public', giving an indication of the aims of the legislation, but section 1 refers, *inter alia*, to dogs of the 'type known as a pit bull terrier'. This is not a recognized definition.
12 'Is this dog a pit bull terrier?', was the relevant question, rather than 'Is it a dog of a kind which society might consider it appropriate to destroy?'
13 It is not suggested here that simply adopting the language of science in legislative drafting would resolve these problems, as this cedes control to one discourse, rather than seeking a negotiated solution to external complexity.
14 H. Walls, 'What is "Reasonable Doubt"? A Forensic Scientist Looks at the Law' [1971] *Criminal Law Review* 458.
15 P. Roberts and C. Willmore, *The Role of Forensic Science Evidence in Criminal Proceedings*, Research Study 11, Royal Commission on Criminal Justice (London, 1993).
16 In Roberts and Willmore, *Forensic Science Evidence*, a forensic scientist said, 'This is

never cut and dried. At the end of the day it's always down to the reporting officer himself to decide whether he thinks the sample of glass matches ... You can talk about standard deviations, computer programs, there are suggestions of guidelines, but at the end of the day it is down to the reporting officer to decide'.

17 *Chard* v. *Chard* [1956] P. 259, put on a statutory footing in relation to petitions for dissolution of marriage by s.19(3) Matrimonial Causes Act 1973 and recognized in relation to the offence of bigamy by s.57 of the Offences Against the Person Act 1861. Cf. s.184 Law of Property Act 1925: if it is uncertain for the purposes of succession to property who was the survivor of two persons dying at the same time, the younger is presumed to have survived the elder.

18 It is beyond the scope of this chapter to consider whether this is a product of the adversarial system, although Jasanoff, *Science at the Bar*, comments that the French system seems better at creating presumptions than common law jurisdictions.

19 'Probabilistic statements, no matter how precise, are often treated as admissions of uncertainty, not to say unreliability' (C. Oddie, *Science and the Administration of Justice*, London, 1991).

20 Luhmann, *Legitimation*; Luhmann, *Soziale Systeme*.

21 For example, confessions obtained in breach of the PACE Codes, under s.78 PACE.

22 An excellent overview of common law admissibility tests for experts is S. Gatowski, S. Dobbin, J. Richardson, C. Nowlin and G. Ginsburg, 'The diffusion of scientific evidence: A comparative analysis of admissibility standards in Australia, Canada, England and the United States and their impact on social and behavioural sciences' (1996) 4 *Expert Evidence* 86.

23 Frekelton described the approach when applied to novel scientific evidence as being one of 'benevolent acquiescence': I. Frekelton, 'Contemporary Comment, When Plight Makes Right, The Forensic Abuse Syndrome' (1994) 18 *Criminal Law Journal* 29.

24 *R* v. *Silverlock* [1894] 2 QB 766.

25 *R* v. *Turner* [1975] QB 834.

26 At least notionally this remains part of the English test, but see *R* v. *Stockwell* (1993) 97 Cr.App.R. 260.

27 Civil Evidence Act 1995; Criminal Procedure and Investigations Act 1996.

28 *Frye* v. *United States* 293 F. 1013 (D.C. Cir. 1923).

29 A similar general acceptance approach has been followed in Australia: *R* v. *Runjanjc* (1991) 53 A Crim. Rev. 362.

30 'Verbal fingerprinting', the concept that one can identify who wrote a text by analysis of the use of language, as in studies which seek to show that Bacon wrote plays attributed to Shakespeare. See 'Editorial' (1992) 1 *Expert Evidence* 79; D. Canter, 'An Evaluation of the Cusum Stylistic Analysis of Confessions' (1992) 1 *Expert Evidence* 93; A. Morton and M. Farringdon, 'Identifying Utterance' (1992) 1 *Expert Evidence* 84.

31 *R* v. *McCrossen* (1992) unreported, 10 July 1991. See 'Editorial' (1992) 1 *Expert Evidence* 79.

32 *Frye* was overtaken by Rule 702 of the 1975 Federal Rules of Evidence, which imposes the test of whether the evidence would 'assist a trier of fact to understand the evidence or determine a fact in issue'.

33 *Daubert* v. *Merrell Dow Pharmaceuticals* (1993) 113 S. Ct. 2786.

34 'Confronting the new challenges of scientific evidence' (1995) 108 *Harvard Law Review*, 1481.

35 Jasanoff, *Science at the Bar*, p.63.

36 See *R* v. *Beland* (1987) 36 CCC (3d) 481, 43 DLR (4th) 641; applied, for example, in *R* v. *Johnston* (1992) 69 CCC (3d) 395 re DNA. But see *R* v. *Mohan* (1994) 89 CCC (3d)

402, 29 CR (4th) 243, (1994) 2 SCR 9, where the Supreme Court adopted a looser test of relevance and necessity.

37 For a detailed exploration of the problems, see Roberts and Willmore, *Forensic Science Evidence*.

38 Roberts and Willmore, *Forensic Science Evidence*.

39 B. Wynne, 'Establishing the rules of law: constructing expert authority', in R. Smith and B. Wynne (eds), *Expert Evidence: Interpreting Science in the Law* (London, 1989), p.23.

40 Others prefer to see it as an ad hoc resolution to conflict, rather than a formation of consensus: for example, C. Jones, *Expert Witnesses* (Oxford, 1994), who sees it as a struggle for supremacy between powerful epistemologies.

41 'Because of its apparent objectivity an opinion that claims a scientific basis is apt to carry undue weight with the trier of fact' (*US* v. *Baller* 519 Fed 2d 463 (1975)).

42 G.Teubner, *Autopoietic Law: A New Approach to Law and Society* (Berlin, 1988).

43 Jasanoff, in *Science at the Bar*, has called this shared language 'science law'.

44 D. Carson, 'Expert Evidence in the Courts' (1992) 1 *Expert Evidence* 13.

45 United Kingdom Environmental Lawyers Association.

46 Such as the FSS Quality Codes.

47 One must be cautious about the proliferation of processes which seek to explain science to judges, effectively asking judges to think like scientists without any critical appraisal of their potentially differing objectives and without questioning the aims and methodologies of science. See, for example, the Federal Judicial Centre's *Reference Manual of Scientific Evidence*.

48 Jasanoff, *Science at the Bar*, p.211. See also Roberts and Willmore, *Forensic Science Evidence*.

49 Section 78A(2), as inserted by the Environment Act 1995.

50 T. Swanson, 'Environmental Economic and Regulation', in O. Lomas (ed.), *Frontiers of Environmental Law* (London, 1991).

51 Authorized under s.78YA(1) of the Environmental Protection Act 1990: 'Consultation on Draft Guidance Note, Department of the Environment' (London, 1996).

52 Such as the *Law Society Code for Expert Witnesses* (London, 1996).

53 See the relative lack of appellate cases concerning the use of DNA evidence, despite the current wider debate about its limitations and use.

54 See, for example, *Qualcast (Wolverhampton) Ltd* v. *Haynes* [1959] AC 743. An employee was injured at work through not wearing safety shoes. The court had to determine whether the tortious duty of care upon the employer was phrased widely, in terms of taking reasonable care for the safety of workmen, in which case whether not encouraging his staff to wear safety shoes was a breach of that duty became a question of fact; or whether the tortious duty was phrased more specifically, so as to include a duty to urge staff to wear protective shoes, the issue then becoming one of law.

55 Roberts and Willmore, *Forensic Science Evidence*.

56 For example, some can be mitigated by court-appointed experts-enhanced pretrial consideration of expert evidence in civil cases.

57 See Luhmann, *Legitimation* and *Soziale Systeme*, for examples.

58 D. Feldman, 'Public Interest Litigation and Constitutional Theory in Comparative Perspective' (1992) *Modern Law Review* 44.

59 *R* v. *Secretary of State for Trade and Industry, ex parte Duddridge* [1995] Environmental Law Reports, 151.

60 See Chapter 9 of the present volume.

61 A decrease in uncertainty does not necessarily equate with a decrease in conflict: J. Graham, L. Green and R. Roberts, *In Search of Safety: Chemicals and Cancer Risk*

(Cambridge, Mass., 1988).

62 Where bodies are established it is important to recognize the lessons from the US experience of Federal Advisory Committees: see S. Jasanoff, *The Fifth Branch* (Cambridge, Mass., 1990).

63 Section 209 of the Water Resources Act 1991 required tripartite sampling. Appeal courts demonstrated a limited capacity for fine-tuning the provisions: see *A-G's Reference (No. 2 of 1994)* [1994] 1 WLR 579, *CPC (UK) Ltd* v. *National Rivers Authority* [1994] *The Times*, 4 August; A. Mumma, 'Use of compliance monitoring data in water prosecutions' (1993) 5 *Journal of Environmental Law* 19.

64 Now incorporated into s.209 by the Environment Act 1995.

65 Roberts and Willmore, *Forensic Science Evidence*.

66 Is case X plausible; not are there other, more plausible, explanations?

67 Carson has argued that the codes have had the opposite effect, creating trial by expert, with the court as 'quality auditors': D. Carson, 'Expert Evidence in the Courts' (1992) 1 *Expert Evidence* 13; D. Carson, 'A Role in Preventing Decision Error' [1990] *Journal of Social Welfare Law* 151.

68 *R* v. *Ward* [1993] 2 All ER 577.

69 D.F. Ross, J.D. Read and M.P. Toglia (eds), *Adult Eyewitness Testimony: Current Trends and Developments* (New York, 1993). For controversy concerning the use of eyewitness memory research, see, for example, E. Ebbesen and E. Konecni, 'Eyewitness memory research: Probative v. prejudicial value' (1997) 5 *Expert Evidence*, 2; A. Yarmey, 'Probative v. prejudicial value of eyewitness memory research' (1997) 5 *Expert Evidence* 89.

70 *DPP* v. *Ping Lin* [1976] AC 574.

71 Judges Rules 1964; *Home Office Administrative Directions* (London, 1978).

72 *R* v. *Westlake* [1979] *Criminal Law Review* 652.

73 *R* v. *Stewart* [1972] 56 Cr.App.R. 272; *R* v. *Kilner* [1976] *Criminal Law Review* 740.

74 Compare the post-PACE cases: *R* v. *Everett* [1988] *Criminal Law Review* 826; *R* v. *Harvey* [1988] *Criminal Law Review* 241.

75 *R* v. *Lattimore* [1975] 62 Cr.App.R. 53. Fisher Report: *Report of an Inquiry by the Hon. Sir Henry Fisher into the circumstances leading to the trial of three persons on charges arising out of the death of Maxwell Confait and the fire at 27 Dogett Road, London, SE6* (London, 1977).

76 See G. Gudjonsson, *The Psychology of Interrogations, Confessions and Testimony* (London, 1992).

77 See note 8, above.

78 Individual defendants will continue to argue that they smoke particularly pure reefers and that hence what would on average make 50 reefers would for them only make 10 and may therefore represent a quality held purely for personal use.

79 Different experts use 'highly likely', to mean different things, for example: see Roberts and Willmore, *Forensic Science Evidence*.

80 See note 4, above.

4 Bayesianism and Proof

Mike Redmayne

Judges and juries, when performing their fact-finding role, have something in common with scientists evaluating theories. Each is concerned with evidence and proof. Just as fact finders analyse evidence in order to decide whether a case is proven to a certain standard, so scientists look to evidence when deciding how strong a case has been made for a theory. While there are no formal standards of proof in science, scientists do want to know whether the available evidence supports one theory better than its competitors, or whether a theory is strong enough for it to be worth spending time and resources pursuing it.

Some commentators believe that fact finders and scientists have something else in common, too. The fact-finding process in law and theory choice in science, it is argued, can both be usefully represented as processes governed by the rules of conventional probability theory. One particular consequence of these rules, a formula called Bayes's theorem, takes centre stage in these attempts to theorize the relationship between evidence and proof. Indeed, so important is Bayes's theorem to this project that the term 'Bayesianism' is used to describe the subjective probability theory involved. This chapter examines some of the problems that face attempts to account for theory confirmation in science through Bayesianism and discusses similar criticisms of the Bayesian model of fact finding in law.[1] This is not intended to be a comprehensive review of the pros and cons of Bayesianism, but it is hoped to show that the problems that emerge in four key areas - the concept of subjective probability, the concept of evidence, prior probabilities and complexity - are not isolated failings. Rather these problems are linked by the distinct lack of realism of the Bayesian model of proof. The concluding sections of the chapter argue for the adoption of a more naturalized theory of proof and attempt to clarify the role that Bayesianism may legitimately play in evidence scholarship.

As a preliminary, it is worth making some observations about the Bayesian project in law in order to demonstrate why the debate about

Bayesianism is important, and to give some idea of the problems facing Bayesianism. It is tempting to think that the process by which fact finders make (or should make) decisions is of little importance. Juries and judges are left to apply their common sense, and the question whether their decision-making process can be modelled by Bayesianism is neither here nor there. This is not entirely true. There are cases, albeit rare ones, where probability theory gets used in court. A recent example is *R* v. *Adams*, where the Court of Appeal delivered a judgment condemning the presentation of Bayes's theorem to a jury in a DNA case.[2] In addition to this, one of the central points of contention in the debate about Bayesianism is just what it means to prove a case, so issues surrounding standards of proof are at stake. A couple of well-known examples illustrate this; they also give a flavour of some of the problems facing the Bayesian project. Consider a tort case where there are two contested issues: negligence and the existence of a duty of care. If the plaintiff proves both these elements to a probability of 0.7 then, applying conventional probability theory, she will lose the case because the conjunction of the elements (assuming independence) is only proven to 0.49. This may be acceptable, but note that adding another contested issue, say causation, raises the standard to which each element must be proved to around 0.79. Another problem is illustrated by the gatecrasher paradox. Suppose that 1000 people attend a rodeo, but only 499 pay. Then, it seems, the rodeo's proprietor can recover the ticket price from any (perhaps all) of those attending, because the probability that any spectator did not pay is greater than 0.5.[3] Bayesians and non-Bayesians alike have put forward all sorts of solutions to these problems, but it is hoped that enough has been said by now to show that there is, at least, a question mark hanging over Bayesian models of proof.

Theory Confirmation in Science and Law

One particularly important aspect of the philosophy of science is the attempt to provide rational criteria for explaining why scientists prefer some theories to others. This task, however, has not proved easy. Attempts, such as that by Carnap, to provide a comprehensive inductive logic for theory choice are now generally regarded as having failed. In the latter part of this century, some philosophers have instead turned to probabilistic accounts of theory confirmation.[4] If a scientist can never be sure that a particular theory is true, she can at least regard it as being more probable than its competitors. Similarly, though she may not feel able to regard a theory as having been definitively falsified, she may regard it as being very improbable. Subjective probability theory offers to give the probabilistic account of theory confirmation a solid foundation. In particular, Bayes's theorem can be used to depict the process through which a scientist evaluates a hypothesis in the light of evidence. Where *p*(*h*) is the probability of the hypothesis, *p*(*e*) is the probability of the evidence and *p*(*h*|*e*) is the probability of the hypothesis given the evidence, Bayes's theorem provides that:

$$p(h|e) = \frac{p(h)\,p(e|h)}{p(e)}$$

A theory of subjective probability is used to operationalize this account of theory confirmation. Subjective probabilities can be interpreted as degrees of belief. Thus, in the above formula, *p*(*h*) is the degree of belief that the scientist has in the hypothesis before taking the evidence into account. The only limitation put on *p*(*h*) by subjective probability theory is a requirement of consistency. Thus, if there are five mutually exclusive and exhaustive theories being considered by a scientist, she may assign any degree of belief she likes to each of them so long as the probability of their conjunction sums to 1. The consistency requirement prevents the scientist from having a Dutch book made against her (a combination of bets on different events where she is guaranteed to lose, whatever the outcome of the events).[5] Thus subjective probability theory is closely linked to a theory of rational belief.[6]

The application of Bayes's theorem to fact finding in law is (at least, initially) straightforward. The fact finder updates her belief in the hypothesis of interest (for example, that the defendant is guilty) by considering each piece of evidence which has been presented during the trial. The more evidence there is that is probable given guilt but improbable otherwise, the higher will be the fact finder's final calculation of the probability of guilt. If this final probability satisfies her conception of guilt beyond a reasonable doubt, she will return a verdict of guilty.

The Notion of Subjective Probability

The difficulties faced by the Bayesian project start with Bayesianism's most basic building block: subjective probability.[7] The concept of subjective probability certainly captures something about our doxastic attitudes: looking out of my window at the grey sky, I think it is very probable that it will rain at some point this afternoon; not having been into my office yesterday, I thought it probable that I would have some e-mail waiting for me when I switched on my computer, but improbable that I would have more than 20 messages. But the phenomenon of credal uncertainty does not demonstrate the existence of subjective probabilities in the Bayesian sense. Even with the trite examples just given, I am unwilling to classify my beliefs with anything more precise than the vague qualifiers, 'probable', 'improbable' and 'very probable'. I am reluctant to supply the numerical probabilities that seem required to get a scheme of subjective probabilities up and running. In response to my reticence, the Bayesian has a number of strategies in order to coax my degrees of belief into the open. For example, by asking me to state the odds at which I would be prepared to take either side of a bet on the relevant event, she can calculate how probable I regard the event as being. There are, however, a number of objections to this manner of operationalizing subjective probability. Suppose I am asked to imagine a bet on whether it will rain in St Petersburg this afternoon. My almost total ignorance of the weather patterns in that city at this time of year would make me reluctant to state any odds at all. Even if I am prepared to state the odds at which I would accept a bet, there will be doubts about whether those odds represent my real degree of belief, because the method of eliciting those odds may have distorted that degree of belief.[8] I may find myself stating odds of evens a lot of the time, because the failure of any other odds to spring to mind leads me to believe, mistakenly, that I am indifferent about the bet. On the other hand, I may find that I never state odds of evens, even when I am truly indifferent, because I have become suspicious of the all too neat symmetry of those odds. Alternatively, my aversion to risk may lead me not to state the odds that would represent my true degree of belief.[9]

These criticisms may seem petty, but underlying them is a more fundamental point. Mark Kaplan has remarked that the Bayesian conception of subjective probability presumes that our mental architecture contains the equivalent of a black box stocked with subjective probabilities just waiting to be elicited. But the objections just considered suggest that there may not be anything lurking within my mind that corresponds to a subjective probability.[10] This sort of objection to the concept of subjective probability has been put on a slightly firmer footing by Alvin Goldman, who suggests that our doxastic attitudes are frequently better represented by binary (true/false) beliefs than by probabilities[11] (beliefs of this sort are anathema to Bayesians[12]). Drawing on connectionist models of reasoning, Goldman argues that a more accurate model of uncertainty is fluctuation between binary belief states, much as our perception of a Necker cube fluctuates between two different interpretations but never settles on either, nor on any state between them.

There is a fairly obvious response to these criticisms of subjective probability. This is to claim that subjective probability theory is not meant to be psychologically realistic, that it is merely meant to offer a normative conceptualization of belief and belief change in response to evidence. Thus, even if the Bayesian concedes that the concept of degree of belief has no real-world equivalent, she might argue that it represents how an ideally rational person would order her beliefs. There are, however, problems in this shift to the normative plane. One difficulty is that the whole point of describing mechanisms by which we can gain access to a person's degree of belief in a proposition seems to be to lend psychological plausibility to the notion of subjective probability. If Bayesians are not really interested in psychology, why do they not simply posit point-valued degrees of belief and be done with attempts to explain how we would arrive at them? It seems that this route is not taken because it would make the whole notion of degrees of belief that much more implausible. And if degrees of belief do not exist, a normative theory which relies on them begins to look otiose.

Quality of Evidence

Another set of problems for the Bayesian project relates to the way Bayesianism describes evidence. A number of commentators – both evidence scholars and philosophers of science[13] – have pointed out that the use of probability figures as the descriptive basis of belief does violence to some common notions about evidence. There is a frequently used illustration of the problem.[14] Consider two different cases: in case (a) you have an opaque urn in front of you containing 100 balls; 50 are black and 50 are white. In case (b) you have a similar urn, but you do not know what the proportion of black and white balls in it is. A ball has been drawn at random from each urn, and you are asked to state the probability that it is white. On the Bayesian interpretation, each case warrants an identical response: the ascription of a probability of 0.5 to *p* (white). But there is a fundamental difference between the two situations: in (a) there is good evidence, whereas in (b) there is almost none. Yet the use of probabilities in the basic Bayesian scheme does not allow us to represent this difference.[15] Metaphorically we might say that evidence is a two-dimensional concept, but that Bayesianism collapses it into one dimension. In this process, something important is lost.

A number of other examples of the poverty of the Bayesian conception of evidence are provided by Peter Achinstein.[16] For a Bayesian, something is evidence for a hypothesis when it increases the probability of the hypothesis. Formally e is evidence for h when $p(h|e) > p(h)$.[17] However e may still be evidence for h when this inequality does not obtain. Consider, first, the so-called 'paradox of ideal evidence'.[18] Suppose that you are asked to assign a probability to the statement, 'the thousandth toss of this coin will yield heads'. You are likely to choose a probability of 0.5. If you now toss the coin 999 times, noting that heads results approximately half of the time, and again estimate the probability of heads on the thousandth toss, you are likely to say 0.5 again. But there seems to be an epistemic difference between these two probabilities, one that is not captured by Bayesianism. Additionally, according to the probabilistic definition of evidence, the 999 tosses are not evidence of how the coin will land on the thousandth toss.

Achinstein provides two other useful examples of the limitations of the probabilistic definition of evidence.[19] These can be fairly easily adapted to a legal context. Suppose that there is a dispute about whether drug D causes side-effect S. To support the hypothesis (*h*) that it does, we might consider epidemiological evidence (*e*); *e*1 is a study of 2000 similar patients, half of whom received D and half of whom did not. Of the 1000 receiving D, 950 had side-effect S, whereas none of the control group did. This, of course, increases the probability of *h*. Consider now *e*2, a second study of the effects of D which is similar to *e*1 in all respects, except that only 850 subjects had S. Considered after *e*1, *e*2 will decrease the probability of *h*. Achinstein argues, however, that *e*1&*e*2 provides stronger evidence for *h* than does *e*1 alone because, together, they report the results of a study of 4000 patients which provides a more convincing basis for believing *h*. Achinstein's second example is similar, but this time the difference between epidemiological evidence *e*1 and *e*2 is not the number of subjects with S, but the manner in which the studies were conducted: *e*2 might be better evidence of *h* even though it does not increase its probability if, for example, *e*2 was evidence of a more carefully conducted study, one in which a number of factors, such as the age, weight and lifestyle of the subjects, were varied. By increasing the variety of relevant evidential factors, *e*2 is better evidence for *h* than is *e*1, yet Bayesianism is notoriously poor at explaining our desire for variety of evidence.[20]

Achinstein concludes that a full understanding of the concept of evidence strength must involve two factors: (a) how much belief it is reasonable to have in *h*, given *e*, and (b) how reasonable it is to have that much belief in *h*, given *e*.[21] A possible response to this problem, from within a Bayesian framework, might use some concept such as second order probability in order to address (b). It seems clear that any coherent Bayesian account of legal proof must resort to something like second order probability in order to explain the standards of proof and to show why examples such as the gatecrasher paradox are so troubling.[22] Supposing that a coherent conceptualization of second order probability could be achieved within the Bayesian framework, it would face two problems. The first would be that it would be significantly more complicated than standard Bayesianism, the simplicity of which is one of the attractive parts of the Bayesian project. The second problem would be that, even with two numbers to characterize the fact finder's doxastic attitude, it is by no means clear that this would suffice as a representation of strength or weight of evidence. As Achinstein notes, 'There are different, potentially conflicting, respects in which evidence can be stronger' and they may 'pull in different directions'.[23]

Prior Probabilities

In order to use Bayes's theorem to update her belief in a hypothesis, a scientist needs a prior probability for the hypothesis: $p(h)$ in the equation above. But how is $p(h)$ to be calculated? Consider the hypothesis 'there is life on Mars', which is to be tested by sending a probe to the planet to perform certain chemical tests, the results of which will be relayed back to earth. If the evidence gained from the probe is not decisive, but provides some support for the hypothesis, the posterior probability of the life on Mars hypothesis will vary considerably, depending on the prior probability accorded to it. Yet this prior probability is obviously something about which scientists may disagree and, owing to this, subjective prior probabilities threaten to undermine the objectivity of science.[24]

The problem of prior probability has received considerable attention in the scientific literature. A common response is that it is not a significant problem because, even if two scientists have very different priors, over time the evidence will 'wash out' the differences in initial starting points. As the evidence builds up in support of a hypothesis, the degrees of belief which the two scientists have in it converge to certainty (alternatively, if the evidence consistently undermined the hypothesis, they would converge to impossibility). The convergence to certainty argument is reassuring at first sight. However it has been questioned whether it is applicable to typical scientific cases,[25] and whether convergence will occur over the medium term, as opposed to the very long term.[26]

If prior probabilities are seen to cause problems in scientific applications of Bayes's theorem, the problems are more acute when we turn to the Bayesian project in law. How can a specific probability be given for the initial likelihood of guilt or liability? Let us concentrate on criminal cases, where the problems appear to be sharpest. Those who are hostile to the Bayesian project have capitalized on the problem of prior probability by asserting that the presumption of innocence must require a prior of zero, which derails the Bayesian scheme from the word go because, no matter how much evidence is considered by the fact finder, the probability of guilt would remain zero.[27] This argument is unconvincing, however. As a rule of evidence, the presumption of innocence simply requires that the prosecution bears the burden of proving its case beyond reasonable doubt.[28] So it does not seem to be inconsistent with the presumption if the fact finder starts the case with a non-zero prior. Instead most Bayesians have presumed that, to reconcile Bayesianism with evidence law, they must show some coherent way in which a low prior could be determined. One approach is to base the prior on the population of possible perpetrators. For example, if a case involves a crime committed in a city with a population of 3 million, the prior would be 1 in 3 million. This approach has been popular, partly because it is readily applicable in DNA cases, which have provided fertile ground for Bayesian analysis. As a heuristic, the population of possible perpetrators analysis is a useful way of showing the interaction between prior and posterior probability, but as an expression of how a fact finder should think about a case it is incredibly artificial. One problem is that there seems to be no good reason for preferring one population figure to another. Why the population of the city in which the crime took place? Why not the population of England? The United Kingdom? Europe? The world? Bayesians eager to show that they are not trampling all over the presumption of innocence might settle on the world population as a sufficiently low prior.[29] But then an awful lot of cases are not going to come anywhere near to being proved beyond reasonable doubt. A more significant problem is that the population solution leaves a large number of cases unaddressed. How do we calculate a prior in a fraud case? Or a murder case where the defendant claims self-defence?

A slightly different proposal has been put forward by Richard Friedman, who, sensitive to some of the above difficulties, proposes that, in order to generate a low enough prior, the fact finder should be asked to put out of her mind the very fact that the defendant has been accused of a crime. This, he suggests, could be brought home to the jury by asking questions such as: 'How probable do you think it is that on July 8, 1994, a comet hit Mercury? Venus? Earth? Mars? Jupiter? Saturn?'[30] But again, once the prior probability has been set this low, it is difficult to see how most cases could be proved by the prosecution beyond reasonable doubt without the presentation of massively more evidence than is habitual. The problem, it seems, is that in order to portray a coherent (and normatively acceptable) process of forensic proof, the Bayesian is forced to create an alarmingly artificial theory.[31] The question of prior probability is one that simply does not arise in traditional evidence scholarship, and that is not a failing on the part of traditional scholars: it simply reflects the way the trial process works in the real world. The failing lies with the Bayesian project, which asks us to provide answers to questions which should not have been asked in the first place.

Complexity

If we suppose that the Bayesian project can overcome the problems described in preceding sections, any real-world application of Bayes's theorem must face still another difficulty. This is that the calculations required to assess the probability of a hypothesis threaten to mire the scientist or fact finder in intractable complexity.[32] To understand why this is so, we must note that, each time a piece of evidence is fed into the theorem, it is not enough simply to update the probability of the hypothesis by conditioning on the new evidence alone. By doing this, we would run the risk of ignoring important dependency relations between the pieces of evidence which would throw our calculation off kilter. Instead we would have to calculate the conditional probability of the new evidence, taking into account not only the hypothesis of interest but also all of the other evidence we have considered.

Complexity can also arise in other ways. If we focus again on real-world applications of Bayes's theorem, we will note that during the process of belief updating through Bayes's theorem the scientist or fact finder may develop a new theory to explain the evidence. In science, this problem has been well put by Harold Brown:

> Contemporary studies of scientific revolutions have provided us with myriad examples of situations in which surprising new hypotheses came to be entertained, including cases in which new hypotheses were introduced in response to new evidence. ... Thus ... even if we have encountered convergence to one of the hypotheses in the set under consideration, we can choose to override this result by returning to the context of discovery and changing the mix of hypotheses and prior probabilities.[33]

An example of a similar situation in legal fact finding was provided by the recent television programme, *Trial by Jury*, which showed the deliberations of a mock jury on a fairly realistically presented case involving a stabbing. During its deliberation, the jury suddenly constructed a new hypothesis (that the defendant had taken his knife out of his pocket before he was thrown to the floor) which had not been put forward by either side during the trial.

The fact that new hypotheses can suddenly emerge alerts us to another way in which complexity arises. For the Bayesian project to work, it must be recognized that in many situations it is no good simply conditioning one hypothesis on the evidence under consideration. Frequently, for both scientists and fact finders, many more hypotheses will be in play. If only one or two are considered, the final probabilities of those hypotheses calculated through the application of Bayes's theorem will be of little use because they will fail to take into account other possibilities which, to the extent that they are probable, detract from the probability of the hypotheses that were considered. Again the Bayesian calculation becomes significantly more complicated once we try to accommodate multiple hypotheses.

The problem of complexity has been addressed by Bayesians in two main ways. Writing about Bayesianism in science, Wesley Salmon has proposed that complexity can be dealt with if we lower our sights.[34] If, rather than attempting to calculate the probability of a hypothesis, we restrict Bayesianism to hypothesis comparison, we may be able to limit complexity. But even this may cause problems if we try to compare the probability of a hypothesis with that of its negation (because its negation is a disjunction of several hypotheses), which leads Salmon to choose, instead, a form of Bayes's theorem which merely attempts to compare the probability of two well-defined but non-exhaustive hypotheses:

$$\frac{p(h1|e)}{p(h2|e)} = \frac{p(e|h1)\,p(h1)}{p(e|h2)\,p(h2)}$$

While this overcomes many of the problems facing the implementation of the Bayesian project, the solution comes at a price: a radically restricted role for Bayesianism in theory confirmation. It is not surprising, then, that some Bayesians are unwilling to pay this price.[35]

Turning to law, we find that a similar strategy has been adopted by two of the leading Bayesian scholars. Bernard Robertson and Tony Vignaux have drawn a number of interesting insights from the application of Bayenianism to evidence law but, like Salmon, they adopt a form of Bayes's theorem which is better suited to hypothesis comparison than to ascribing a uniquely determined probability to a hypothesis.[36] The hypotheses they choose in their illustrations are generally those attributed to the parties in the presentation of their cases. While this has considerable heuristic potential in much of their work, the simplification tells against considering this form of Bayes's theorem to be an adequate model of legal proof.[37]

A second Bayesian response to the complexity problem is one which we came across briefly earlier. It is to shift to the normative plane, denying that any claim is being made about the real-world application of Bayesianism. However the reason why the problems of complexity are significant is that, as reasoners, we find ourselves in a 'finitary predicament'.[38] Both our time and our cognitive resources are limited, and these limitations have obvious repercussions for our standards of rationality. The normative and the possible cannot be separated as easily as some Bayesians would claim. There are parallels here with arguments sometimes made against utilitarianism as an adequate model for moral choice. Bernard Williams has noted that utilitarianism makes

> enormous demands on supposed empirical information, about people's preferences, and that information is not only largely unavailable, but shrouded in

> conceptual difficulty; but that is seen in the light of a technical or practical difficulty, and utilitarianism appeals to a frame of mind in which technical difficulty, even insuperable technical difficulty, is preferable to moral unclarity, no doubt because it is less alarming. ... Utilitarianism ... is alarmingly good at combining technical complexity with simple mindedness.[39]

Bayesianism seems to be in a similar predicament. And if we try to cut back on complexity by reducing the amount of information we need to make either the Bayesian or the utilitarian calculation, we will reach a result in which we will have no good reason to have much confidence.

Naturalised Models of Inference

It should by now be apparent that there are a number of criticisms of the Bayesian project. If these have a common factor, it is the unrealistic assumptions made in order to operate the Bayesian scheme: it is assumed that we are able to probabilify our doxastic states, assign prior probabilities to hypotheses and accomplish incredibly complex calculations. These assumptions simply do not fit easily into what we know about the way either scientists or fact finders undertake decision making under uncertainty in the real world. Perhaps the Bayesian project's main problem, then, is that it starts in the wrong place. Bayesianism is 'top-down' modelling: starting from the assumption that inference should be governed by the probability axioms, it attempts to fill in the details, only to find that they sit uneasily with human cognitive practices. Instead it may be that we would do better by starting from the bottom, using what we know about our inferential practices to develop a model of proof.

Some recent work in the philosophy of science has taken this approach, heeding W.V. Quine's admonition: 'Better to discover how science is in fact developed and learned than to fabricate a fictitious structure to similar effect.'[40] No more than a brief sketch of some of the developments in this field is possible here. At the outset, it is worth noting that there is little evidence that scientists reason like Bayesians, or that they use Bayes's theorem to judge the merits of their theories – this despite the fact that many scientists are sophisticated probabilists.[41] Ronald Giere has argued that, instead, case studies suggest that scientists act like satisficers. Rather than pursuing every implication of a theory and comparing it to all possible competitor theories (as they would if attempting to determine a unique probability for the theory), they simply seek a reasonable fit between theory and data.[42] Giere suggests that probability judgments do play some role in theory choice: when gauging the strength of a theory in the light of evidence, scientists will attend to the conditional probability of the evidence given the theory, but will not follow this through into full-blown Bayesianism by then attempting to calculate the probability of the hypothesis given the evidence.

Two other empirically based models of theory confirmation in science draw on connectionist theories of cognition. Paul Thagard has developed an explanation-based model of theory choice which he has applied to case studies in the history of science.[43] The fundamentals of this model are that scientists judge theories by their ability to explain the available evidence. A theory is more credible than others to the extent that it explains more of the evidence, does not conflict with any pieces of evidence, and provides a simpler explanation than its rivals (the more a theory resorts to auxiliary hypotheses, the less credible it is). Analogical reasoning also plays a role in Thagard's model: a theory will be judged to be more credible if it is similar to other successful theories. Elements of a connectionist model of scientific theories have also been described by Paul Churchland.[44] Churchland has suggested interpretations of 'theory' and 'explanation' modelled on vector transformations in neural networks; in his model, the important cognitive action takes place at a sublinguistic level. He suggests that it is unrealistic to view theories (as the Bayesian does) as sets of sentences that can be manipulated by rules.

One of the merits of these empirically based perspectives on theory confirmation in science is that they do not ask too much of scientists. They presume that scientists can evaluate theories without comparing them to all possible rival theories in the probability space. In addition, because these perspectives do not portray rule-based reasoning as the paradigm of all good reasoning, they are better able to account for some of the virtues of human reasoning, such as speed and flexibility. However attempts to naturalize the philosophy of science in this manner are open to a number of criticisms. An objection to an empirically based theory such as Giere's is that it may leave us with no standards with which to criticize poor scientific reasoning.[45] Thagard's and Churchland's theories are open to many of the criticisms of connectionism: they are based on neuroscientific research which may be superseded, and Churchland's work in particular indulges in some fairly heavy-handed reductionism, because it presumes that all meaningful mental states must be reducible to neural states.[46] These are important objections. To the extent that they are applicable to legal models of proof, they are addressed below.

The leading empirical research on legal fact finding, conducted by Nancy Pennington and Reid Hastie, suggests that fact finders use explanation-based decision making (EBDM).[47] Though Pennington and Hastie's model is not explicitly connectionist, EBDM shares a number of features with Thagard's model of 'explanatory coherence':[48] the key feature of both is that fact finders construct theories and test them by their ability to explain the evidence which has been presented. To be convincing, an explanation must be coherent (internally consistent and consistent with schema drawn from the fact finder's experience); it should also have good coverage (accounting for all of the evidence) and have a degree of uniqueness (it will be less convincing to the extent that alternative explanations can account for the evidence). Some commentators have suggested that EBDM can be reconciled with a Bayesian model of proof:[49] if we envisage explanations as hypotheses, then it is argued that we can think of a fact finder conditioning each hypothesis on the evidence in order to compare their probabilities. This interpretation of EBDM, however, misses an important point: the empirical evidence supporting EBDM does not suggest that fact finders do engage in probability assessments of the explanations they have constructed, even on a holistic scale.[50] How, then, do fact finders decide whether an explanation has been proved to a particular standard of proof? It should be conceded that, to date, this is one of the least well elaborated aspects of EBDM. Nevertheless, some pointers can be offered. It seems likely that in many cases only one coherent explanation of the evidence will emerge, so there would be no need to perform a probabilistic assessment. In other cases, there may be two or more competing explanations, and the fact finder must choose between them, but this process need not be probabilistic. In a criminal trial, a fact finder might treat acquittal as a default verdict, to be chosen if a prosecution explanation does not satisfy the attributes of coherence, coverage and uniqueness to a sufficient degree. Alternatively the fact finder might concentrate on defence explanations, and acquit the defendant on finding a reasonable explanation of the evidence consistent with innocence. To the extent that induction plays a role, it may be eliminative rather than probabilistic: the fact finder will eliminate explanations or pieces of evidence which make little sense and pay no attention to them, even though they may minimally probabilify an explanation.

Theories of Proof

Debates about the role of Bayesianism in legal fact finding have been going on now for a number of years.[51] Many of the criticisms of the Bayesian project made in this chapter have been put forward in these debates in some form or another. Despite this, proponents of Bayesianism do not view these criticisms, most of which rely on the empirical inadequacy of Bayesianism, as being especially convincing. In this section an attempt is made to probe the different attitudes to theories of proof that seem to underpin these very different attitudes to Bayesianism.

A recent strategy among Bayesians involved in the legal debates has been, rather than to attempt to refute the criticisms of Bayesianism, to argue that the results of Bayesian scholarship prove its validity. In the words of David Kaye: 'The proof of the value of this approach lies in the pudding, and [Bayesianism] has produced some treats in the kitchen.'[52] It is true that the application of probability theory to evidential problems appears to have yielded some interesting insights. To give just two examples, it has clarified the reasoning (and lack of reasoning) underlying the use of character evidence to impeach witnesses;[53] it has also proved valuable in the analysis of expert evidence.[54] The use of Bayes's theorem as an analytical tool does not, however, demonstrate its adequacy as a theory of proof (meaning, in this context, a theory of what it means to prove a case to the appropriate standard). In any case, many of the insights yielded by Bayesian analysis do not depend on Bayesianism (though this is *not* to deny that Bayesian analysis is extremely useful as a means of clarifying the arguments); as recent research has shown, at the turn of the century forensic scientists were making the distinctions now said to have been revealed by Bayesian analysis, without, of course, using Bayes's theorem.[55] Furthermore many interesting insights have been gained through non-Bayesian analysis, yet Bayesians do not claim that this demonstrates the validity of those perspectives as theories of proof.[56] Although Bayesianism does offer a theory of proof – that standards of proof can be considered as subjective probabilities, set at values to be determined by utility theory – this is just what is controversial about Bayesianism.

Underlying these disagreements about the usefulness of Bayesian theory is, one suspects, a deeper disagreement, which centres on the extent to which a theory of proof should reflect human cognitive capacities and natural reasoning processes. Many Bayesians brush aside empirically based criticisms of Bayesianism on the grounds that they are irrelevant. Bayesianism, they argue, is not meant to be a descriptive theory of processes of proof, but a normative or idealized theory. The point that there is an interaction between the normative and the descriptive has been touched on several times in this chapter, but never fully resolved. Below, three reasons for naturalizing a theory of forensic proof are offered.

1 A theory of proof should reflect the cognitive capabilities of human fact finders.[57] This seems to be accepted by most Bayesians, who have responded to criticisms about the intractability of Bayesian calculations by proposing ways of simplifying Bayesianism. But, if we take 'cognitive capabilities' to include the ability to express the subjective probabilities required by Bayesianism, then doubts about the basis of those probabilities are a significant problem.

2 Because we use human fact finders, a theory of proof should reflect human cognitive practices. As a result of this, EBDM is currently the most appropriate basis on which to build a model of proof. Unless we can be sure that fact finders reason probabilistically, or in a manner that is equivalent to probabilistic reasoning, we should be aware that changing the rules of evidence to conform to probability theory might be detrimental, because it would lead to a mismatch between the cognitive behaviour of fact finders and the task they are asked to perform.

3 A theory of proof should not be used to justify a decision irrespective of the processes that produced it. Recently, Richard Friedman has claimed that, 'when thinking well ... fact finders reach results that are roughly consistent with those they would reach if they were to apply probability theory rigorously'.[58] This shift to what might be termed counterfactual Bayesianism seems to be designed to avoid criticisms based on (1) and (2) above, because it makes no claim to either describe or prescribe the process used to make decisions. However it seems futile to evaluate beliefs without reference to the way in which they were formed.[59] If X comes to believe *y* through a non-Bayesian process, but would have believed *y* had she used a Bayesian process, her decision would not be justified by Bayesian standards. Similarly, if X comes to believe *z* through a non-Bayesian process, the fact that she would not have believed *z* had she used a Bayesian process is not, in itself, a ground for criticism. Criticism would only be appropriate if X could be shown how, in practice, she could use a Bayesian process to improve her reasoning[60] - and here all the difficulties of using Bayes's theorem in a real-world setting re-enter the picture. In short, if Bayesianism is to be used as an evaluative standard, it must be used to evaluate processes, not results.

Bayesianism as a Tool

It has been argued above that Bayesianism is an inadequate theory of proof because it does not reflect the cognitive practices of human decision makers. But that is very different from arguing that Bayesianism can never be useful as a tool for evidence scholars. One danger in developing a theory of proof which is too firmly rooted in empirical evidence about human cognitive practices is that it will ignore the fact that human beings are remarkably good at extending their cognitive capabilities. For example, William Bechtel has criticized Churchland's reductionist strategy in the philosophy of science because it presumes that all meaningful manipulation of theories must be explained at the neural level.[61] This, Bechtel argues, ignores the fact that scientists frequently use tools such as algebra, diagrams and the like in order to further their understanding of theories; probability theory could, of course be added to this list.

Probability theory may, then, be validly used by evidence scholars in some contexts. As was acknowledged above, in this manner Bayesianism has contributed to some important insights into evidence doctrine. Might Bayesianism also be a useful tool for fact finders?[62] It is possible that, if we provided fact finders with some instruction in probability theory, we might improve their decision making. But the desire to use Bayesianism in such contexts would not override the empirically based criticisms outlined above because, 'unless the mind has a suitable structure, it cannot *use* tools properly'.[63]

Conclusion

This chapter has reviewed some of the criticisms of Bayesianism as a model of theory confirmation in science and of proof in law. There are many criticisms of the Bayesian project, but those that have been focused on have made it possible to develop a consistent theme: that Bayesianism's main failing is that it is a model of inference that bears little relation to ordinary cognitive practices. We have seen that subjective probability, the building block of Bayesianism, is a dubious concept. If we grant Bayesianism its subjective probabilities, then it runs into trouble with its one-dimensional concept of evidence. Bayesian explanations of prior probability exemplify the unrealistic nature of the whole enterprise, while attempts to avoid complexity leave us with an impoverished model.

As these are substantial criticisms, what might explain the popularity of Bayesianism? Two reasons are worth highlighting. Just as utilitarianism is attractive because it appears to offer a neat moral theory, so the popularity of Bayesianism is partly due to 'the allure of a precise mathematical tool - the probability calculus - which dangles the prospects of a tidy and elegant theory'.[64] The idea of a rule-based system of inference is beguiling, but that does not make it right.[65] Another reason for Bayesianism's popularity is that it does work in some contexts. In science, Bayesianism works in statistical inference where fixed parameters make its application relatively straightforward; much more problematic is its application as a model of inference and theory choice.[66] In law, Bayesianism has proved to be a useful analytical tool; but that does not make it an appropriate theory of proof.

The burden of the argument in this chapter has been that a theory of proof should be firmly based on empirical knowledge. At present, the best available evidence suggests that fact finders use explanation-based decision making, and it does not seem that this model can easily be reconciled with probability theory. So what does this mean for the way we analyse the rules of evidence? Any answer to that question would require a detailed inquiry which which will not be pursued here. But analysis of such academic favourites as the paradoxes of proof apart, there may be no very deep implications of the sort of non-Bayesian model outlined here. Evidence law has left the question, 'What does it mean to prove a case?' largely to fact finders in individual cases. Given the complexity of this topic, and the difficulty of developing rules of inference, that is doubtless wise.

Notes

1 This approach is similar to that adopted by Ron Allen in a recent paper, in that it draws parallels between criticisms of Bayesianism in the philosophy of science and in law. See Ronald J. Allen, 'Rationality, Algorithms and Juridical Proof: A Preliminary Inquiry' (1997) 1 *International Journal of Evidence and Proof* 254. As Allen demonstrates, scrutiny of the philosophy of science literature reveals that there are deeper problems for the Bayesian project than those that have been at the forefront of the legal debates.

2 [1996] 2 Cr.App.R 467. The judgment is discussed in detail in Mike Redmayne, 'Presenting Probabilities in Court: The DNA Experience' (1997) 1 *International Journal of Evidence and Proof* 187.

3 For some interesting empirical research, which suggests that fact finders do have significant problems in accepting that a case has been proved in these sorts of circumstances, see Gary L. Wells, 'Naked Statistical Evidence: Is Subjective Probability Enough?' (1992) 62 *Journal of Personality and Social Psychology* 739.

4 For a brief account of the problem of induction, and the emergence of Bayesianism, see Colin Howson and Peter Urbach, *Scientific Reasoning: The Bayesian Approach* (2nd edn, La Salle, 1993), ch. 1.

5 In spite of this, consistency is a remarkably weak requirement: I may have a consistent belief set even though all my beliefs are false. Alternatively I might have an inconsistent belief set, even though the majority of my beliefs are true.

6 While there are Dutch book arguments for consistency of beliefs at any particular moment in time, it should be noted that there is no Dutch book argument which requires a person to update her beliefs through using Bayes's theorem. See Colin Howson, 'Theories of Probability' (1995) 46 *British Journal for the Philosophy of Science* 1, 9-12.

7 The criticisms that follow draw particularly on Mark Kaplan, 'Bayesianism Without the Black Box' (1989) 56 *Philosophy of Science* 48.

8 See Jon Elster, *Ulysses and the Sirens: Studies in Rationality and Irrationality* (Cambridge, 1979), pp.129-30.

9 See Richard W. Miller, *Fact and Method: Explanation, Confirmation and Reality in the Natural and Social Sciences* (Princeton, 1987), pp.331-3.

10 Kaplan, 'Black Box'. Kaplan notes that these objections still hold when Bayesianism is relaxed to allow subjective probabilities to be interpreted as probability distributions rather than point-valued probabilities. His conclusion, however, is not that we should give up the concept of subjective probability completely; instead he suggests that we should accept it as a regulative ideal which we should adopt whenever we have a coherent set of preferences for the beliefs in question. This would substantially restrict

the scope of Bayesianism. It would almost certainly count against its use by fact finders in all but the simplest cases.

11 Alvin I. Goldman, *Epistemology and Cognition* (Cambridge, Mass., 1986), pp.324–43. For a similar conception of uncertainty as transition between states of certainty, see Gerd Gigerenzer *et al.*, *The Empire of Chance: How Probability Changed Science and Everyday Life* (Cambridge, 1989), pp.225–6. The authors suggest that uncertainty might be measured by frequency of transition.

12 An example is provided by Ward Edwards, in 'Comment' (1986) 66 *Boston University Law Review* 623: 'no real-world proposition ... has probability 1; I would not assign probability 1 to the proposition that my name is Edwards'.

13 See, for example, P. Gärdenfors and N. E. Sahlin, 'Unreliable Probabilities, Risk Taking and Decision Making' (1982) 53 *Synthese*, 361; Alex Stein, 'Judicial Fact-finding and the Bayesian Method: The Case for Deeper Scepticism about their Combination' (1996) 1 *International Journal of Evidence and Proof* 25.

14 For example, Kaplan, 'Black Box', 55. The example is similar, of course, to the 'is it raining in St Petersburg?' question posed above.

15 Second order probability might be used to address this problem. This possibility is examined below.

16 Peter Achinstein, 'Concepts of Evidence', in Peter Achinstein (ed.), *The Concept of Evidence* (Oxford, 1983); *The Nature of Explanation* (New York, 1983), ch. 10; 'Stronger Evidence' (1994) 61 *Philosophy of Science* 329.

17 In fact, in law things are a little more complex than this. The probabilistic definition of evidence corresponds to the measure of probative value suggested in Richard D. Friedman, 'A Close Look at Probative Value' (1986) 66 *Boston University Law Review* 733. However most other legal Bayesians define evidential relevance in terms of the likelihood ratio: $p(e \mid h) \mid p(e \sqcap h)$; where numerator and denominator of this ratio are not identical, the evidence is considered relevant (see, for example, Richard Lempert, 'Modeling Relevance' (1977) 75 *Michigan Law Review* 1021). At first sight, the likelihood ratio is not open to the criticisms which follow, but this is because it describes relevance from the point of view of a judge deciding issues of admissibility rather than from the point of view of the fact finder combining pieces of evidence. Even where evidence is relevant on the likelihood ratio analysis, the fact finder must still decide whether it changes her degree of belief in the hypothesis in issue, and the evidence may be redundant if it merely replicates evidence that has come before. Unless $p(h \mid e) > p(h)$ the evidence has no probative value for the fact finder.

18 See Karl Popper, *The Logic of Scientific Discovery* (London, 1959), p.407.

19 Achinstein, 'Stronger Evidence', 331–9.

20 See Peter Achinstein, 'Variety and Analogy in Confirmation Theory' (1963) 30 *Philosophy of Science* 207.

21 Achinstein, 'Stronger Evidence', 343.

22 Very few of those involved in the debate about Bayesianism in evidence law have attempted to develop a concept of second order probability in order to address the shortcomings of orthodox Bayesianism. Richard Friedman has taken a step in this direction, in 'Answering the Bayesioskeptical Challenge' (1997) 1 *International Journal of Evidence and Proof* 276, but his proposal remains sketchy. Although only peripherally concerned with the legal debates, James Logue has developed a system of second order probability as a means of analysing probabilistic resilience and has suggested that this provides solutions to some of the legal problems. See James Logue, *Projective Probability* (Oxford, 1995), pp.87–95, 150–54.

23 Achinstein, 'Stronger Evidence', 349.

24 The subjectivity of Bayesianism prompted Clark Glymour to reject it as a model of theory choice. See Clark Glymour, 'Why I am not a Bayesian', in David Papineau (ed.), *The Philosophy of Science* (Oxford, 1996).

25 Mary Hesse, *The Structure of Scientific Inference* (London, 1977), pp.115–16.

26 See Malcolm R. Forster, 'Bayes and Bust: Simplicity as a Problem for a Probabilist's Approach to Confirmation' (1995) 46 *British Journal for the Philosophy of Science* 399, 411.

27 For example, L. Jonathan Cohen, 'The Problem of Prior Probabilities in Forensic Proof' (1982) XXIV *Ratio* 71.

28 There is, arguably, a second element to the presumption: that the fact finder should decide the case only on the evidence presented to her during the trial, in other words, that she does not fill in evidential gaps in the prosecution case. This requirement, however, is rather indeterminate because, unless the fact finder brings some outside knowledge to the case, none of the evidence presented will make any sense at all. Alex Stein, in Ronald J. Allen *et al.*, 'Probability and Proof in *State* v. *Skipper*: An Internet Exchange' (1995) 35 *Jurimetrics Journal* 277, 283, has also suggested that the presumption 'has a broader significance' than being a restatement of the burden and standard of proof, but the evidential implications of any such significance remain opaque.

29 For example, Richard Lempert, 'The New Evidence Scholarship: Analyzing the Process of Proof', in Peter Tillers and Eric D. Green (eds), *Probability and Inference in the Law of Evidence: The Uses and Limits of Bayesianism* (Dordrecht, 1988), p.77. Lempert suggests 'that in all cases ... the prior probability of the matter in question be set at an odds of one to one less than the number of actors in the world ... I see no other empirically justified starting point'.

30 Richard D. Friedman, in 'Probability and Proof in *State* v. *Skipper*', 296.

31 Though, for more subtle Bayesian attempts to describe the belief state which a fact finder should have before hearing any evidence, see Simon Blackburn, 'Review of *The Probable and the Provable*' (1980) 44 *Synthese* 149; Logue, *Projective Probability*, pp.152–3. Both commentators use the concept of second order probability to describe a non-committed initial belief state.

32 For recognition of the complexity problem in science, see Hesse, *Scientific Inference*, p.111. Hesse notes that 'calculation of both posterior probabilities and likelihoods presupposes that not only initial probabilities over all hypotheses and evidence statements are known, but also that initial probabilities of all *conjunctions* of hypotheses and evidence are known'. In law, the complexity point has been particularly stressed by Craig Callen, for example in 'Cognitive Science, Bayesian Norms and Rules of Evidence' (1991) 154(A) *Journal of the Royal Statistical Society* 129. One implication of complexity is that no human – nor even any computer – can ever be a perfect Bayesian. See Daniel N. Osherson, 'Judgment', in Daniel N. Osherson and Edward E. Smith (eds), *Thinking: An Introduction to Cognitive Science, Volume Three* (Cambridge, Mass., 1990), pp.79–82.

33 Harold I. Brown, 'Reason, Judgement and Bayes's Law' (1994) 61 *Philosophy of Science* 351, 359–60.

34 Wesley Salmon, 'Rationality and Objectivity in Science, *or* Tom Kuhn Meets Tom Bayes' in Papineau (ed.), *The Philosophy of Science*.

35 John Earman, *Bayes or Bust? A Critical Examination of Bayesian Confirmation Theory* (Cambridge, Mass., 1992), pp.171–3.

36 See, for example, Bernard Robertson and G.A. Vignaux, 'Extending the Conversation About Bayes' (1991) 13 *Cardozo Law Review* 629.

37 I have developed this criticism at greater length in Mike Redmayne, 'Science, Evidence

and Logic' (1996) 59 *Modern Law Review* 747.

38 See Christopher Cherniak, *Minimal Rationality* (Cambridge, Mass., 1986).

39 Bernard Williams, 'A Critique of Utilitarianism', in J.J.C. Smart and Bernard Williams, *Utilitarianism: For and Against* (Cambridge, 1973), pp.137, 149. For a more detailed development of this critique, see Onora O'Neill, 'The Moral Perplexities of Famine Relief', in T. Regan (ed.), *Matters of Life and Death* (Philadelphia, 1980). O'Neill notes that, 'if it turns out that the comprehensive data that utilitarians need are *usually* not available, then the attraction fades. We are left with indecision rather than precision, even in matters of justice' (p.285).

40 W.V. Quine, 'Epistemology Naturalized', *Ontological Relativity and Other Essays* (New York, 1969), p.78.

41 As Ronald Giere observes, one does not find statements of the odds on particular theories in any of the physics journals: Ronald N. Giere, *Explaining Science: A Cognitive Approach* (Chicago, 1988), p.156. See also Miller, *Fact and Method*, p.269, who notes that 'Bayesian Inference to the preferred alternative has not resolved, even temporarily, a single fundamental scientific dispute'. This is not to deny that Bayesian statistics are used effectively in many fields, but there is a large difference between Bayesian statistics and Bayesian confirmation theory: as regards the former, Bayesianism is used against strictly defined background assumptions, but these are lacking when it is applied to theory confirmation. See Forster, 'Bayes and Bust'.

42 Giere, *Explaining Science*, pp.161–78.

43 'Explanatory Coherence' (1989) 12 *Behavioral and Brain Sciences* 435. For a summary, see Alvin I. Goldman, *Philosophical Applications of Cognitive Science* (Boulder, 1993), pp.39–51.

44 Paul M. Churchland, 'On the Nature of Theories: A Neurocomputational Perspective' and 'On the Nature of Explanation: A PDP Approach', *A Neurocomputational Perspective: The Nature of Mind and the Structure of Science* (Cambridge, Mass., 1992).

45 See David Stump, 'Naturalized Philosophy of Science With a Plurality of Methods' (1992) 59 *Philosophy of Science* 456, 458.

46 For some cogent criticisms, see Susan Haack, *Evidence and Inquiry* (Oxford, 1993), ch. 8.

47 See Nancy Pennington and Reid Hastie, 'The Story Model for Juror Decision Making', in Reid Hastie (ed.), *Inside the Juror: The Psychology of Juror Decision Making* (Cambridge, Mass., 1993). Although the Pennington/Hastie model is more commonly referred to as the 'story model', I prefer 'explanation-based decision making' as I am uneasy about some of the connotations of 'story model', such as the implication that fact finders pay relatively little attention to evidence. Pennington and Hastie use the phrase 'EBDM' to describe the model in recent work, such as 'The OJ Simpson Stories' (1996) 67 *University of Colorado Law Review* 957.

48 In 'Explanatory Coherence', 449–53, Thagard describes the application of his model to legal fact finding.

49 For example, Bernard Robertson and G.A. Vignaux, 'Probability – The Logic of the Law' (1993) 13 *Oxford Journal of Legal Studies* 457.

50 See Pennington and Hastie, 'Story Model'. For the finding that mock jurors spend little time discussing reasonable doubt, see Reid Hastie, Steven Penrod and Nancy Pennington, *Inside the Jury* (Cambridge, Mass., 1983), p.170. For research showing that subjects in a mock tort case will return a judgment of non-liability when their subjective probability of liability is greater than 0.5, see Wells, 'Naked Statistical Evidence'.

51 For a review of the main trends in these debates, see John Jackson, 'Analysing the New Evidence Scholarship: Towards a New Conception of the Law of Evidence' (1996) 16

Oxford Journal of Legal Studies 309.

52 David H. Kaye, in 'Probability and Proof in *State* v. *Skipper*', 305. The 'proof of the pudding' metaphor has proved popular among contributors to the special issue of the *International Journal of Evidence and Proof* on Bayesianism and Juridical Proof 253–360.

53 Richard D. Friedman, 'Character Impeachment Evidence: Psycho-Bayesian [!?] Analysis and a Proposed Overhaul' (1991) 38 *University of California at Los Angeles Law Review* 637.

54 Bernard Robertson and G.A. Vignaux, *Interpreting Evidence: Evaluating Forensic Science in the Courtroom* (Chichester, 1995).

55 F. Taroni, C. Champod and P.A. Margot, 'Were Earlier Criminalists Pioneers of Bayesianism in Forensic Science?', paper presented at the Third International Conference on Forensic Statistics, Edinburgh, July 1996.

56 For example, cognitive science (Craig R. Callen, 'Hearsay and Informal Reasoning' (1994) 47 *Vanderbilt Law Review* 43) and Baconian probability, which alerted us to the significance of 'weight' or, at least, some analogous component of proof (L. Jonathan Cohen, *The Probable and the Provable*, Oxford, 1977).

57 This first reason only requires minimal naturalism. On different degrees of 'naturalism', see Haack, *Evidence and Inquiry*, pp.118–20.

58 Friedman, 'Answering the Bayesioskeptical Challenge'.

59 See Goldman, *Epistemology*, pp.87, 90–91.

60 A similar point is often made in response to those who claim that humans are irrational, or poor reasoners, because in various experiments they have been shown to violate Bayesian norms. The response is that this is better interpreted as a failure of learning rather than as a failure of reasoning, just as it may be better to interpret an inability to divide 20,367 by 73 as a failure in learning (or recalling) the algorithm for long division rather than as a failure to reason well. See Goldman, *Philosophical Applications*, pp.30–31; Giere, *Explaining Science*, p.174.

61 William Bechtel, 'What Should a Connectionist Philosophy of Science Look Like?', in Robert N. McCauley (ed.), *The Churchlands and Their Critics* (Oxford, 1996). See also Giere, *Explaining Science*, pp.172–8, for the argument that probability theory is a model that may be useful to scientists.

62 I have myself – somewhat cautiously, to be sure – suggested that Bayesian analysis may be useful in some cases. See Redmayne, 'Presenting Probabilities'.

63 Goldman, *Epistemology*, p.5.

64 Ibid., p.328.

65 For a detailed critique of rule-based conceptions of rationality, see Harold I. Brown, *Rationality* (London, 1988).

66 See Forster, 'Bayes and Bust'.

5 Expert Games in Silicone Gel Breast Implant Litigation

Sheila Jasanoff

Legal historians have noted the relatively late appearance of institutionalized medicolegal knowledge and practices in Anglo-American judicial proceedings.[1] Here at the end of the 20th century, however, the American legal system suffers if anything from a surfeit of expertise. Courts today are awash with scientific evidence, generated largely at the behest of the litigating parties. Forensic science figured crucially in a series of high-profile criminal cases during the 1990s: the identification of telephonic voices (New York State Judge Sol Wachtler's threatening calls to his ex-mistress); handwriting (White House aide Vince Foster's suicide note and the Jon-Benét Ramsey ransom letter); typewriting (Theodore Kaczynski's authorship of the Unabomber manifesto); blood spatters (O.J. Simpson's glove, shoes and car); traces of chemical explosives (the Oklahoma City bombing); intercranial bleeding and 'shaken baby syndrome' (the murder trial of British au pair Louise Woodward). In civil cases, scientific evidence underpins claims of damage from drugs, diet pills, medical devices, electromagnetic fields, environmental pollutants and a host of other hazards, imagined or real. Expert evidence is invoked not only to prove guilt and causation, but also to establish baselines of acceptable behaviour in far-flung domains of professional endeavour, as in cases involving medical malpractice, insider trading, scientific misconduct, nursing, babysitting or child abuse.

As if driven by the law of supply and demand, forensic science, the cluster of scientific specialisms dedicated to the investigation of legally relevant matters of fact, has undergone massive growth and diversification in the past few decades. Indicators of professionalization, such as treatises, journals and associations, have not lagged far behind. A recent 1241-page treatise on scientific evidence testifies to the breadth and depth of this transformation. Its index lists, under a single letter of the alphabet, topics as disparate as 'semen', 'shoewear', 'skeleton', 'skidmarks' and 'smothering'.[2] Similarly hardly an academic discipline has not been called upon at one time or another to satisfy the legal system's insatiable thirst for certified knowledge. Sociologists and philosophers of science, for example, testified against the constitutionality of an Arkansas creationist law,[3] and specialists in ancient philosophy debated the constitutionality of an anti-gay rights referendum in the state of Colorado.[4]

The sudden efflorescence of experts and expertise in legal settings has brought with it a rising concern about the lines of demarcation between genuine and spurious experts, between mere claims of expert knowledge and the real thing. The fairness, not to say the perceived competence, of the legal process depends on its ability to make just such demarcations, but the capacity of courts to do so credibly is increasingly in doubt. For some, the problem reduces to a search for rules or criteria with which courts should be able to distinguish, quite generally, between legitimate science and its meretricious lookalikes.[5] Others have put their faith in process over rules and urged courts to assess the state of knowledge through wider use of specially appointed experts or panels. But such formulaic solutions, as has been argued elsewhere,[6] fail to make allowances for the contingencies that govern the production of scientific evidence. In the great majority of modern legal controversies, relevant expertise is not to be had for the asking, conveniently displayed in well-marked packages in the grand supermarket of science. Like every other aspect of a litigant's story, expert evidence too must be painstakingly pieced together from disparate, contradictory, incomplete and changeable sources.[7] Its function from the start is to support or contest particular accounts of something gone wrong in the world; normative and epistemological commitments are therefore inseparably woven together into expert evidence.

How then should courts tackle the demarcation problem of distinguishing between 'good' and 'bad' expert testimony? If appeal to external scientific authority is excluded in principle, whether in the form of absolute rules or of authoritative processes, clarification has to be sought within the very settings where evidence is made, through a deeper understanding of the mechanisms by which experts gain or lose credibility in the eyes of the law. Expertise is best viewed for our purposes as the end product of a complex game – equipped with its own distinctive moves, countermoves, rhetorics and practices – which can be simultaneously played by multiple players (such as judges, juries, lawyers, scientists, witnesses and professional communities) at varied locations, inside and outside the courtroom. This dynamic model helps us to sort and compare the divergent claims of expertise that come before the courts in complex litigation, such as the silicone gel breast implant (SGBI) lawsuits that have flooded US courtrooms since 1977.[8] Appreciation of the model, finally, provides a basis for refining the judgments that should govern the admissibility of expert evidence in legal proceedings.

How to Tell an Expert

In everyday life, expertise strikes us as an unproblematic phenomenon with clearly defined boundaries. The word 'expert' has, to begin with, a respectable pedigree in the English language. According to the *Oxford English Dictionary*, Chaucer already spoke of a person 'in science so experte' and of 'Maystres ... That were of lawe expert and curious'. We have, besides, quite clear intuitions about how to use the term in ordinary speech. A cook, a salesman or a piano tuner, for instance, can be designated 'expert' for simply measuring up to certain conventional performance standards. By contrast, it seems reductionist to pin the label 'expert' on a violinist, mathematician or theatre critic, whose craft transcends any predetermined repertoire of rules. Yet we readily concede that artists, inventors and technicians all possess some form of expertise. Rule 702 of the US Federal Rules of Evidence (Testimony of Experts) begins to tease apart some of these intuitive judgments by acknowledging the varied ways in which expertise can be constituted. Persons may be recognized as experts in the courtroom by virtue of 'knowledge, skill, experience, training, or education'; once they are so certified, they need not, like laypeople, limit their testimony solely to matters known through direct, personal experience. Expertise, as conceived by the law, clearly encompasses the special sort of competence that we term 'science', but it is a significantly broader concept.

While granting that there are varied cognitive and experiential pathways to expertise, Rule 702 does require all would-be experts to show some level of learning or mastery beyond the ordinary. Expertise is not a state to be claimed at will. Yet, in the landscape of contemporary legal disputes, it seems that almost any kind of human experience can be converted, if only temporarily, into a domain of possible expertise. Scientists, used to operating within tightly drawn boundaries of professional authority,[9] find this catholic embrace of expertise unsettling, to say the least. Is the courtroom, then, the proverbial country of the blind where even the one-eyed man is king? The answer, of course, is no. The legal system has as great a stake in distinguishing admissible from inadmissible claims of expertise as science itself. In testing the credibility of experts, the law reaffirms its own credibility. The ways in which it does this, however, are all its own, conditioned by the legal system's peculiar needs, constraints and purposes. Consequently the law's techniques for evaluating scientific evidence do not map neatly onto science's modes of testing knowledge claims. Contrary to conventional wisdom, these discrepancies do not make the law anti- or un-scientific; they merely accentuate the necessary distance between legal and scientific fact finding.

Formal screening of experts has long been a component of legal proceedings. The American federal system determined admissibility for 70 years in accordance with an otherwise obscure 1923 appeals court decision, *Frye* v. *United States*,[10] which decreed that the science underlying expert testimony had to be 'sufficiently established to have gained general acceptance in the particular field in which it belongs'. The *Frye* rule proved difficult to administer consistently, and over time different interpretations of 'general acceptance' took hold in different jurisdictions around the country. Despite this lack of uniformity, the basis for screening experts did not attract much attention outside the legal community until the 1993 Supreme Court decision in *Daubert* v. *Merrell Dow Pharmaceuticals, Inc.*,[11] which many hailed as the case that would liberate federal courts from an onslaught of 'junk science'. *Daubert* overruled *Frye*, holding that it had been superseded by the legislatively enacted Federal Rules of Evidence. Federal courts, the Supreme Court declared, should henceforth subject offers of expert testimony to two basic tests: that of 'fit', or relevance, and that of scientific reliability. To assist the lower courts in applying the latter test, the court proposed four criteria: (a) did the evidence rest on a tested and falsifiable theory or technique; (b) had the underlying science been peer reviewed; (c) what was the technique's error rate, if known; and (d) recapitulating *Frye*, was it generally accepted?

In the glare of publicity surrounding *Daubert* and the efforts to apply it, the moves that legal actors make in constructing experts and expertise have become much more transparent than they were in the shadowy *Frye* regime. Federal judges appear substantially less inclined in the post-*Daubert* era simply to defer to the parties' experts. Rather courts have sought actively to test the relevance and reliability of expert testimony, through proceedings in which expertise is dynamically constructed and deconstructed. Some of the tests applied in screening experts are explicit and rule-like, as *Daubert* contemplated, and have become the subject of vigorous debate and commentary. Others are tacit, invisible, contingent and so unreflectively applied that they elude systematic inquiry. At the same time, the screening process has become palpably more interactive. Judges do not unproblematically apply the legally sanctioned demarcation criteria to a well-defined set of factual possibilities. Instead they (and, where applicable, their appointed experts) respond to specific, situated and strategic moves made by the litigants to establish some expert claims and deconstruct others. By piecing together these cross-cutting manoeuvres, we gain insight not only into what counts as expertise in American law but also into the merits of competing approaches to demarcating expertise.

The Game of Expertise

The making of expertise within the legal process can usefully be conceptualized as a kind of game in which experts and their claims struggle for credibility in the eyes of the fact finder. As in any game, some of the moves have to be made in accordance with prescribed rules; others are left to the players' wit and imagination. Figure 5.1 lays out the central parameters of the expertise game on an imaginary board divided into four quadrants by a horizontal and a vertical axis. The horizontal axis - labelled *experience* - accommodates moves designed to professionalize the knowledge claimed by expert witnesses. It is not enough for experts simply to embody personal trustworthiness, although this of course is a *sine qua non* of witnessing more generally. In order to claim the special prerogatives that the law accords them, experts have to embody in their own persons the collective judgments of a discipline, occupation or profession. Their success depends on establishing a double claim on the fact finder's trust: not only as individuals, but also as representatives of certified specialist communities. Correspondingly their credibility can be undermined by attacking either their personal or their professional integrity.

The vertical axis - labelled *objectivity* - designates efforts to move expert evidence from the pole of untested or subjective observation (for example, eyewitness testimony) towards that of scientific fact. Expert testimony gains special force when it is seen as conforming to scientific standards. The expert's personal biases and faults then diminish in significance, although (as will be clear in later examples) the personal dimension never completely disappears. An expert who represents science speaks for a reality presumed to be beyond mere individual experience. The more scientific the claim, the less open it is to personalized attack. Its objectivity is underwritten by science's cultural authority. Following *Daubert*, however, judicial scrutiny can less readily be avoided simply by asserting that testimony is based on reliable science. The labels 'scientist' and 'scientific' have become resources to be strategically deployed, defended and fought for vis-à-vis the judge as well as the opposing party. The vertical axis in Figure 5.1 delineates the moves by which witnesses' claims can either be made to look more like science or else methodologically deconstructed and rendered inadmissible as scientific testimony.

Together, the two axes define the basic strategic spaces in which expertise can be asserted or challenged. Proceeding clockwise from the top left, the first three quadrants all represent spaces in which expertise can be plausibly claimed, but on varying grounds: in quadrant 1, the goal is to enhance the objectivity of lay experience by stressing its skilled, disciplined or knowledgeable character; in quadrant 2, moves are designed to tie expertise

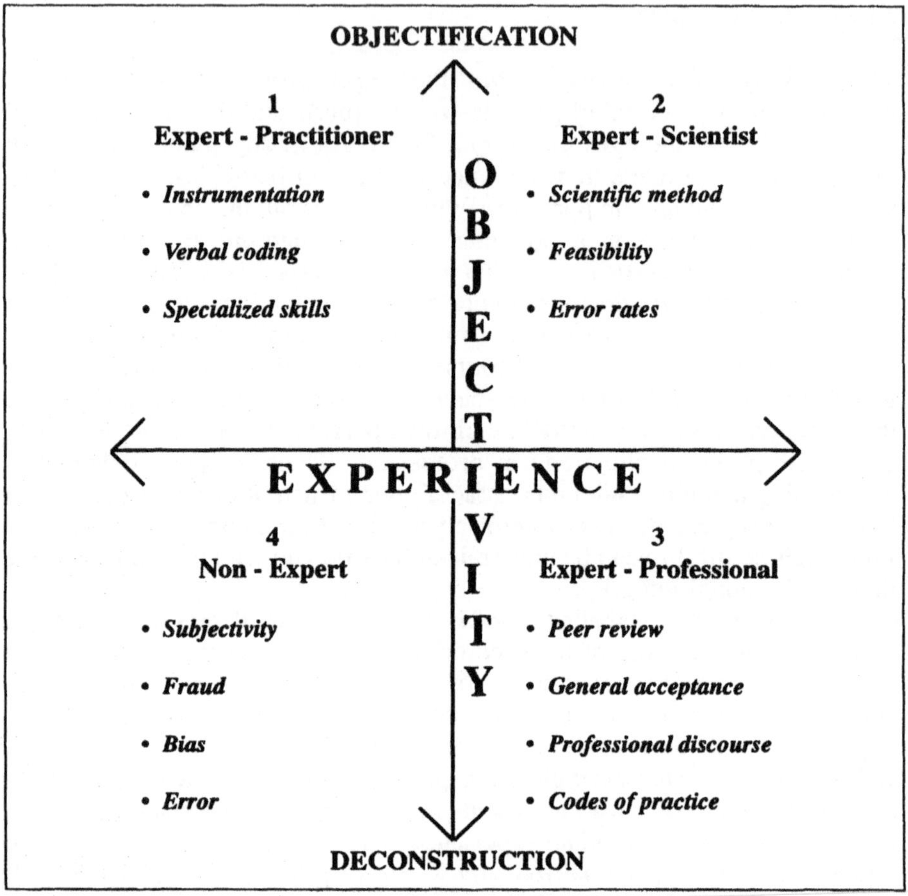

Figure 5.1 Game board of expertise

explicitly to scientific methods and the objectivity of science; in quadrant 3, expert claims are linked to the judgment and experience of professional communities, but not necessarily to science. In quadrant 4, by contrast, the permitted moves are largely deconstructive: to deprive experts of the resources of specialized 'knowledge, skill, experience, training or education'. The would-be expert is reduced here to the status of a lay witness of no special skill and questionable personal integrity. To succeed in the expertise game, players must press their claims as far as possible in the direction of scientific objectivity and accredited professional experience. In challenging expert claims, the goal is just the opposite: to move claims into quadrant 4, that is, back towards the poles of subjective knowledge and individual experience. Only when pressed into this space can expert claims be said to meet neither the relatively stringent tests of scientific reliability nor the broader measures of professional expertise.

Interpreted within the model of the expertise game, *Daubert* acquires a more complex meaning than it has been accorded by most commentators. It is not, as is sometimes asserted, simply an injunction to judges to 'think like scientists'. Rather, *Daubert* outlines a programmatic view of the possible means by which allegedly expert claims can be moved along one or the other major axis of knowledge certification. The criteria proposed by the Supreme Court are consistent in this respect with the eclectic approach to expertise taken by the Federal Rules of Evidence. *Daubert* implicitly recognizes that expert knowledge, for legal purposes, is not coextensive with scientific knowledge. Of the four *Daubert* criteria, only two (testability and error rates) refer specifically to moves along the *objectivity* axis, by which experts lay claim to scientific reliability; the other two criteria (peer review and general acceptance) refer to moves along the axis of *experience*, from personal to professional, but not necessarily scientific, knowledge.

Daubert did not aim to provide comprehensive rules for establishing expertise and it should not be construed as having done so. The model of the expertise game helps identify some of the gaps in the criteria. 'Falsifiability', for instance, is derived from the philosopher Karl Popper's model of experimental science and has little relevance for other forms of scientific activity. Furthermore none of the criteria explicitly takes account of the role of material resources - such as instruments, reagents, test animals, photographs, software or computerized databases - in producing 'objective' scientific knowledge, even though their pervasiveness in scientific practice is now widely acknowledged.[12] Similarly no mention is made of professional codes or formal research protocols that can be used to underwrite claims of professional knowledge. The criteria, finally, assume a degree of autonomy on the part of judges that does not square with the interactive and locationally dispersed character of the expertise game. The opinion shows neither a reflexive awareness of the judicial role in constructing different meanings of admissibility nor a sensitivity to the ways in which legal discourse might be incorporated into the production of supposedly objective scientific statements. We will return to these points below in connection with the moves made by litigating parties in the SGBI cases.

Playing by the Rules

The layout of Figure 5.1 allows cases involving expert claims to be sorted into four 'bins', defined on the one hand by the source of the claimed experiential authority (personal or professional) and on the other by the choice to defend or contest claims of facticity (objectification or deconstruction). In each bin or quadrant, a finer characterization can be produced by describing the specific pathways followed in building up or tearing down the claims of expertise. Was the expert's experience shown to conform to impartial professional standards or was it challenged as idiosyncratic, wrong or biased? Was expert knowledge validated by the test of falsifiability or by that of general acceptance? The metaphor of sorting into bins scarcely does justice to the intricate dynamics of actual cases, which involve simultaneous, competing moves by several actors. In the game of expertise, the contest rarely takes place along preordained positions and stationary battle lines. Winning strategies more often require flexible accommodation to choices made by other players claiming superior scientific or professional authority.

The broad category of toxic tort cases, for instance, can be seen in the light of this analysis as composed of contests between plaintiffs' experts wishing to position themselves in quadrant 2 (upper right), or failing that in quadrant 1, and defendants seeking to press their opponents into quadrant 4 (lower left). An instructive example is *Christopherson* v. *Allied Signal Corp.*,[13] in which a suit was brought on behalf of a deceased worker at a battery manufacturing plant in Waco, Texas. The plaintiffs claimed that Christopherson had contracted a rare and fatal form of small-cell colon cancer as a result of exposure to nickel and cadmium fumes at his workplace. The only expert testimony provided for the plaintiff was based ultimately on an affidavit by a co-worker, whose testimony the court rejected as lacking sufficient markers of reliability: 'We find particularly telling', the court opined, the 'admission in his deposition that he did not know the chemical composition of the fumes nor the mix of chemicals in the impregnation and soak tanks'.[14] Other missing elements included quantitative data on the size of the plant and the soak area, the ventilation system and the dosage and duration of exposure; all these could presumably have been gathered through appropriate instrumentation, but not through unmediated observation. Faced with these gaps, the court concluded that the co-worker's subjective experience of his working conditions could not be packaged as expert testimony.

Skilful deployment of instruments can help clothe individual observations in the guise of credible expertise (quadrant 1), even when no professional warrant is available for particular ways of seeing. Thus, in *People* v. *Marx*,[15] a 1975 California criminal case, a court admitted evidence of bite marks on the victim's body although such testimony was not supported by an 'established science of identifying persons from bite marks'. The court applauded the prosecution experts' 'enthusiastic response to a rare opportunity to develop or extend forensic dentistry into the area of bite mark identification'.[16] Especially persuasive in the court's view was the fact that the experts 'did not rely on untested methods, unproven hypotheses, intuition or revelation. Rather, they applied scientifically and professionally established techniques - X-rays, models, microscopy, photography' to produce data that were independently 'verifiable by the court'.[17] Accordingly the court felt competent to rule that the novel uses of these techniques by prosecution experts raised no serious issues of admissibility.

Not only material instruments, but discursive strategies can be used to rerepresent personal observations as knowledge grounded in professional experience (quadrant 3). In the first Rodney King trial, for example, an 'expert' on police practice persuaded the jury to see a videotape of police violence as experienced policemen allegedly would have seen it. He accomplished this sleight of vision by verbally coding the movements of the victim's body: almost invisible changes in the position of arms, legs and buttocks were classified by these means as 'aggression', calling forth, in turn, such graduated and calculated responses as 'assessment periods', 'escalations of force', 'kicks' and 'blows'.[18] Similar verbal coding has been used with greater and lesser success to convert visual tests of car drivers' sobriety, such as 'horizontal gaze nystagmus', into techniques of expert policing.[19] Appeal to contingently constructed, yet seemingly impersonal, assessment rules can equally be made the basis for rejecting expert claims. An example that gained considerable notoriety in the United States was the idealized code of practice against which the criminalist Denis Fung was measured and found wanting under cross-examination by Barry Scheck in the O.J. Simpson trial. A lesser known but no less revealing example is the list of 'qualifications of expert witnesses in ancient Greek thought' produced by the philosopher Martha Nussbaum in connection with her testimony in the Colorado gay rights trial; by codifying the prerequisites for responsible classical scholarship, she hoped to place some interpreters (and interpretations) of Plato outside the pales of credible expertise.[20]

In quadrant 4 (lower left), we find strategies for moving claims down the objectivity axis, through deconstruction of their scientific merit, or back along the horizontal axis from professional to personal, and hence not qualifying as expertise. Since *Daubert*, for example, sceptical deconstruction of peer review appears to be gaining ground. In a federal district court case, *Valentine* v. *Pioneer Chlor Alkali*,[21] the court rejected an expert's testimony on the neuropathological effects of chlorine inhalation even though he had published an article in a peer-reviewed journal. In explaining its decision, the court produced its own demarcation criterion. Editorial peer review, the judge concluded, was not legally cognizable as 'true' peer review:

'Militating against forensic use of editorial peer review as a proxy for genuine critical examination of purported scientific evidence is the fact that the average referee spends less than two hours assessing an article submitted to a biomedical journal'.[22] When the *Daubert* case itself was reconsidered following the Supreme Court's 1993 decision, the Ninth Circuit Court of Appeals engaged in a similar construction of case-specific demarcation criteria. To strengthen the case for admissibility, it held, scientific evidence should be based where possible on 'pre-litigation research', which is 'less likely to have been biased toward a particular conclusion by the promise of remuneration'. Such a foundation would help to counter charges that the evidence in question 'is not science at all, but litigation'.[23] This ad hoc and unsupported rule was adopted with alacrity by the SGBI defendants, as we shall see below.

Personal integrity is another possible focus of attack in quadrant 4. This is where cross-examination can be deployed to great effect, by revealing personal bias, misconduct, financial interest or inconsistency on the part of individual experts. In the courtroom, the expert's personal credibility is always at stake and the claimed authority of science guarantees no protection against such probing. In *Blum* v. *Merrell Dow Pharmaceuticals, Inc.*,[24] for example, a products liability case involving the drug Bendectin, a Pennsylvania trial judge pointed to defects in the defence experts' professional integrity (evidence of bias in peer review) as well as personal integrity (corporate funding of research) as the basis for downgrading their credibility.

The testimony demonstrated that articles were inserted in 'peer review' journals, without review by independent authorities, but edited by lawyers; that 'peer review' journals published, as valid, the results of 'less than good studies'; that articles were rejected for publication by prestigious journals before being published in the 'peer review' journal, *Teratology*. The testimony exposed scientific literature created for purposes of legal defence. The testimony revealed a sycophantic relationship between 'scientists' and their funding source: the defendant, Merrell Dow.[25]

With this range of illustrations in mind, let us turn now to the construction of expertise by players in the litigation concerning breast implants.

The SGBI Litigation: Birth of a Mass Tort

Silicone gel breast implants were first introduced into the American market in the early 1960s as substitutes for earlier, less satisfactory devices, such as wax, fabric, directly injected silicone, synthetic sponges or saline-filled implants. The new product was favoured for its appearance, physical stability and apparent non-reactivity. By the 1970s, SGBIs were in wide use for cosmetic breast augmentation as well as for breast reconstruction following cancer surgery. Some 20 years later, reasonable estimates for the number of women with breast implants ranged between one and two million, with more precise figures probably not ascertainable.[26] SGBIs were marketed before the enactment of the 1976 Medical Device Amendment to the Federal Food, Drug and Cosmetic Act which required safety and efficacy testing for all implants. Information about the devices' safety was therefore largely the product of anecdotal and ad hoc post-market reporting by users, medical professionals and the media, a problem that was later to plague both plaintiffs and manufacturers. After 1976, SGBIs were subject to review by advisory panels to the Food and Drug Administration (FDA), the regulatory agency whose task it was to decide whether to demand additional testing or to leave the devices on the market. By all indications, FDA exercised its review power lackadaisically and without serious conviction throughout the 1980s.

Starting in the late 1980s, the breast implant story took surprising new turns. There were, to begin with, incontrovertible reports of rupture and leakage from the implants, accompanied by local inflammation, painful scarring, contraction and hardening of the surrounding breast tissue. Even intact implants were prone to 'bleeding', permitting small quantities of silicone to escape and be gradually disseminated through the body. For many women, the localized responses alone were severe enough to necessitate surgical removal of the implants, a procedure that some underwent more than once in the hope of finding a workable solution. More troubling were the increasing reports of so-called 'connective tissue diseases' (CTDs), a collection of auto-immune disorders afflicting the joints, skin and internal organs that included such conditions as lupus, scleroderma and rheumatoid arthritis. Complaints of this gravity could not stay hidden. In December 1990, the CBS television reporter Connie Chung produced a segment on breast implants on her show, *Face to Face with Connie Chung*. She offered 'shocking' revelations of implant-induced disease and charged the FDA with lax regulation and failure to inform women of the risks to their health. Concurrently suits by women with implants began to reach the courts in substantial numbers and with large financial consequences. In December 1991, a federal jury awarded an unprecedented $7.34 million (including $6 million in punitive damages) to a California woman who claimed that she had developed 'mixed connective tissue disease' because of her implants.[27]

Partly in response to these events, regulatory pressure on SGBIs tightened in the early 1990s. Dr David A. Kessler, then FDA Commissioner and an ardent public health activist, requested the agency's General and Plastic Surgery Devices Panel to assess the safety of breast implants. The panel's scientific review, rounded out with three days of contentious, highly charged hearings in November 1991, concluded that not enough information was available to establish the safety of the devices, but that they should remain on the market pending further study. On 6 January 1992, however, Kessler requested a voluntary moratorium on the use of SGBIs to permit the review of additional data obtained from manufacturers in the course of litigation. In its report of April 1996, the FDA advisory panel reaffirmed that the connection between silicone gel and CTDs was not yet scientifically established but recommended restrictions on access to implants while clinical trials were conducted.[28] Acting on these recommendations, the FDA immediately restricted the use of implants to reconstruction after cancer surgery; the agency also proposed strict guidelines for new clinical trials of SGBIs.[29]

The moratorium and its aftermath confirmed many implant recipients' worst suspicions about their health complaints, and the steady trickle of SGBI lawsuits around the country soon turned into a torrent. Manufacturers and plaintiffs alike were caught up in one of the most distinctive, frustrating and messy inventions of the modern American legal system: the mass toxic tort. The total number of SGBI claimants was known to exceed 440 000. Dow Corning Corporation, the market leader in implant sales, recognized that extreme measures were needed to deal with its potential liability. Settlement emerged as the most attractive option for Dow Corning as well as its major competitors. By late 1994, federal procedures for multi-district litigation were used to consolidate some 9600 claims for pretrial proceedings in the Northern District of Alabama. In September of that year, Chief Judge Samuel C. Pointer, Jr shepherded the parties into a $4.25 billion global settlement, with Dow Corning agreeing to pay some $2 billion of that amount.[30] For some months, it seemed that the controversy might actually close, but that impression proved to be illusory.

Several factors contributed to the unravelling of the first SGBI settlement in the following months. To begin with, too many plaintiffs opted not to participate in the global settlement, including most of the Texas claimants, accounting for almost one-quarter of the total number of litigants. Faced with massive uncertainty about the extent of its liability, Dow Corning filed for bankruptcy in May 1995. Science, too, began to emerge as a separate force in the SGBI story, as data became available from the first systematic studies of women with breast implants. On 16 June 1994, the *New England Journal of Medicine* (*NEJM*) published the results of the first clinical trial investigating the correlation between silicone implants and connective tissue diseases.[31] Conducted by the respected Mayo Clinic in Minnesota, this retrospective cohort study compared 749 women who had received SGBIs between 1964 and 1991 with twice that number of women in a control group and found no statistically significant increase in CTDs among the former. The Nurses' Health Study, a Harvard-based survey of some 100 000 present and former nurses, appeared to confirm the Mayo Clinic findings, as did several other studies that followed. As both litigation and scientific research inexorably continued, judges and litigants had to decide how to accommodate the emergent and allegedly independent voice of science into their legal strategies. The model of the expertise game provides a useful framework for analysing the resulting manoeuvres on all sides.

Law Meets Science: Experts in Action

Of the many different fora, both state and federal, in which SGBI lawsuits continued to make headway, two attracted special notice for their innovative approach to expert testimony. The first, *Hall* v. *Baxter Healthcare Corp.*,[32] unfolded in a federal district court in Oregon under Judge Robert E. Jones; the other was the federal multi-district litigation, MDL-926, which continued to play out in Judge Pointer's court in Birmingham, Alabama after the breakdown of the original settlement. Central to both proceedings was the attempt to construct an authoritative picture of implant-related disease, a problem that both courts addressed by appointing independent scientific panels to review and sift the available evidence. As of late 1997, the Pointer panel was still conducting its inquiry, whereas Judge Jones had made legal history in *Hall* by ruling inadmissible all of the plaintiff's evidence supporting the claim of silicone-induced CTD. For our purposes, however, it is the contrast between the two court-initiated processes and associated moves by litigants that is of greatest interest. Differences in the strategies adopted by the judges and the parties in the two courts provide compelling insights into the game-like character of legal expertise: even in the post-*Daubert* era, remarkably few moves are fixed in advance, and the scientific stories constructed in the courts bear the unavoidable stamp of judicial predilection.

In Search of Neutrality

In appointing independent experts to assist them, courts are institutionally concerned, first and foremost, to ensure neutrality with respect to the outcome of the lawsuit. Financial connections with the parties are an immediate disqualifier, as is - ordinarily - evidence of overly close professional or personal relations between experts and parties. Both the *Hall* and the MDL-926 proceedings took pains to screen the court-appointed experts against outright bias, but the methods chosen were far from identical. To identify suitable experts (ultimately, four in number) for the panel in *Hall*, Judge Jones appointed a single special master, Dr Richard T. Jones, who was as it happens the judge's cousin, but also a highly regarded emeritus professor of biological sciences at Oregon Health Sciences University.[33] Judge Pointer's approach was considerably more measured and elaborate. He took over from a group of judges in New York the idea of appointing a *panel* of special masters to designate the MDL-926 expert panel. Six distinguished academic scientists and law professors, each carefully screened for possible hidden financial interests in the case, eventually advised Judge Pointer on the selection of his four expert panellists.

To what extent did these processes actually guard against bias? One notes immediately that *cognitive* bias or interest apparently received less attention from both judges than possible pecuniary interests. The plaintiffs in *Hall*, for example, argued that Judge Jones himself was a source of bias potentially overriding any efforts to secure the neutrality of his expert advisers. The judge's wife had been satisfactorily fitted with implants following cancer surgery in the late 1970s, a fact that Judge Jones acknowledged but did not see as sufficient to warrant recusing himself:

> That doesn't mean that I will admit all evidence as proffered or exclude all evidence as proffered. I will just look at whatever the state of the art is. And that keeps moving all the time, as we all know. But I did want to make that disclosure. And if that creates any problems for anybody, why that's up to you. But I am not going to recuse myself on these cases because of that.[34]

This public confession evidently secured the judge's personal credibility, although his subsequent decision to exclude all of the plaintiffs' evidence was widely seen as unorthodox, unprecedented and a likely overstepping of the admittedly fuzzy line between permissible judicial screening and impermissible judicial fact finding.

A more interesting issue of potential cognitive bias arises in connection with the divergent mapping of the relevant scientific fields by the two expert panels. The *Hall* panel included an epidemiologist, a rheumatologist, an immunologist–toxicologist and eventually a polymer chemist;[35] the MDL-926 panel also covered the areas of epidemiology, rheumatology, immunology and toxicology, but not polymer chemistry.[36] Such differences in scientific coverage are not exactly unprecedented in the annals of evidentiary proceedings. Under the *Frye* rule, courts had frequently disagreed in identifying the 'particular fields' in which novel scientific evidence belonged. Could the reliability of polygraphy, for example, be adequately certified by skilled polygraphers or was additional testimony required from one or more scientific fields, such as neurology, psychiatry and physiology?[37] No clear consensus ever emerged, and excessive scope for judicial boundary drawing came to be recognized as a weakness of *Frye*.

Proceedings designed to establish definitive causal stories under *Daubert* give rise to similar dilemmas. The choice of experts and the fields they represent cannot be dismissed as merely incidental: it goes to the heart of what the fact finder views as contested or as taken for granted. The absence of a chemist on the MDL-926 panel signalled, in effect, that questions about the chemical properties of silicone gel did not merit 'neutral' review. Yet a substantial part of the plaintiffs' argument in *Hall* and other SGBI cases has centred on silicone chemistry, with analogies drawn between silicone gel and silica, a substance known to be associated with auto-immune diseases in exposed workers.[38] Were the two courts, we may ask, seeking to adjudicate the 'same' case through their differently constituted expert panels?

Framing Choices: An 'Atypical' Disease?

That question resonates all the more forcefully when one considers the framing of the plaintiffs' health claims in the two proceedings. Frustrated by epidemiological studies that found no significant increase in CTDs among implant users, plaintiffs' groups began to claim by the early 1990s that science was pursuing the wrong questions and therefore coming up with irrelevant answers. SGBIs, they contended, were not in the main associated with 'classic' CTDs, such as lupus and scleroderma, but with a more insidious and ill-defined set of 'atypical connective tissue disorders' (ACTDs). Included in this group were ailments that might reflect disorders of the immune system - chronic fatigue, headaches, hair loss, night sweats, swelling, joint pains - but that also occur with some frequency among women in ordinary life. Furthermore the cluster of conditions labelled ACTDs presents serious difficulties for 'objective' medical diagnosis, since the primary evidence of these symptoms' occurrence tends to be the reporting of them by victims. The imprecision of the conditions, together with their high background or 'normal' incidence, make ACTDs a particularly elusive target for epidemiological study.

Not surprisingly, important players in the SGBI cases have sought in various ways to establish - or disestablish - the claims of expert knowledge concerning ACTDs. Marcia Angell, the executive editor of *NEJM* and a vocal advocate of legal adherence to scientific standards, dismissed complaints of 'atypical' disease on the ground that they are impossible to pin down for purposes of scientific study:

> The problem of vague or shifting definitions of disease continues to plague the study of breast implants. When a study fails to find an increased risk of certain diseases or symptoms in women with implants, adherents of the theory that implants cause disease are quick to suggest that the diseases in question are different. It is impossible to study whether something causes illness, however, unless the illness is clearly described. Otherwise, it cannot be consistently diagnosed and its relation to breast implants cannot be examined. This sort of situation is what Karl Popper, the philosopher of science, had in mind when he said that a scientific hypothesis had to be 'falsifiable' to be meaningful.[39]

In terms of the expertise game, Angell's strategy is to deconstruct ACTD claims as both unscientific (not 'falsifiable') and subjective (not backed up by professionally accredited observation). 'Scientific', in her lexicon, is virtually synonymous with 'epidemiological', a position she articulated even more forcefully in an *amicus* brief, submitted jointly with *NEJM*, to the US Supreme Court in an unrelated case, *General Electric Co.* v. *Joiner*. The brief argued that general causation in toxic tort cases is a 'necessary proxy' for specific causation and can only be established through 'observational epidemiological research'.[40] This move sought to accomplish three important goals at once: to elevate the scientific and professional standing of epidemiology; to render irrelevant the evidence on specific causation, including the less institutionalized, 'new' research on biological markers and bioplausibility favoured by plaintiffs;[41] and to move into quadrant 4 of Figure 5.1 the results of self-reporting studies, such as a study of over 400 000 women health professionals (Women's Health Study) which did find evidence of increased risk of CTDs and which, not surprisingly, has been extensively cited by plaintiffs' experts.[42]

Angell's moves to deconstruct ACTDs and elevate the status 'observational epidemiology' make perfect sense when seen against the backdrop of wider struggles for authority in scientific medicine. The epidemiology that Angell defends, and for which *NEJM* serves as an authoritative mouthpiece, falls distinctly on the 'fastidious' side of the 'pragmatic–fastidious' boundary that the sociologist of science Stephen Epstein identified in his study of the politics of AIDS research.[43] 'Fastidious' science, as Epstein describes it, seeks clean study designs, with low ambiguity, in the hope of producing equally clean results; 'pragmatic' research, by contrast, is more willing to accommodate life's 'messy' realities in study designs, with consequently less clearly interpretable results. As Epstein notes, moreover, these stylistic preferences are not random within medicine but reflect deeper cleavages about the authority and status of 'pure' academic research as opposed to 'messy' clinical practice. The problem for claimants in toxic tort cases is that fastidious approaches are unlikely to detect many of the symptoms they complain of: increased incidence in diseases of ordinary life or diffuse syndromes, often lacking 'objective' markers, and attributable to the synergistic interaction of multiple, poorly understood risk factors. Starkly put, the very atypicality of the SGBI plaintiffs' condition removes it from the investigative purview of 'normal' epidemiological science.

None of the participants in *Hall* explicitly challenged the concept of a single, universally applicable, gold standard for epidemiological research, although such an argument might well have benefited the plaintiffs. Instead the parties confronted the expert panel and the court with diametrically opposed visions of the nature, causes and scientific indicators of ACTDs. The defence argued, on the one hand, that claims concerning ACTDs were (as Angell also insisted) untested and untestable; on the other hand, they cited acknowledged authorities such as FDA's Kessler to support the position that there was no solid scientific evidence tying ACTDs to breast implants. The plaintiffs, by contrast, claimed that epidemiology was too blunt an instrument to establish a definitive relationship between silicone and ACTDs. They therefore presented collateral expertise with respect to biomarkers and other indicators of bioplausibility to shore up their causal argument (see below).

Judge Jones in the end affirmed the defendants' contention that ACTD was 'at best an untested hypothesis', overlooking in the process the more shaded assessment offered by his own epidemiology expert, Dr Merwyn Greenlick.[44] Judge Pointer, cutting a different path, instructed the MDL-926 expert panel to consider the relationship between breast implants and both classic and atypical manifestations of connective tissue disease or immune system disorders; his order listed some 40 separate conditions whose possible link to silicone exposure the panel was asked to review.

Standards of Admissibility

Players in the SGBI expertise game have diverged not only with respect to their framing of the central issues in the case but also in their representations of the standards governing admissibility. While ostensibly conforming to *Daubert*'s ruling precepts, plaintiffs and defendants in *Hall* offered the expert panel radically different readings of what the case means and how it bears on particular types of evidence. Generally the defendants sought to hold the plaintiffs' experts to the relatively restrictive moves along the *objectivity* axis, whereas the plaintiffs embraced the more enabling moves along the *experience* axis also sanctioned by *Daubert*.

The contrasts between the two strategies emerged clearly in the summation videotapes prepared by the two sides as part of their closing argument. The defendants' presentation was shot through with references to both *Daubert* opinions, whose criteria were invoked, separately and together, as definitive tests of scientific reliability. Mary Wells, the chemistry expert, opened her argument with a brief 'sag demonstration' to make visible the issue of 'fit'. Allowing the gel to sag out of an upturned jar, Wells contended that none of the plaintiffs' evidence about silica was relevant because it did not concern the kind of substance actually used in implants. She quickly went on to list the *Daubert* criteria, including the 'prelitigation research' criterion announced by the Ninth Circuit in *Daubert II*. The plaintiffs' evidence on silicone chemistry, Wells argued, failed to meet any of the criteria and hence was inadmissible. The fact that witnesses for the plaintiffs, specifically Chris Batich and Leonico Garrido, possessed apparently solid professional credentials was simply irrelevant: 'The plaintiffs have not met their burden of proof to establish that the testimony of Dr. Batich or Dr. Garrido is scientific knowledge as required by *Daubert*. The fact that a scientist wants to speak does not mean that the words he speaks are supported by science.'[45] Similarly Jane Thorpe, the epidemiology expert, adopted language from *Daubert II* in asserting, 'Plaintiffs have failed to show in some objectively verifiable way that the experts have chosen a reliable scientific method and followed it faithfully. ... Atypical disease is a label for non-disease.'[46]

In his closing argument, Michael L. Williams, the chief trial attorney for the plaintiffs, tried for his part to avoid, through careful boundary work, the potentially trumping effect of the negative epidemiological studies relied on by defendants. He began by stressing the absence of research on the condition specifically complained of by the plaintiffs, that is, *atypical* CTDs. A review article by Kessler and other FDA scientists provided grist for his mill, especially the conclusion that 'research is also needed to further address the potential for a long-term association between silicone implants and rare or atypical connective tissue disease syndromes'.[47] Setting aside most of the available epidemiologic findings as irrelevant (because focused only on 'classic' CTDs), statistically weak or flawed, Williams created space for a wider range of expert testimony, including biomarker studies and studies of occupational exposure to silica. The existing epidemiology on ACTDs, his argument ran, provided enough indication of risk to take the plaintiffs' case across the threshold of admissibility, but it was not dispositive on its own. Under these circumstances, any reasonable medical scientist would look to additional sources of information – animal studies, biomarker studies, occupational studies, clinical experience – and this was precisely what he asked the court to do.

Significantly Williams neither mentioned *Daubert* by name nor invoked the criteria. This strategy comported well with the plaintiffs' overarching goal of getting as many as possible experts, and their fields, accepted as both relevant and reliable. Williams wanted the court to take a holistic view of a large body of evidence, none of it compelling on its own, but all of it together conveying a telltale impression of smoke, with smouldering fires behind. Relying implicitly on *Daubert*'s injunction that admissibility decisions should be made on the basis of an expert's methodology, not the expert's conclusions, Williams showed from the record that panel members had found the plaintiffs' experts to be reputable scientists using ordinary methods.[48] Another argument used to justify the introduction of non-epidemiological evidence bordered on the equitable notion of estoppel. Williams asserted that pharmaceutical companies had not seen fit before 1991 to conduct clinical trials of silicone implants. They had based their claims about the safety of SGBIs on the very kinds of indirect evidence that they now sought to exclude from the courts. This was not fair. What had historically been the industry standard should now be the standard applied to the plaintiffs' evidence as well.

Williams hereby sought to make the industry's moral integrity and past behaviour part and parcel of the scientific admissibility determination. In less subtle ways, this was the same strategy that SGBI activist groups were following in fora other than the courts. A particularly splashy campaign was waged by the Command Trust Network (CTN), an information clearing house co-founded by former cancer patient Sybil N. Goldrich. CTN placed its advertisements in such highly visible locations as the Op-Ed page of the *New York Times*. All of them carried in bold letters the message, 'Dow Corning Knew', followed by varying graphic charges, such as 'silicone breast implants rupture', 'silicone breast implants leak' and 'silicone compounds kill roaches'. The moral message was not lost on juries. On 18 August 1997, for example, a Louisiana jury found that Dow Chemical had failed to test silicone properly for use in the human body and had misled a group of 1800 women about the health risks posed by the substance;[49] however, the dissolution of the Louisiana class action in December 1997 left the ultimate impact of this decision unclear.

Form and Function

It should be noted, finally, that the moves in the expertise game are shaped in substantial part by the processes used to elicit expert advice and testimony. A deposition, a pretrial hearing, a panel review or an actual trial each offers distinctive opportunities and constraints for the presentation of evidence. Differences in process between the expert panels in *Hall* and MDL-926, in particular, were significant enough to have a detectable impact on each one's assessment of the available evidence. As noted earlier, the four *Hall* panellists were selected by a single technical assistant to Oregon's Judge Jones. More importantly, they were not court-appointed experts in the sense contemplated by Rule 706 of the Federal Rules of Evidence; instead Judge Jones elected to insulate them from testifying at trial and from possible cross-examination by designating them as technical advisers to the court. Once appointed, the panel operated like a kind of science court, asking questions of the parties' witnesses and watching videotaped summations of the evidence. Only after they had written their reports to the court were the advisers questioned by counsel for the parties. All of the resulting records informed Judge Jones's decision to exclude the plaintiffs' expert evidence.

Larger in scope and possible impact, the MDL-926 process resembled in some respects more a regulatory proceeding than a science court. Judge Pointer, as we have seen, screened the prospective panel members with a sharper sense of public accountability than his counterpart in Oregon. The expert panel was formally appointed pursuant to Rule 706; its members therefore may be called upon to testify at trial, supplementing the testimony of the party experts. There was from the beginning a strong sense that, if the MDL-926 process 'worked', it could serve as a model for other mass tort cases. Consequently a more self-reflective attitude prevailed than in the Oregon court; for instance, Judge Pointer collaborated with research staff at the Federal Judicial Center with an eye to creating an adequate documentary record of the proceedings. The multi-district expert panel met the parties' experts in July 1997 in a three-day hearing in Birmingham, Alabama. Borrowing directly from the regulatory model, the panel also held a shorter hearing with unaffiliated scientists in Washington, DC in November 1997. In keeping with its potential policy-steering role, the panel was asked to comment not only on the possible causal connection between SGBIs and auto-immune disease, but also on whether opinions contrary to its conclusion's could be viewed as 'legitimate and responsible disagreement' within the profession.[50]

While it is still too early to evaluate the full impact of these procedural choices, it is safe to conclude that they did influence the parties' strategic options. Judge Pointer evidently took pains to emulate the non-adversarial format of many regulatory hearings.[51] His objective, presumably, was to promote a dispassionate but thorough airing of conflicting viewpoints, with as little lawyerly grandstanding as possible. The summation videos in *Hall*, by contrast, encouraged partisan representations and were designed, particularly on the defendants' side, to take advantage of the visual medium. Williams, presenting the plaintiffs' case, maintained a low-key, almost professorial demeanour, but (as described above) he used the opportunity to impugn the integrity of the industry position. The defence engaged in more obvious stage management, from the choice of tough-talking, severely attired women to make the case for implant manufacturers, to a television clip of Commissioner Kessler denying, in a February 1996 interview on *Frontline*, that there was any evidence supporting the association between silicone and typical or atypical connective tissue diseases. The defendants' epidemiology presentation closed dramatically, with a damaging quotation from one of the plaintiffs' own experts, Dr Goldsmith, whose disembodied words commanded, for several seconds, both the viewer's attention and the video screen: 'At the moment, I must suggest to you that the evidence looks to me as if it's just that, that it's a possibility, and I would have to characterize it as less than 50 per cent. That would be where I am at the moment.'[52]

Conclusion

The SGBI example highlights a very general conclusion about the nature of expertise in the American legal system: what counts as legitimate expertise for purposes of the law is not determined by means of unambiguous rules applied impartially and without variance by solomonic judges. Expertise, rather, is the product of a dynamic process that actively engages a multiplicity of legal actors in constructing, validating and certifying particular knowledge claims as more authoritative than others. On the game board of expertise, players can marshall a complex array of resources – material, discursive, social and moral – in support of their moves to highlight some viewpoints as more knowledgeable than others. Credibility can be gained, most commonly, through moves that seek to professionalize and objectify the assertions of expert witnesses. Correspondingly doubt can be sown and trust undermined through moves that emphasize possible subjectivity and bias in the expert's position. The spaces in which the expertise game is played extend, moreover, well beyond the confines of particular lawsuits, into the more public worlds of television, books, newspapers, public lectures, the Internet, regulatory politics and even unrelated litigation.

Through a comparison of two expert advisory proceedings, in *Hall* v. *Baxter* and the federal multi-district litigation, we have seen further that *Daubert*, far from bringing uniformity to evidence law, has opened up wide new avenues for the exercise of judicial discretion. The gatekeeping power that judges enjoy in the post-*Daubert* era allows them considerable latitude to shape the moves made by other players in the expertise game and to decide, finally, whose moves to countenance as credible or authoritative. Subjective judicial preferences govern in important ways the process of selecting experts, the framing of relevant evidentiary issues, the choice of applicable scientific standards and the procedural framework for soliciting expert evidence. While the parties and their experts also retain independent agency, their moves are controlled to varying degrees by the presiding judge's prior commitments concerning science and expertise. As a result, courts are no more likely to achieve impartiality in interpreting *Daubert* than they were in construing its forerunner, *Frye*. Indeed the SGBI case suggests that, instead of imbuing judges with a deeper appreciation of what makes science 'scientific', *Daubert* has merely provided a powerful new set of rhetorical resources for masking the unexamined assumptions of courts, litigants and even experts.

If expertise is contingently and strategically constructed within the confines of specific legal disputes and, worse yet, if it incorporates the biases and prejudices of presiding judges, where does this leave the legal system's search for reliable expert knowledge? Are all demarcation efforts doomed to failure, with *Daubert* representing only the latest misguided initiative to separate, once for all, scientific fact from fraud and fantasy? The model of the expertise game seems at first to offer only discouraging answers, for it stresses the malleability of expertise, the role of agency and artifice in representing expert knowledge and the inevitable tie-ins between cognitive and normative realities. There is, however, a more optimistic way to read *Daubert* in the light of the proposed model: not as a hopelessly idealized, and unworkable, formula for truth finding, but as an invitation to reflect on and make transparent the foundations of expert credibility. A lawsuit involving scientific evidence becomes, under this reading, an occasion for the 'fact finder' to choose between alternative frameworks of justification. To the extent that a relativizing model for looking at expertise lays bare the moves underlying expert claims and positions, it can only facilitate the task of comparison.

Justice, it is said, should not only be done but be seen to be done in liberal societies. Courts are important fora for the ritual and public affirmation of a polity's commitment to truth and moral order. Increasingly, as well, courts are being enrolled as agents of civic education in societies in which ordinary citizens live most of their lives comfortably detached from the complex machinery of scientific and technological production.[53] *Daubert* bestowed on judges the power to make some of this backstage apparatus more visible in the wake of technological failures, by requiring litigants to display to others the foundations of their supposed expert knowledge. Unavoidably, however, as the SGBI cases illustrate, judges themselves both set the scene and act upon the stages prepared for the litigants' expert contests. For courts to lose sight of their own role in the expertise game – to be seduced into mistaking the play for objective reality – remains the greatest threat to justice.

Notes

1 Michael Clark and Catherine Crawford (eds), *Legal Medicine in History* (Cambridge, 1994).
2 Andre A. Moenssens, James E. Starrs, Carol E. Henderson, and Fred E. Inbau, *Scientific Evidence in Civil and Criminal Cases* (4th edn, Westbury, NY, 1995).
3 *McLean* v. *Arkansas Board of Education* 529 F. Supp. 1255 (1982).
4 Martha C. Nussbaum, 'Platonic Love and Colorado Law: The Relevance of Ancient Greek Norms to Modern Sexual Controversies' (1994) 80 *Virginia Law Review* 1515–1651; Robert P. George, '"Shameless Acts" Revisited' 9 *Academic Questions*, (1995–6), 24–42.
5 See, in particular, Peter Huber, *Galileo's Revenge: Junk Science in the Courtroom* (New York, 1991); Kenneth Foster and Peter Huber, *Judging Science: Scientific Knowledge and the Federal Courts* (Cambridge, Mass., 1997).
6 Sheila Jasanoff, *Science at the Bar: Law, Science and Technology in America* (Cambridge, Mass., 1995).
7 For a compelling account of this process in the context of toxic torts litigation, see Jonathan Harr, *A Civil Action* (New York, 1995).
8 In 1977, a Texas jury awarded $170 000 to a plaintiff claiming injury from breast implants in what may have been the first such successful lawsuit in the country. See Joseph Nocera, 'Fatal Litigation' (1995) *Fortune*, 16 October, 13–15.
9 Thomas F. Gieryn, 'Boundaries of Science', in Sheila Jasanoff, Gerald E. Markle, James C. Petersen and Trevor Pinch (eds), *The Handbook of Science and Technology Studies* (Thousand Oaks, Cal., 1995), pp.393–456.
10 293 F. 1013 (D.C.Cir. 1923).
11 509 U.S. 579 (1993).
12 See, for example, Bruno Latour and Steve Woolgar, *Laboratory Life: The Construction of Scientific Facts* (Princeton, 1986).
13 939 F.2d 1106 (5th Cir. 1991).
14 Ibid., at 1113.
15 54 Cal.App.3d 100 (1975).
16 Ibid., at 107.
17 Ibid., at 111.
18 Charles Goodwin, 'Professional Vision' (1994) 96 *American Anthropology* 606–33.
19 See Jasanoff, *Science at the Bar*, pp.60–61.
20 Nussbaum, 'Platonic Love', 1607–22.
21 921 F.Supp. 666 (D.Nevada 1996).
22 Ibid., at 675.
23 43 F.3d 1311 (9th Cir. 1995), at 1317–18.
24 No. 1982 (Court of Common Pleas of Philadelphia County, Civil Trial Division), 1996.
25 *Blum*, at 70 (Appendix B).
26 Marcia Angell, *Science on Trial: The Clash of Medical Evidence and the Law in the Breast Implant Case* (New York, 1996). See also California Legislature, Senate Committee on Health and Human Services, *Hearing on the Safety of Silicone Breast Implants*, Sacramento, Cal., 5 February 1992.
27 *Hopkins* v. *Dow Corning Corp.* Case C88-4703-TEH (ND Cal. 1992). See also Angell, *Science on Trial*, p.55.
28 Council on Scientific Affairs, American Medical Association, 'Silicone Gel Breast Implants' (1993) 270 *JAMA*, 2602–6.
29 David A. Kessler, 'The Basis of the FDA's Decision on Breast Implants' (1992) 326 *New*

England Journal of Medicine, 1713–18.

30 Joseph Sanders and D.H. Kaye, 'Expert Advice on Silicone Implants: *Hall* v. *Baxter Healthcare Corp.*' (1997) 37 *Jurimetrics Journal* 113–28.

31 S. Gabriel *et al.*, 'Risk of Connective Tissue Diseases and Other Disorders after Breast Implantation' (1994) 330 *New England Journal of Medicine*, 1697–1702.

32 947 F.Supp. 1387 (D.Or. 1996).

33 See Sanders and Kaye, 'Expert Advice'.

34 *Andrews, et al.* v. *Bristol-Myers, et al.* U.S. District Court Case No. 94-258-JO, Status Conference Hearing Transcript, 4 April 1996, pp.41–2.

35 Sanders and Kaye, 'Expert Advice', The experts were Dr Merwyn R. Greenlick of Oregon Health Sciences University (epidemiology), Dr Robert F. Willkens of the University of Washington (rheumatology), Dr Ron McClard of Reed College (chemistry) and Dr Mary Stenzel-Poore of Oregon Health Sciences University (immunology).

36 The MDL-926 experts were Betty Diamond, an immunologist, Barbara Hulka, an epidemiologist, Peter Tugwell, a rheumatologist and epidemiologist, and Nancy Kerklivet, a toxicologist: 'Scientific Justice', *The Economist*, 26 July 1997, p.69.

37 For further discussion of this example, see Sheila Jasanoff, 'Judicial Construction of New Scientific Evidence', in Paul T. Durbin (ed), *Critical Perspectives on Nonacademic Science and Engineering* (Bethlehem, P.A. (ed.)), pp.220–24.

38 For a description of the chemical profile of SGBIs, see AMA Council on Scientific Affairs, 'Silicone Gel Breast Implants', p.2603; see also Angell, *Science on Trial*, p.106. On the theories of Nir Kossovsky concerning the molecular properties of silicone, see Gary Taubes, 'Silicone in the System' (December 1995) *Discover*, 65–75.

39 Angell, *Science on Trial*, p.104.

40 Brief of *Amici Curiae*, in the *New England Journal of Medicine*, and Marcia Angell, M.D., in Support of Neither Petitioners Nor Respondents, *General Electric Co.* v. *Joiner* No. 96-188, US Supreme Court, October 1996.

41 See, for example, Taubes, 'Silicone in the System'.

42 Charles H. Hennekens *et al.*, 'Self-reported Breast Implants and Connective Tissue Diseases in Female Health Professionals: A Retrospective Cohort Study' (1996) 275 *JAMA* 616.

43 Stephen Epstein, *Impure Science: AIDS, Activism and the Politics of Knowledge* (Berkeley, 1996), pp.255–6.

44 See Sanders and Kaye, 'Expert Advice', 120.

45 *In re Silicone Gel Breast Implant Litigation*, Defendants' Response Videotape, August 1996.

46 Ibid. Compare text of *Daubert II*, 43 F.3d at 1319.

47 Barbara G. Silverman *et al.*, 'Reported Complications of Silicone Gel Breast Implants: An Epidemiologic Review' (1996) 124 *Annals of Internal Medicine* 755.

48 Williams has made this point even more forcefully in unpublished writing since the decision in *Hall*: 'Two facts shock everyone not familiar with the record. First, plaintiffs' experts had world-class qualifications; they included the heads of the Departments of Rheumatology and Immunology at Oregon Health Sciences University and U.C. Davis Medical School, and dozens of other Ph.D.'s and board-certified M.D.'s. ... These highly respected medical school department heads are *not* junk scientists' (personal communication from Michael L. Williams, 13 August 1997).

49 *Spitzfaden* v. *Dow Corning Corp.* 92-2589 (Orleans Parish Civil District Court).

50 Sanders and Kaye, 'Expert Advice', 125.

51 Scientific Justice', p.69. Public hearings of this type permit a wide range of opinion to be expressed without premature polarization or hardening of views. For further

discussion of these points, see Sheila Jasanoff, *The Fifth Branch: Science Advisers as Policymakers* (Cambridge, Mass., 1990).

52 Testimony of Dr David Goldsmith, quoted on Defendants' Video Summation, August 1996.

53 Jasanoff, *Science at the Bar*, pp.215–17.

6 DNA Evidence in the Courtroom: A Social-Psychological Perspective

Jason Schklar

Introduction

DNA profiling and other kinds of scientific evidence are playing an increasingly important role in criminal investigations and court proceedings.[1] As the 'DNA wars' draw to a close and the admissibility of certain DNA profiling techniques becomes less controversial,[2] an important question still remains: are jurors able to understand the complex scientific and inherently probabilistic testimony that accompanies a DNA match report? Although some scholars opine that jurors are incapable of evaluating complex scientific evidence,[3] others argue that jurors perform this role adequately.[4] There is also concern that jurors will attribute an air of 'mystic infallibility' to scientific evidence[5] or a 'special aura of credibility' to a scientific witness,[6] or that jurors will be unduly influenced by overtly probabilistic evidence because it exudes an 'aura of precision'.[7] This latter sentiment resembles the court's remarks in *People* v. *Collins* that mathematics is 'a veritable sorcerer in our computerized society' who threatens to 'cast a spell' over triers of fact.[8]

In the opinion of a social psychologist, whether jurors can evaluate scientific evidence appropriately is an empirical question – one that Joseph Sanders correctly notes is only minimally informed by relevant data.[9] This belief is shared by the National Research Council, which recommended that 'behavioral research should be carried out to identify any conditions that might cause a trier of fact to misinterpret evidence on DNA profiling and to assess how well various ways of presenting expert testimony on DNA can reduce such misunderstandings'.[10] The purpose of this chapter is to review what limited behavioural research exists on the issue of juror reactions to

DNA evidence and to supplement these findings with a sampling of what social psychological theory has to offer.

The DNA Match Report

When a trial involves DNA evidence, jurors are generally presented with testimony about the way in which the crime scene DNA evidence was collected and how the crime lab processed the evidence and tested for any matches between the various crime scene and comparison samples. Jurors are then told that a match was found between some of the crime scene DNA evidence and the defendant's or victim's own DNA in a manner that tends to incriminate the defendant either by including the defendant as a possible donor of the DNA sample left behind by the perpetrator (for example, a semen stain left on the victim's panties) or by including the victim as a possible donor of a DNA sample that connects the defendant to the crime (for example, a blood stain in the trunk of the defendant's car). Although this chapter generally refers to the situation in which the defendant's DNA allegedly matches some crime scene DNA, the discussion applies more broadly to any instance of an apparently incriminating DNA match.

By itself, a reported match conveys little information of probative value to the trier of fact. Jurors must consider the possibility that the match was declared even though the defendant did not commit the crime. This section outlines the two main ways that this is possible: a match can be erroneously reported even though the defendant was not the true source of the crime scene DNA evidence, and a defendant might be the true source of the crime scene DNA evidence in a manner consistent with his or her innocence.

How Can There be a Reported Match when the Defendant is Not the True Source?

There are at least three ways a match can be declared when the defendant is not the true source of the crime scene DNA evidence. First, even though no two individuals (except identical twins) have the exact same DNA, it is possible that the DNA profile of the crime scene evidence could match another person's DNA as well as that of the true contributor owing to random chance. The probability of a match being declared due to random chance is called the 'random match probability' (RMP) and it is calculated by population geneticists using their knowledge of specific allele frequencies in existing DNA databases. Depending on the DNA typing technique used and the rarity of the DNA profile, the size of the RMP can be vanishingly small - sometimes in the range of one in several billion.[11]

Second, the DNA test results can be inaccurately interpreted. When there is uncertainty regarding whether or not a match should be declared between two DNA profiles, examiner bias may lead the forensic analyst to see what he or she expects to see: a match.[12] This kind of decision maker bias has been well documented by social psychologists in a variety of contexts.[13] Although recent advances in DNA technology and interpretation have reduced the likelihood of this kind of error, in principle it is still possible whenever human interpretation is required.[14]

Third, human error in the processing of evidence in the DNA laboratory can lead to an incorrect match report. Although some forensic scientists have argued that it is impossible to obtain a false positive match using current DNA technology,[15] the few published proficiency test reports belie this claim.[16] The probability that a match report was declared as the result of a human error in the DNA lab is known as the laboratory error rate (LE).

How Can an Innocent Defendant be the True Source of a Match Report?

There are at least two possible ways that an innocent defendant can be the true source of the crime scene DNA evidence. First, consider the example of a man who is found murdered in his bed, and a subsequent DNA analysis reveals that his wife is a possible donor of several strands of hair found in the bed sheets. Given that the two shared the same bed during the course of their marriage, there is a completely innocuous reason for the wife's DNA to be found at the crime scene. An inclusionary DNA match does not necessarily translate into incriminating evidence.

Second, both negligence and intentional efforts can implicate an innocent defendant. Sloppiness during evidence collection can lead to cross-contamination between evidence and comparison samples. Alternatively, DNA samples can be planted at the crime scene by, for example, a personal enemy or a police investigator under pressure to clear a case. Obviously a DNA match report based on evidence that has been contaminated or planted can hardly be considered proof of a defendant's guilt.

To summarize, clearly there are differences between a reported match and a true match,[17] and between an inclusionary match report and an incriminating match report. The question the social psychologist asks is whether jurors are sensitive to these differences.

Explaining What We Do Know: What Do Jury Simulation Studies Tell Us?

What little empirical research has been conducted by psycho-legal scholars (social and otherwise) on jurors' evaluations of DNA evidence generally falls into the category of jury simulation (also known as 'mock jury') research. This involves the presentation of trial vignettes to jury-eligible adults ranging from a convenient (albeit not very representative) sample of undergraduates to more difficult to obtain (yet more representative) sample of people who are at a court house waiting to serve on a jury. Most of these trial vignettes are presented in written format, although some studies have been conducted using elaborate videotaped trial simulations that are quite realistic. After study participants (also known as 'mock jurors') review the trial materials they are individually asked to render a verdict and to answer several questions regarding their impressions of the case. In some studies mock jurors are instructed to deliberate as a group, and their deliberations are recorded and analysed along with the jury verdict.

To summarize what we know about juror evaluations of DNA evidence from a social psychological perspective, we will draw on the findings of five relevant published jury simulation studies as well as some data that my adviser, Professor Shari Diamond, and I have collected over the past two years. First the main findings of the two approaches researchers have used to assess jurors' use of probabilistic DNA evidence are outlined, and then the few unsuccessful efforts that have been made to improve jurors' decisions are documented.

Approach One: Bayes's Theorem

A major approach studying lay reactions to probabilistic DNA evidence used Bayes's theorem to estimate the degree to which jurors should revise their belief that the defendant committed the crime given some incriminating trace evidence such as blood, semen or hair fibre. The general methodology used in these Bayesian updating studies[18] includes three steps. First, mock jurors quantify their initial belief that the defendant is guilty (prior probability of guilt estimate) immediately after they receive some incriminating non-probabilistic evidence and before they receive the probabilistic evidence. Second, mock jurors are presented with the incriminating probabilistic evidence (always a match report and an RMP-type estimate in these studies). Third, mock jurors quantify their revised belief that the defendant is guilty (posterior probability of guilt estimate) given the incriminating probabilistic evidence. Bayes's theorem is then used to calculate how much jurors should have been influenced by the incriminating trace evidence on the basis of their prior probability of guilt estimates and the size of the RMP. This normative estimate is then compared with mock jurors' actual posterior probability estimates of guilt to examine whether they overweighted, underweighted or appropriately weighted the incriminating probabilistic evidence.

Research employing this methodology has revealed a number of patterns indicating how people process probabilistic information. Most importantly, although people are sensitive to variations in the size of the RMP, they tend to underweight this piece of probabilistic information in their decisions. Jurors do not sufficiently increase their belief that the defendant committed the crime given their prior probability estimate and the size of the RMP. This is consistent with Saks and Kidd's claim, based on their review of the relevant social psychological literature, that people generally give probabilistic information less weight in their decisions than is logically warranted.[19] It also contradicts the concerns raised by Tribe that mathematical evidence will unduly influence jurors because of its aura of precision.[20]

Another finding in the Bayesian updating studies is that occasionally people misperceive the meaning of the RMP estimate. Consider a juror who estimates that the probability that the defendant committed the crime was .20, based on the non-DNA evidence before learning of an incriminating DNA match report. The juror then learns that the probability that the match could have occurred due to random chance (RMP) was .05. Assuming that the juror uses only the RMP to update his or her belief, the participant should arrive at a posterior probability of guilt estimate of 0.83 according to Bayes's theorem.[21]

However some people erroneously adopt the so-called 'Prosecutor's Fallacy' and misperceive the RMP as the posterior probability that the defendant is not guilty instead of the conditional probability that the defendant's DNA matches the crime scene DNA, given that the defendant is not the true source. Using the above example, a victim of the Prosecutor's Fallacy would have a posterior probability of guilt estimate of .95 – much higher than the normatively appropriate .83 – on the basis of the erroneous inference that there is only a .05 probability that the defendant was not the person who committed the crime.

On the other hand, some people erroneously adopt the so-called 'Defence Attorney's Fallacy' and consider the probability that the defendant is guilty to be equivalent to one in the number of people in a suspect population who could have also contributed the crime scene evidence. Using the earlier example of a .20 prior probability of guilt and a .05 RMP, if a crime occurs in a town of 10000 people the juror who succumbs to the Defence Attorney's Fallacy would reason that the defendant is only one of 500 potential donors of the crime scene evidence and would conclude that the probability that the defendant committed the crime was one in 500, rather than the appropriate Bayesian probability of .83.

It is important to note that these two errors have not been found to occur with any great frequency. Only about 2 per cent of the mock jurors in the Goodman study succumbed spontaneously (that is, without coaxing from the attorneys or expert witnesses) to the Prosecutor's Fallacy,[22] and no one succumbed to the Defence Attorney's Fallacy. These errors were only slightly more frequent when either the attorneys[23] or the expert witnesses[24] employed one of the fallacies to explain the meaning of the RMP.

Approach Two: Combining Separate Probability Estimates

Using a different approach, Jonathan Koehler and his colleagues examined whether mock jurors could combine RMP and LE information appropriately in cases in which one estimate was extremely small and the other estimate was many orders of magnitude larger.[25] Mock jurors were presented with zero, one or two estimates of the probability that a match was declared between some crime scene evidence and the defendant, even though the defendant was not the source of the crime scene evidence. Mock jurors in the two separate estimates condition received both an extremely small RMP estimate (one in a billion) and a much larger LE estimate (two in a hundred).[26] Notice that, given the two separate estimates, the probability that a match was declared as a result of either random chance or human error is equal to the sum of the probability of either one occurring (or one in a billion plus two in a hundred which equals approximately two in a hundred) minus the probability of their joint occurrence (which, assuming the two events occur independently, is minuscule – two in a hundred times one in a billion). In essence the two in a hundred LE figure 'dwarfs' the RMP estimate of one in a billion, rendering it almost meaningless.

If people understood that the much larger LE estimate essentially 'dwarfed' the much smaller RMP estimate, mock jurors who received both estimates should have (a) convicted the defendant as often as their counterparts who were not told the size of the separate RMP and LE estimated but were given a single normatively combined estimate of two in a hundred, and (b) convicted the defendant less often than jurors who received only the much smaller RMP estimate. However mock jurors who received separate RMP and LE estimates convicted the defendant as often as – and, in Study 2, more often than – their counterparts in the single estimate (RMP only) condition, and significantly more often than people who received a single normatively combined estimate of two in a hundred that the match occurred as the result of either random chance or human error. These findings led Koehler and his colleagues to conclude that mock jurors were prejudicially influenced by the extremely small – yet essentially irrelevant – RMP of one in a billion when they should instead have focused on the much more likely LE of two in a hundred.

Efforts to Help Jurors

Efforts to help jurors perform as better Bayesians have not been successful. In a study by David Faigman and A.J. Baglioni, all mock jurors received an expert's Bayesian explanation of how to weight the probabilistic information associated with the blood typing evidence.[27] It was found that people generally misunderstood and ignored this testimony and still ended up underutilizing the probabilistic evidence as compared to Bayesian norms. In a more recent study by Brian Smith and his colleagues, some mock jurors received Bayesian training by an expert witness, while the rest of the mock jurors did not.[28] No difference was obtained between the two groups in terms of performance relative to Bayesian norms, and in all cases mock jurors tended to underweight the probabilistic evidence.

In a slightly different attempt to improve jurors' use of probabilistic evidence, Jane Goodman presented mock jurors with probabilities using different formats (for example, mathematical odds, like one in a thousand, versus a percentage, like 1 per cent), and with and without bar graphs to represent visually the test results.[29] Unfortunately none of these efforts had any effects on verdicts or helped mock jurors become better Bayesians.

An initial effort to help jurors combine extremely small RMP and much larger LE estimates correctly has also failed to improve juror performance. Shari Diamond and I tested a new experimental condition in which an expert witness gave mock jurors a simple instruction about how separate RMP and LE estimates should be combined (that is, by summing them and subtracting the probability of their joint occurrence).[30] We replicated the basic pattern of results from the original study conducted by Koehler and his colleagues: mock jurors who received two separate RMP and LE estimates of one in a billion and two in a hundred convicted the defendant significantly more often than those who received a single normatively combined estimate of two in a hundred. The addition of the simple combination instruction did not counteract the effect of the two separate estimates: mock jurors in this experimental condition convicted the defendant as often as their counterparts who had received the two separate estimates without the combination instructions.

Explaining What We Do Not Know: What Can Social Psychological Theory Tell Us?

All of the published studies reviewed so far have focused on the way jurors evaluate quantitative RMP and LE estimates. This seems like a reasonable approach given the fact that the National Research Council has consistently recommended that jurors be provided with separate quantitative estimates of RMP and LE when an incriminating match report is introduced into evidence.[31] However a variety of other factors may influence jurors' evaluations of a DNA match report. Do jurors attribute a sense of 'mystic infallibility' to forensic science evidence? When jurors are not presented with any LE information, do they simply assume that the test results are error-free? Do jurors consider the possibility that the match report was due to either the contamination or planting of evidence by the police? Do jurors consider whether the crime scene DNA evidence could have really been left by the defendant in a manner consistent with his or her innocence?

In the absence of empirical data that bear directly on these questions, existing social psychological theory may provide some tentative answers. What we know about trials involving DNA evidence is that they involve complex scientific and probabilistic testimony, there is likely some ambiguity and difference of opinion about key factual issues, and there are inevitably questions jurors may have that are unanswered by the evidence presented by the parties. This kind of decision making under conditions of uncertainty and less than perfect knowledge is exactly what social psychologists study. For instance, social psychological theory and research reveals that, when people are required to evaluate ambiguous or incomplete information, their decisions tend to be guided by what their background experiences lead them to expect,[32] what their mental representations – called schemata – are for a given event or social role,[33] or what they believe makes the most coherent narrative story.[34] Also, when people are required to evaluate information that is too complex for them to understand, they may turn to simple heuristic cues or rules of thumb to make decisions.[35] This section outlines how these social psychological principles might provide some additional insight into the way jurors evaluate DNA match reports.

Reported versus True Matches

The recent release of the Inspector General's report on the FBI crime laboratory confirmed many of the serious allegations of sloppiness and unethical behaviour agent Frederick Whitehurst levelled against a number of forensic scientists.[36] The findings of this report were well publicized in the mainstream media,[37] providing a vivid and frightening example of what other scholars researching laboratory proficiency have known for years: forensic science test results in a number of areas are appallingly inaccurate and unreliable.[38] Although no published study has measured jurors' naive expectancies of how likely a DNA match report could have occurred as a result of LE, some evidence indicates that people think human errors in the DNA lab are more likely than proficiency test results have revealed. In a study conducted to assess naive expectancies of how accurate and error-prone DNA test results are, undergraduates estimated the probability that a match report occurred as a result of LE was about one in ten.[39] These estimates of LE are between five and 100 times greater than DNA crime lab proficiency testing has revealed.[40]

The notion that expectancies about LE might play a role in juror decisions casts previous empirical findings in a new light. First, one can reconsider the apparent underweighting of the RMP estimates in the Bayesian updating studies: were jurors underweighting the RMP information, or were they considering the possibility that the lab tests were not error-free? It is possible that at least part of the reason mock jurors did not adjust their posterior probabilities to the extent that Bayes's theorem would predict is that they were influenced by their uninformed estimates of LE which may have been larger than the RMP estimates with which they were provided.

In addition mock jurors' uninformed expectancies about LE may partially explain the finding in the study by Koehler and his colleagues that mock jurors who received both RMP (of one in a billion) and LE (of two in a hundred) estimates convicted the defendant slightly more often than their counterparts who had only received a RMP estimate (and no LE).[41] Perhaps providing mock jurors with an LE estimate had the unintended effect of increasing confidence in the DNA profiling results because the LE estimate with which mock jurors were presented was smaller than what they had naively expected.[42]

Do jurors attribute a sense of 'mystic infallibility' to forensic science evidence? Do they consider forensic scientists to be honest and unbiased? General attitudes toward science and scientists may influence how jurors make decisions based on complex scientific information that is difficult to comprehend. To the extent that jurors are distrustful of science and scientists, they may be less likely to believe that the results of a DNA match report represent a true match. I assessed undergraduates' attitudes toward science using a questionnaire that tapped beliefs about the objectivity of science and scientists and found that these beliefs were correlated with perceptions of DNA evidence.[43] Specifically people who were more distrustful of science and scientists were more likely to believe that a match report could have occurred as the result of a lab error and were less willing to convict a hypothetical defendant when DNA was the only piece of incriminating evidence.

Shari Diamond and I replicated these findings in a more involved mock jury study.[44] Undergraduates acting as mock jurors had filled out the attitudes towards science and scientists questionnaire between eight and ten weeks before they participated in this study. In the experimental session, mock jurors read a brief trial scenario in which a defendant was on trial for sexual assault, and the main inclusionary evidence was a match between a semen stain left at the crime scene and the defendant's own DNA. Mock juror attitudes towards science were again significantly positively correlated with defendant culpability judgments, even after statistically controlling for the influence of the non-DNA evidence. Also mock jurors who believed that the crime scene DNA truly did originate from the defendant (that is, the reported match was a true match) had significantly more favourable attitudes towards science than mock jurors who were either unsure that the defendant was the true source of the DNA evidence or who believed that the defendant was definitely not the true source of the DNA evidence. These findings contradict the opinion held by some legal scholars that jurors uncritically accept scientific evidence because of its perceived infallibility and instead indicate that variability in jurors' attitudes towards science can affect whether they believe that a reported match is in fact a true match.

Inclusionary versus Incriminating Match Reports

Jurors' background and experiences can affect their opinion as to whether they consider an inclusionary DNA match report to be incriminating evidence. For example, when we first replicated the original study by Koehler and his colleagues, we asked mock jurors to list the reasons behind their verdict choices. The case had involved the murder of a woman who had been physically abused by her husband in the past. DNA extracted from blood scrapings underneath the wife's fingernails was reported to match the husband's DNA. Several of the mock jurors who decided to acquit the husband reported that they were not influenced by the DNA match. They reasoned that the blood could have been left from prior abuse and that the woman could have been killed by someone else. Perhaps this reasoning is related to one's experiences with or knowledge of non-lethal domestic violence.

In the study Shari Diamond and I conducted,[45] we assessed mock jurors' attitudes toward the causes of rape using Margaret Burt's rape myth acceptance (RMA) questionnaire.[46] Higher rape myth acceptance is associated with victim blame: that is, believing that the victim 'asked for it' by her actions or appearance. In this study, higher rape myth acceptance was associated with not guilty verdicts and perceptions that the presentation of the DNA match report – the main piece of evidence against the defendant – was unfair, inaccurate and unhelpful. Restated, background attitudes about the causes of sexual assault appear to be related to the degree to which people interpret an inclusionary DNA match report as incriminatory evidence.

Jurors may also have expectancies about the trustworthiness of police officers who conduct criminal investigations and criminalists who collect DNA samples from the crime scene. These expectancies may be based on a variety of sources of information, including both media-generated stories and personal experiences with the legal system. For instance, in the United States, members of African American and other non-white communities have traditionally felt disenfranchised with the legal system and have viewed the police with suspicion and distrust.[47] This distrust may explain the finding that African American and Hispanic or Latino mock jurors in the study that Shari Diamond and I conducted were much more likely than Caucasians to believe that the DNA match report was a result of intentional tampering.[48] Non-white participants' median estimate of the probability that the DNA match report was a result of intentional tampering was one in a thousand, while for whites it was one in a hundred thousand. Although mock juror ethnicity did not significantly predict verdict preferences, mock jurors' estimate of the likelihood that the match report was a result of intentional tampering was positively related to their culpability judgments. Thus it appears that expectancies about the trustworthiness of police investigators is related to how willing people are to believe that the defendant is innocent despite evidence of a reported match between the defendant's DNA and some crime scene evidence.

Jurors' Reliance on Simple Heuristics and Rules of Thumb

Koehler and his colleagues reasoned that the extremely small RMP estimates may have unduly influenced jurors because people did not understand how the much larger LE should have qualified their decisions.[49] Instead mock jurors may have relied on their intuitive sense of which estimate was more important, or how they thought the two quantitative estimates should be mathematically combined. Specifically they hypothesized that mock jurors may have afforded more inferential weight to the more extreme and vivid RMP estimate, as is suggested by the vividness hypothesis,[50] or that they may have incorrectly combined the RMP and LE by averaging them together, as originally suggested by Richard Lempert.[51] Shari Diamond and I subjected these two potential decision heuristics to further empirical scrutiny and found that neither fitted the data very well. It seemed more likely that mock jurors were either multiplying the two estimates together or perhaps engaging in some other evaluation strategy we were unable to assess.[52]

The Implications of Jurors' Expectancies

It should be emphasized that jurors' expectancies are not necessarily accurate reflections of the real world. Expectancies can be shaped by things like the media, the community one lives in and other idiosyncratic life experiences – all of which may result in a biased picture of the world. Both litigants and the courts need to consider the implications of jurors' uninformed expectancies because they can potentially shape verdict preferences in unfavourable and normatively undesirable ways. From the perspective of a litigant, juror expectancies can represent either a benefit or a burden, depending on whether they are favourable or unfavourable to the litigant's case. Accordingly attorneys may try and influence the pool of juror expectancies when selecting a jury. However this process is unlikely to be extremely productive as, even though attorneys show some ability to exclude unfavourable jurors,[53] the existing empirical literature suggests that the ability to predict jury behaviour on the basis of the information typically available during jury selection is quite limited in most cases.[54] Consequently attorneys should focus on presenting evidence during the trial that will help combat and perhaps replace unfavourable juror expectancies.

From the perspective of the court, to the extent that people's expectancies are not so dogmatic as to preclude them from fairly evaluating the evidence, a heterogeneous pool of juror experiences offers a nice double bonus. Because a variety of background characteristics such as culture, ethnicity, gender and socioeconomic status influence juror expectancies, a heterogeneous jury will likely be seen as a representative jury that legitimately represents a cross-section of the community. A heterogeneity of juror experiences and expectancies has also been found to improve the quality of jury deliberations by encouraging a more thorough evaluation of the evidence.[55]

Conclusions

Often criticisms have been raised about jurors' competency to evaluate scientific information, yet ironically this criticism is not well grounded scientifically. The main goal of this chapter was to explore one facet of science and the law by offering a social psychological discussion of jurors' reactions to probabilistic DNA evidence. Although our knowledge of the way jurors use (and misuse) probabilistic DNA evidence is improving, we do not know much about what other factors jurors consider in their decisions – except for a few predictions based on social psychological theory and some anecdotal empirical evidence. Future research needs to explore new ways to help guide jurors' use of RMP and LE information, as they do not appear to be getting it right and a simple instruction does not appear to help. We also need to investigate jurors' uninformed expectancies more systematically in order to identify the factors people appear to weigh when deciding whether a reported match is a true match, or whether an inclusionary match is perceived to be incriminating evidence. Finally we need to examine how jurors pool their knowledge and expectancies when they deliberate as a jury. No published study to date has examined how group discussion might influence reactions to DNA evidence.

To conclude, it has been shown that social psychologists are well suited to address the issue of jury comprehension in a scientific way. We offer empirically validated theory and methodologically rigorous training to the issue of jury decision making. This is what social psychology as a science has to offer law.

Notes

1 National Research Council Committee on DNA Forensic Science, *An Update, The Evaluation of Forensic DNA Evidence* (Washington, DC, 1996); J.L. Peterson, J.P. Ryan, P.J. Houlden and S. Mihaljovic, 'The Uses and Effects of Forensic Science in the Adjudication of Felony Cases' (1987) 32 *Journal of Forensic Sciences* 1730.

2 E.S. Lander and B. Budowle, 'DNA Fingerprinting Dispute Laid to Rest' (1994) 371 *Nature*, 735; National Research Council, *An Update*.

3 D.E. Bernstein, 'Junk Science in the United States and the Commonwealth' (1996) 21 *Yale Journal of International Law* 123; P.W. Huber, *Galileo's Revenge: Junk Science in the Courtroom* (New York, 1991).

4 R.J. Allen and J.S. Miller, 'The Common Law Theory of Experts: Deference or Education?' (1993) 87 *Northwestern University Law Review* 1131; N.J. Vidmar and R.A. Schuller, 'Juries and Expert Evidence: Social Framework Testimony' (1989) 52 *Law and Contemporary Problems* 133.

5 *United States* v. *Addison* 498 F.2d 741 (1974).

6 E. Imwinkelried, 'The Standard for Admitting Scientific Evidence: A Critique from the Perspective of Juror Psychology' (1982–3) 28 *Villanova Law Review* 554

7 L. Tribe, 'Trial by Mathematics: Precision and Ritual in the Legal Process' (1971) 84 *Harvard Law Review* 1329.

8 *People* v. *Collins* 60 Cal., 2d 319 (1968).

9 J. Sanders, 'From Science to Evidence: The Testimony on Causation on the Bendectin Cases' (1993) 46 *Stanford Law Review* 79.

10 National Research Council, *An Update*, pp.6–34.

11 J. Goodman, 'Jurors' Comprehension and Assessment of Probabilistic Evidence' (1992) 16 *American Journal of Trial Advocacy*, 361; J.J. Koehler, A. Chia and S. Lindsay, 'The Random Match Probability in DNA Evidence: Irrelevant and Prejudicial?' (1995) 35 *Jurimetrics Journal* 33.

12 W.C. Thompson, 'Evaluating the Admissibility of New Genetic Identification Tests: Lessons from the "DNA War"' (1993) 84 *Journal of Criminal Law & Criminology*, 22; W.C. Thompson, 'Subjective Interpretation, Laboratory Error and the Value of Forensic DNA Evidence: Three Case Studies' (1995) 96 *Genetica* 153.

13 R. Nisbett and L. Ross, *Human Inference: Strategies and shortcomings of social Judgement* (Newark, NJ, 1980).

14 National Research Council, *An Update*.
15 For examples, see J.J. Koehler, 'Error and Exaggeration in the Presentation of DNA Evidence at Trial' (1993) 34 *Jurimetrics Journal* 21; Thompson, 'Evaluating the Admissibility'.
16 See Koehler *et al.*, 'The Random Match Probability', National Research Council Committee on DNA Technology in Forensic Science, *DNA Technology in Forensic Science* (Washington, DC, 1992); National Research Council, *An Update*.
17 I borrow this distinction between a *reported* match and a *true* match from Koehler *et al.*, 'The Random Match Probability'.
18 These studies are D. Faigman and A.J. Baglioni, 'Bayes' Theorem in the Trial Process' (1988) 12 *Law and Human Behavior* 1; Goodman, 'Jurors' Comprehension'; B.C. Smith, S.D. Penroad, A.L. Otto and R.C. Park, 'Jurors' Use of Probabilistic Evidence' (1996) 20 *Law and Human Behavior* 49; W.C. Thompson and E. Schumann, 'Interpretation of Statistical Evidence in Criminal Trials' (1987) 11 *Law and Human Behavior* 167.
19 M.J. Saks and R Kidd, 'Human Information Processing and Adjudication: Trial by Heuristics' (1980) 15 *Law & Society Review* 123.
20 Tribe, 'Trial by Mathematics'.
21 This assumes that the probability that a correct match report would be declared if the defendant was the true source of the crime scene evidence is 1.0, which, according to Faigman and Baglioni, 'Bayes' Theorem' and Koehler *et al.*, 'The Random Match Probability', seems reasonable.
22 Goodman, 'Jurors' Comprehension'.
23 Thompson and Schumann, 'Interpretation of Statistical Evidence'.
24 Smith *et al.*, 'Jurors' Use of Probabilistic Evidence'.
25 Koehler *et al.*, 'The Random Match Probability'.
26 Actually mock jurors were presented with an LE of either two in a hundred or one in a thousand. Because size of the LE did not affect conviction rates, I only mention the two in a hundred estimate to streamline the presentation of these results.
27 Faigman and Baglioni, 'Bayes' Theorem'.
28 Smith *et al.*, 'Jurors' Use of Probabilistic Evidence'.
29 Goodman, 'Jurors' Comprehension'.
30 J. Schklar and S.S. Diamond, 'Juror Reactions to DNA Evidence: Errors and Expectancies', manuscript in preparation based on Schklar's master's thesis.
31 National Research Council, *DNA Technology*; National Research Council, *An Update*.
32 Nisbett and Ross, *Human Inference*.
33 J.E. Alcock, D.W. Carment and S.W. Sadava, *A Textbook of Social Psychology* (2nd edn, London, Ontario, 1991).
34 N. Pennington and R. Hastie, 'Evidence Evaluation in Complex Decision Making' (1986) 51 *Journal of Personality and Social Psychology* 242; N. Pennington and R. Hastie, 'Explaining the Evidence: Tests of the Story Model for Juror Decision Making' (1992) 62 *Journal of Personality and Social Psychology* 189.
35 A.H. Eagly and S. Chaiken, *The Psychology of Attitudes* (New York, 1993); R.E. Petty and J.T. Cacioppo, *Communication and Persuasion: Central and Peripheral Routes to Attitude Change* (New York, 1986).
36 US Department of Justice/Office of the Inspector General Special Report, 'An Investigation into Laboratory Practices and Alleged Misconduct in Explosives-Related and Other Cases' (Washington, DC, 1997).
37 For some examples, see 'The Unscientific F.B.I. Lab' (*New York Times* 17 April 1997, p.A34); 'Lab Report' (*Washington Post*, 19 April 1997); 'Poor Lab Work Gives Both FBI, Justice a Black Eye' (*USA Today*, 17 April 1997, p.A14); N. Gibbs, 'Under the

Microscope' (149 *Time*, 28 April 1997), p.28.

38 Peterson *et al.*, 'Uses and Effects'; R. Jonakit, 'Forensic Science: The Need for Regulation' (1991) 4 *Harvard Journal of Law and Technology* 109; M.J. Saks and J. Koehler, 'What DNA "Fingerprinting" Can Teach the Law About the Rest of Forensic Science' (1991) 13 *Cardozo Law Review* 361.

39 J. Schklar, 'Naive Beliefs About Science and Reactions to DNA Evidence', paper presented at the 1996 Biennial American Psychology/Law Society Conference in Hilton Head, South Carolina, March 1996. This was also mock jurors' modal uninformed LE estimate in a pilot study Shari Diamond and I conducted using the original Koehler *et al.*, 'The Random Match Probability' stimulus materials.

40 Koehler *et al.*, 'The Random Match Probability'; National Research Council, *An Update.*

41 Koehler *et al.*, 'The Random Match Probability'.

42 I would like to thank Shari Diamond for originally sharing this perceptive insight with me.

43 J. Schklar, 'Naive Beliefs About Science'.

44 Schklar and Diamond, 'Juror Reactions'.

45 Ibid.

46 M.R. Burt, 'Cultural myths and support for rape' (1980) 38 *Journal of Personality and Social Psychology* 217.

47 See Bureau of Justice Statistics, *Sourcebook of Criminal Justice Statistics* (Washington, DC, 1994) for an illustration of the gap between white and non-white or black Americans' opinions about police overreaction to crime, confidence in the police and ethical standards of the police.

48 Schklar and Diamond, 'Juror Reactions'.

49 Koehler *et al.*, 'The Random Match Probability'.

50 Nisbett and Ross, *Human Inference.*

51 R. Lempert, 'DNA, Science and the Law: Two Cheers for the Ceiling Principle' (1993) 34 *Jurimetrics Journal* 41.

52 Schklar and Diamond, 'Juror Reactions'.

53 H. Zeisel and S.S. Diamond, 'The Effect of Peremptory Challenges on Jury and Verdict' (1978) 30 *Stanford Law Review* 491.

54 S.S. Diamond, 'Scientific Jury Selection: What Social Scientists Know and Do Not Know' (1990) 73 *Judicature* 178.

55 See C.L. Cowan, W.C. Thompson and P.C. Ellsworth, 'The Effects of Death Qualification on Jurors' Predisposition to Convict and on the Quality of Deliberation' 8 *Law and Human Behavior* 53; N. Pennington and R. Hastie, 'Practical Implications of Psychological Research on Juror and Jury Decision Making' (1990) 16 *Personality and Social Psychology Bulletin*; S.S. Diamond, J.D. Casper, A. Marshall and J. Schklar, 'Deliberative Processes and Democratic Decisionmaking: Listening to the Jury', paper presented at the Annual Meeting of the Law & Society Association in Glasgow, Scotland, July 1996.

7 The Social Production of Rape Trauma Syndrome as Science and as Evidence

Shirley A. Dobbin and Sophia I. Gatowski

The goal of this chapter is to illustrate the sociopolitical origins and processes which shape the production of science and the production of scientific evidence. By examining rape trauma syndrome (RTS) evidence in the United States, we aim to provide an example of some of the social and political factors that shape the ongoing production of evidence for the court. We also address the manner in which RTS evidence is used by the law and some of the sociopolitical consequences of the use of such evidence for the law, for the individuals involved and for society in general. This discussion of the social production of a psychological syndrome as 'science' and as 'evidence' will be necessarily brief; the purpose is to highlight some of the issues involved in the production processes.

Drawing upon the general tenets and assumptions of the social construction of science,[1] we assume that social problems and social issues are created through collective definition and mediated through experience and language.[2] We also propose that legal evidence is socially produced through a process of evidence entrepreneurship.[3] According to this theoretical paradigm, 'expert evidence industries' incorporate various levels and types of expert evidence production, entrepreneurship and advocacy.[4] For example, within a given evidence industry are the 'producers', those who actually produce scientific evidence (for example, scientists, technicians and clinicians), and 'product champions', those who promote the use of the scientific idea as evidence (for example, grassroots organizations, attorneys and experts).[5] The review of RTS evidence presented herein highlights the socially negotiated emergence of RTS, both within the therapeutic and scientific arenas, as well as in the general social consciousness surrounding rape and its aftermath. This review serves to highlight the interaction and negotiation among various 'product champions' or 'claims makers' (such as, grassroots women movements, rape crisis personnel, clinical practitioners and researchers) and policy makers that shape the ongoing production of RTS as 'science' and as 'evidence' for use in the courtroom.

We begin with a definition of RTS, followed by a discussion of the emergence of RTS in its historical and legal context. Then we turn to an examination of the general evidentiary issues surrounding the admissibility of RTS evidence and the increasing debate in the United States over whether or not such evidence should be, and can be, considered 'scientific' evidence. Finally we critically examine the functions and consequences, both anticipated and unanticipated, of the use of RTS as evidence in criminal rape trials.

Before proceeding any further, it is important to note that the purpose of this chapter is not to call into question the therapeutic utility of RTS, although it is important to recognize that therapeutic and legal processes and goals are different and not necessarily compatible. Moreover this chapter does not call into question the experiences of rape victims, nor does it trivialize the aftermath of rape for victims.

Rape Trauma Syndrome

Rape trauma syndrome (RTS) is defined as a stress response pattern of the victim following forced, non-consenting sexual activity.[6] It consists of somatic, cognitive, psychological and behavioural symptoms resulting from an active stress reaction to a life-threatening situation. RTS is generally conceived of as a two-phase syndrome: (a) the acute phase and (b) the reorganization phase.[7]

The Acute Phase

According to clinical research, the first stage begins about the time the victim is released or escapes from her attacker and is characterized by disorganization. Depending upon the degree of the attack, the victim may experience feelings of shock or disbelief, alternating with fear and anxiety. It is generally believed that a victim may develop one of two styles of coping with her emotions: an expressive style in which she displays her feelings by crying, sobbing or smiling, or a controlled style in which she masks her feelings behind a calm, composed or subdued appearance. Whichever style she may develop, questions concerning her feelings about the incident may elicit a wide gamut of responses, ranging from fear, humiliation and embarrassment, to anger, revenge and guilt.

The Reorganization Stage

The second phase of RTS typically begins two to three weeks after the attack and is characterized by reorganization. During this phase, common symptoms expressed by someone suffering from RTS are recurrent and intrusive recollections of the event, markedly diminished interest in one or more significant activities, feelings of detachment or estrangement from others, sleep disturbances and memory impairment or trouble concentrating. Eventually the victim begins the process of accepting that the rape is part of her life experience and her focus on the rape as a central defining characteristic lessens. It is at this point that the individual is said to have moved from being a 'victim' to being a 'survivor'.

The Emergence of Rape Trauma Syndrome as 'Science' and as 'Evidence'

The emergence of RTS and rape reform laws in general can be traced to the women's movement, particularly in the United States.[8] In the early and mid-1970s women began organizing and speaking out about rape and violence against women. Women publicized the extent of the violence done to women and protested the insensitive practices and procedures used by police and the judicial and medical systems.

The first rape crisis centres were opened by grassroots activists in the early 1970s. These centres sprung from clear political roots and were run by volunteers, often women who had themselves been raped. These centres were explicitly designed as alternatives to a system perceived to be hostile and oppressive towards women who had been raped. These 'speak-outs', rallies, support groups and crisis centres became public symbols of women's solidarity and power. By speaking out publicly, women demanded a recognition of the prevalence of violence against women and an end to the stigma associated with rape. Women fought so that victims of rape would be taken seriously and treated sensitively by police, hospitals, prosecutors and courts and they worked to reform rape laws that stood as obstacles to the conviction of rapists.

The Early Research

As women began to speak publicly about their experiences of rape and battering, the mental health profession began to take notice. Until 1970 there was virtually no professional literature at all on women's reactions to rape. However, as the increasingly vocal women's movement forced society to pay attention to rape and its aftermath by stressing that rape was neither fabrication, fantasy nor aberration, the research establishment responded to accommodate this 'new reality'. The first article on women's response to rape, published in 1970 by two public health workers, concluded that rape victims showed specific, predictable responses to rape.[9] Based upon interviews with 13 young white women, Sutherland and Scherl described a generalized stress reaction in which women initially experience an acute reaction, which includes fright, shock and disbelief, followed within a few days or weeks by a seeming adjustment to the attack. After several weeks or months, argued Sutherland and Scherl, rape victims become depressed and seek emotional support.

In 1974, in what is generally recognized as one of the most influential articles in the field, Ann Burgess, a professor of nursing, and Lynda Holmstrom, a professor of sociology, redefined the generalized stress reaction of rape victims as a 'syndrome'.[10] The Burgess and Holmstrom research was based on a study of 92 adult rape victims who had sought treatment at a Boston City Hospital. The initial sample was made up of 146 patients who came to the emergency ward reporting that they had been raped. The authors divided the patients into three main categories: (a) victims of forcible rape (either attempted or completed rape, but usually the former); (b) victims in situations to which they were an accessory owing to their inability to consent (this category was made up almost entirely of women and girls who were perceived as lacking the emotional or cognitive development to be able to consent or not consent); and (c) victims of sexually stressful situations (defined as sexual encounters in which the woman initially consented but which ultimately went beyond her expectations and ability to control).

It is worth noting that the second and third categories of patients included women and girls who reported being raped but were eliminated from the study that resulted in the creation of 'rape trauma syndrome'. And, as Stefan[11] notes, no commentator has ever discussed why the originators of RTS discounted the stories of over one-third of the women and girls who came to an emergency room reporting they had been raped. Professor Stefan also questions why, in the third category, many of these stressful sexual situations were not defined as rape, since most of them involved non-consensual sex as defined by the women. Nevertheless the Burgess and Holmstrom study is often cited as proof of the scientific validity of RTS, both in the research literature and in case law. In contrast to the activists who spoke of 'taking back the night' and 'speaking out against violence towards women', Burgess and Holmstrom underscored the importance of the 'therapeutic management of the victim'.

Following the Burgess and Holmstrom study, research flourished, examining the aftermath of rape. Rape victims' post-rape reactions became the subject of numerous research efforts. Many other studies have expanded upon the research of Burgess and Holmstrom and suggest that each victim's reaction depends on factors such as her age, her personality, the circumstances surrounding the rape and the relationship between the victim and the assailant.[12] Some studies have also suggested that the stress reactions exhibited by rape victims are also exhibited by victims of other violent crimes, and that many of the symptoms exhibited by the women are exhibited by others who have also experienced severe stress reactions. As this body of research grew and developed, RTS gained increased recognition in the psychiatric and psychological disciplines, and the concept became widely accepted by the clinical community.

Although RTS caught on very quickly, it was not without its critics in the scientific field. Many criticisms were centred around the researchers' failure to follow traditional methodological practices for conducting such studies.[13] For example, sampling procedures were not described, potential sample bias was not addressed, control or comparison groups were not used, standardized psychometric testing instruments were not used and the reliability of measuring devices was not documented. Moreover these studies usually only assessed and described the experiences of women who sought treatment in a hospital emergency room immediately after being raped, yet the vast majority of women (estimates vary between 80 and 90 per cent) never officially report their rape. The reactions of women who are too frightened or too ashamed to report being raped, or who know they will not be believed, or who may not put the name of rape to their experience, or may not expect others to, are not a part of these studies – in other words, the more typical rape victim is not included in studies of RTS. Recognizing the methodological weaknesses of the earlier studies, recent and more methodologically sound studies have generally supported the early finding and conception of RTS. Nevertheless it is important to note that the purpose of these studies was not to establish a causal link between rape and specific, clinically observable symptoms; rather these early studies attempted to improve therapeutic intervention for rape victims by mental health professionals. That is, RTS research had the goal of improving RTS as a therapeutic tool, not, necessarily, of improving it as a fact-finding tool to prove that a rape occurred.

With the increasing attention and involvement of the professional psychiatric establishment in rape research, the early sociopolitical focus on empowering women who had been raped shifted towards a more individual focus on the rape victim herself. That is, the original focus on rape (for example, why it occurs, how to decrease its prevalence and how to empower women who had been raped) shifted to a focus on rape victims and their reactions to their rape experience. The 'victim services' model began to challenge the explicit political perspective of the earlier crisis centres and support group organizations. Where before rape survivors counselled rape victims, now mental health professionals considered women who had survived a rape to be inappropriate counsellors who might become 'overinvolved' with their patients and lose their objectivity.

The refocus of rape crisis centres was fuelled by increasingly available federal and state dollars. The National Center of the Prevention and Control of Rape was created in 1976 and housed in the United States National Institute of Mental Health. As a result, rape crisis centres were transformed into more agency-like structures with paid professionals on staff, devoted to treating individual victims. By the mid-1980s 'the original model of the rape crisis center [was] virtually extinct'.[14] A national survey in the early 1980s of rape crisis centres found, for instance, that over half were no longer involved in direct political action work of any kind.[15]

The shift in attention from a sociopolitical focus to a focus on rape victims and their post-rape behaviour was solidified in 1980 when the American Psychiatric Association incorporated post-traumatic stress disorder (PTSD) into the *Diagnostic and Statistical Manual of Mental Disorders* (DSM). While not mentioned explicitly in either DSM-III or DSM-IIIR, RTS has been explicitly recognized as a classic form of PTSD. Indeed, as Steketee and Foa note,[16] rape victims constitute the largest single group of PTSD sufferers. The essential feature of the post-traumatic stress disorder is the 'development of characteristic symptoms following a psychologically traumatic event that is generally outside the range of usual human experience'. Although DSM-IV has deleted the phrase 'outside the range of usual human experience' from the classification of PTSD, rape is still classified as a form of PTSD with war, bombings and natural disasters like hurricanes, floods and volcanic eruptions.[17] According to the DSM, following a traumatic event, people develop symptoms which may include hyperalertness, exaggerated startle response, difficulty sleeping, recurrent nightmares, depression and anxiety. Symptoms may emerge immediately after the traumatic event or develop after a latency period of up to one year. Symptoms may impair an individual mildly, or to the extent that every aspect of his or her life is affected. The adoption of PTSD by the American Psychiatric Association as an official diagnosis recognized in the DSM was 'an important event that helped to legitimate RTS as a psychiatric syndrome'.[18] Not only was it a milestone in the social production of RTS as acceptable science, but it was also a significant step in the designation of RTS as acceptable evidence for the courtroom.

The Legal Context

During the 1970s a combination of forces led to the revision of rape laws.

Women's groups and crisis centre advocates maintained that women's legal rights required revision and that current legal procedures were ineffective as a deterrent for rape.[19] Moreover police and prosecutors viewed rape as a law and order issue and likewise supported reform.[20] State legislators and law reformers provided further support by considering rape in a broader framework. The feminist movement and law and order groups concern with escalating rape statistics, the emergence of empirical research disproving much of the myth and misconceptions about rape and supporting RTS as a psychiatric diagnosis, and the increase of women in the legal profession created a climate conducive to effecting change in rape laws and the method for adjudicating rape cases.[21]

For example, rape shield statutes designed to protect rape victims from psychological trauma associated with public disclosure of prior sexual activities were enacted in every state in the United States.[22] Consistent with the pattern of state action, in 1978 the United States Congress enacted Rule 412 of the Federal Rules of Evidence (FRE) which excludes from evidence all reputation and opinion testimony concerning a rape complainant's prior sexual conduct, while allowing for the limited admissibility of evidence of the complainant's specific sexual acts. In addition, most states no longer require the corroboration doctrine, a doctrine that requires independent corroborative proof for identification, penetration and lack of consent.[23]

Reform has also focused on the reconceptualization of rape itself. The traditional view pictured only a woman as the victim of rape and a man as the perpetrator. State legislatures have, for example, revised statutes to make rape a gender-neutral offence in recognition of situations of homosexual rape, lesbian rape and a woman raping a man. Reform efforts have also focused on the abolition of the spousal exemption for rape, with the purpose of eliminating the discriminatory denial to married women of the same protection of individual privacy rights that unmarried women possess.[24] The current conceptualization of the 'reasonableness' of behaviour, and how it influences crimes of sexual assault and sexual harassment, has also been questioned. For example, some commentators argue that current standards of reasonable conduct (including both the 'reasonable person standard' and the 'reasonable woman standard') perpetuate gender myths about what constitutes appropriate female behaviour.[25]

The introduction of RTS testimony into the court, with the goal of increasing conviction rates, was also a major part of this reform effort. To date, 20 state supreme courts have considered the admissibility of evidence of the complainant's PTSD or RTS at a criminal rape trial. All but four have permitted the introduction of such evidence, usually with limitations on the purposes for which it can be used. For example, the testimony of experts in the area of RTS has been offered to rebut defences of consent or fabrication through evidence of post-assault trauma 'symptoms' such as nightmares, sleeplessness and fear of being alone; and to explain 'counterintuitive' behaviour such as being calm and composed, failing to report the rape for days or even months, recanting or giving contradictory testimony, continuing to see the defendant and failing initially to identify the assailant or remember some parts of the assault or its aftermath. Courts have recognized that in this context RTS testimony may be particularly useful in 'disabusing the jury of some widely held misconceptions about rape and rape victims, so that it may evaluate the evidence free of the constraints of popular myths'.[26] Expert testimony on RTS has likewise received judicial sanction in cases involving child victims.[27] Yet, while well entrenched in the medical and psychiatric literature, RTS is a phenomenon that has not been fully accepted in the courts and its admissibility remains somewhat controversial.

The Admissibility of RTS Evidence in American Courts

The general evidentiary issues surrounding the admissibility of RTS expert testimony revolve around whether or not the probative value of RTS testimony outweighs its potential for prejudice and confusion; whether or not the testimony can be considered reliable; what qualifications and experiences qualify someone as an expert on RTS; whether or not testimony on RTS invades the providence of the jury and provides an opinion on the ultimate issue; and whether or not RTS testimony constitutes hearsay. Courts across the United States have reached conflicting conclusions on each of these issues.

For example, a number of courts have found that RTS evidence has probative value,[28] while other courts have rejected RTS evidence on the grounds that it was likely to mislead the jury by implying that the witness was in fact raped – 'the use of the rape trauma syndrome by definition implies that the victim witness was indeed raped, otherwise why would she suffer from RTS?'[29] When RTS is offered as proof that a rape occurred, the evidence has generally been excluded. Indeed some courts have argued that RTS evidence should be excluded as it was developed as a therapeutic tool to understand and treat rape victims, not as a method for assessing whether a rape has occurred. Relatedly some courts have excluded RTS evidence on the grounds that it carries with it an implied opinion that the victim was telling the truth.[30] For example, in *State* v. *Taylor* the court noted that the psychiatrist went too far in expressing his opinion that the victim suffered from RTS as a consequence of the specific incident at issue and that this conclusion vouched too much for the victim's credibility and 'supplied verisimilitude for her on the critical issue of whether the defendant did rape her'.[31] Others have ruled that, although RTS evidence corroborates the victim's claim of rape, thereby supporting or bolstering the credibility of the victim, it nevertheless assists the jury in understanding some aspects of the behaviour of rape victims and is therefore admissible as long as expert testimony does not include comment on the truthfulness of the victim's charge.[32] RTS evidence has also been rejected on the grounds that it constitutes hearsay when victims see psychiatrists in preparation for trial rather than as an ongoing part of treatment. Other courts have found that RTS testimony does not constitute hearsay when based on data personally received by the testifying expert.

While some courts have found significant factual foundation for testimony about RTS, finding that it is generally reliable and sufficiently acceptable within the scientific community,[33] others have found that RTS has not reached a level of reliability that surpasses the commonsense evaluations of jurors in deliberation, and have therefore rejected such evidence.[34] Still other courts, however, have ruled that, when issues of consent are raised by defence, RTS testimony does not invade the providence of the jury since the expert is subject to cross-examination and the jury determines what weight, if any, the evidence should receive.

There is also some debate about what kinds of qualifications and experience qualify someone as an expert on RTS for the purpose of giving testimony in court. Indeed testimony on RTS has been offered through a variety of experts - psychiatrists,[35] psychologists,[36] psychiatric nurses,[37] psychology graduate students,[38] social workers,[39] directors or workers at rape crisis shelters[40] and police officers[41] - but just how someone becomes an expert on RTS is still unclear.

RTS and Daubert *v.* Merrell Dow Pharmaceuticals, Inc.

The United States Supreme Court decision in *Daubert* v. *Merrell Dow Pharmaceuticals*[42] defined a new standard for American federal (and most state) courts to use in determining the admissibility of scientific evidence under Federal Rule of Evidence 702, which governs the admissibility of 'scientific, technical or other specialized knowledge'. *Daubert* outlines four guidelines that the judiciary should consider when considering the admissibility of scientific evidence: (a) determining the 'falsifiability' of a theory, (b) the 'known or potential error rate' associated with applications of a theory, (c) whether the findings have been subjected to peer review and publication, and (d) the 'general acceptance' of the science being offered.

The *Daubert* decision has generated a great deal of scholarship in legal and scientific arenas. For example, should the standard be applied differently to different forms of science? What differentiates scientific knowledge from technical or other specialized knowledge? To date there has been no guiding principle to allow courts to distinguish between what constitutes scientific expert testimony and what constitutes technical or other specialized knowledge. There is currently considerable debate in the United States over whether or not psychological syndrome evidence, and indeed much social and behavioural science evidence, should and can be considered 'scientific' knowledge.[43] In this respect district courts have generally followed three different formulas for applying *Daubert*. Some have interpreted the *Daubert* decision narrowly and applied it only to scientific evidence; others have applied the decision more broadly and used the *Daubert* criteria for judging the admissibility of all expert testimony; still others have taken a middle ground, assuming a *Daubert*-like duty to judge the admissibility of all expert testimony but using different criteria depending on the type of expert.[44] Current debates have also called the role and legitimacy of psychological testimony into question. As Faigman notes, 'Psychology's future place in the trial process thus appears to depend on determining the scientific nature of psychology, a daunting task indeed.'[45]

If syndrome evidence is to be subjected to sophisticated admissibility standards for scientific evidence, will the evidence be able to stand up under scientific scrutiny? Many commentators have argued that applying the *Daubert* guidelines to syndromal evidence, such as RTS, may result in the inadmissibility of such syndromes.[46] Indeed some psychological testimony, including RTS, may not be testable at all in the sense meant by Karl Popper,[47] and by the *Daubert* decision. For example, clinical syndromes are, by their very nature, inherently unfalsifiable and they are typically used post hoc to promote an explanation for post-event behaviour. Moreover syndrome claims are often mutually contradictory and not subject to disproof. That is, if many victims of different traumatic events display common stress reactions (as is suggested by the research) then how can we draw any definitive conclusion regarding the cause of the stress reaction, especially in cases where there are no other witnesses to the traumatic event (as is usually the case in rape) and where there may be no other corroborative evidence (physical evidence and so on)? It is also obviously difficult to calculate potential error rates for this kind of evidence. Many commentators suggest that widespread acceptance of questionable syndrome evidence that has limited scientific reliability and questionable probative value may result in a high number of false positives (that is, identifying a woman as a victim of rape and the defendant as a rapist) because such evidence is overly prejudicial. The risk of making a false positive error with syndrome evidence may arise for several reasons: for example, because *Daubert* is supposed to be a more liberal standard than the previous *Frye*[48] general acceptance test (it is worth noting that whether *Daubert* is a more liberal or a more conservative standard is also debated) and because there is general social or political support for the syndrome, or at least for the perceived consequences of successfully using the syndrome claim.[49]

Others argue that psychological syndromes, and certain other forms of social and behavioural science evidence, should not be subjected to strict Popperian-like scientific guidelines. These commentators argue that psychology, as well as other forms of social science, are not truly 'scientific' and therefore the *Daubert* guidelines do not apply.

We would argue that social and behavioural science, including psychology, is science. And, while social and behavioural science differs in some fundamental ways from the physical and biological sciences, there are some common principles and methods that underscore all scientific work. Therefore, when evaluating the scientific merits of social and behavioural science evidence, including psychological syndromes, it should be held to the standards of 'good science'. What becomes problematic is that *Daubert*-like criteria represent an overly traditional and mechanized view of science, one based upon falsification and objectification, and do not reflect an understanding that all science is contextualized and socially constructed. *Daubert*-like guidelines do, however, represent a practical guide that can be used by the judiciary, and to a certain extent the jury, to evaluate proffered scientific evidence or testimony. But what needs to be recognized is that 'good science' acknowledges its social and political origins.

The Development of an Evidence Industry

It is clear that, from the early 1980s, an 'evidence industry' developed to promote the relevance and utility of RTS for the court. As the preceding discussion demonstrates, members of the psychiatric profession, as well as rape counsellors and social workers, acted as 'product champions' to promote the utility and relevance of RTS for use as evidence in the courts; many feminist scholars promoted the admissibility of RTS as a type of rape reform because the introduction of RTS, they argued, recognized the painful and distressing after-effects of rape and, therefore, brought the reality of the victim back into the courtroom. It was also argued that RTS helped jurors to understand what appears to be unreasonable or unusual behaviour on the part of the victim and helps to alleviate the impact of rape myths and stereotypes (such as the myth that, if a woman did not report the rape immediately, she was fabricating the rape). And, with the recognition of RTS by the American Psychiatric Association in the DSM and a substantial body of 'scientific' research supporting the claim of a generalized syndrome, product champions became powerful advocates for the admissibility of RTS.

In turn, attorneys and experts have become 'evidence entrepreneurs' promoting the use of RTS in certain types of cases. For example, in *State* v. *Bledsoe*,[50] in which the admissibility of RTS was appealed to the California State Supreme Court, an amicus brief was filed by the California Women Lawyers Association on behalf of the prosecution. The brief maintained that the evidence with respect to RTS met the criteria of general acceptance in the relevant scientific community and, therefore, should be admitted.[51] As the use of RTS as evidence became more common, the use of mental health professionals, ranging from psychiatrists to rape counsellors, became increasingly prevalent in rape trials, especially those in which consent was at issue, which is almost all of the trials.

An important part of the development of this evidence industry is the potentially differential ability of parties to produce evidence. As Cooney suggests,[52] litigants vary systematically in their ability to attract evidence at various stages in the legal system, this is true in the processing of rape cases. For example, it is well documented that most rape cases are never pursued to the trial stage; in fact, most are never reported or, if reported, most are not actively pursued by the police and prosecutor's office.[53] Typically it is only the high status victim who has her case actively pursued throughout all levels of the criminal justice system. Status in this context not only refers to time and financial resources, it also refers to the social characteristics of the alleged victim and the degree to which she approximates the ideal of a 'real victim' of a 'real rape'.[54] The concepts of 'real victim' and 'real rape' reflect social stereotypes about appropriate behaviour for women and their relationship to men and our general societal recognition that a true rape is one involving a stranger where there is physical evidence to corroborate the claim of rape. Thus, one can argue, victims who more closely approximate the 'real victim' of a 'real rape' are able to attract scientific evidence more easily than women who may have engaged in questionable 'risky' behaviours (such as accepting a ride from someone met at a bar or walking home alone at night), who are from lower socioeconomic backgrounds,[55] or who have been allegedly raped by an acquaintance. Moreover it is typically higher status victims who can afford the high status psychological examinations conducted by highly qualified professionals. The women who receive the diagnosis of RTS and are perceived to need treatment are generally white, middle-class women – the same kinds of women who politicized the issue 20 years ago. Although indigent women, especially poor minority women, are more likely to be raped,[56] they are rarely identified as victims of RTS (that is, they are less likely to report being raped and hence are less likely to receive diagnosis).

Intimacy variables, as they relate to the relationship between the expert and the alleged victim, may also play an important role in the production process. For example, rape crisis counsellors and therapists tend to have an ongoing therapeutic relationship with the victim, whereas high status psychiatrists are often just called in to conduct a diagnostic assessment of the alleged victim prior to trial. It has been suggested that greater intimacy ties between the client and the expert may be detrimental in the trial context,[57] yet the proffer of psychological or psychiatric testimony in the court by experts who have not had any continued therapeutic relationship with the individual is becoming increasingly criticized.

The Functions and Consequences of Rape Trauma Syndrome

While research on women's reactions to rape and prosecutors' use of rape trauma syndrome in the court has been conducted in good faith to try to validate women's pain and to convict rapists, its consequences for women, both individually and collectively, are far-reaching.[58]

For a given case the introduction of RTS can be a strategic move offered to win the case and to convict a rapist. But it is questionable whether or not the admission of RTS testimony actually results in higher conviction rates or a higher probability of conviction. Typically only the 'best' rape cases (the strongest cases) go to trial and they are usually winnable on several grounds.[59] It is therefore difficult to determine what role RTS plays in a successful prosecution. Moreover, as Faigman notes, 'the vague and unfalsifiable premises that constitute the typical syndrome or profile in use today, for ostensibly beneficent and liberal ends, can be easily reversed and used by the abusers'.[60] The introduction of RTS testimony threatens to reintroduce psychiatric examinations of the rape victim, defendants' access to the woman's medical and psychiatric records, admission of evidence of the victim's past sexual behaviour and even corroboration requirements. The woman's past history (past sexual history generally, as well as past sexually traumatic events and pre-existing disorders) becomes relevant evidence for the defendant to offer the fact finder. Such a reintroduction of the woman's past history and behaviour is exactly what rape shield laws were enacted to counter.[61] Therefore the introduction of RTS testimony has the potential of revictimizing the victim again and reinforcing the perception that the justice system is unfair and insensitive to women who have been raped.[62]

RTS assumes that there are certain specific and predictable responses to being raped, but what if the complainant does not suffer from RTS? The absence of RTS symptoms in the alleged rape victim is a defence for a rape defendant: she does not suffer from RTS, therefore she must not have been raped. In other words, because a woman does not display symptoms of RTS she must have consented and her claim of rape must be false.[63] Moreover the reliance on RTS to rebut defence claims of consent shows that women are still not believed in court. Women who accept and enact victimhood and have access to 'objective' professionals who can vouch for their emotional or physical disturbance will be believed, but those victims who are not inclined to seek professional help or have no access to it because of economic or other pressures have little or no credibility. As Stefan argues, 'the presentation of RTS evidence does not solve the problem of women's lack of credibility; it concedes it'.[64]

In addition to constructing all of a woman's anger, distress and pain after being raped as arising from the rape itself and erasing the role of family, police, hospitals and the trial process in magnifying her pain and redirecting her anger toward herself, RTS has turned the reaction itself - the 'symptoms' - into behaviour at best pitied and at worst condemned. The elements of rape victims' struggle and survival disappear in many articles on RTS, which appear quite distant and judgmental: 'Professionals working on women who had been assaulted predominately view injured parties as victims requiring rescue and draw on psychological theories of victimization which emphasize dependence, low self-esteem, learned helplessness and other personality deficits.'[65] For example, words like 'fear' are replaced by words like 'phobia', with all of that word's connotations of irrationality. As Kelly notes, 'most research on sexual violence has neglected, or indeed at times misread, women's acts of resistance and challenge which display strength and determination'.[66]

It is also argued that RTS removes women's rape experience from its social and political context. The use of 'scientific' evidence to remove or obscure social and political context or consequences constitutes, in Stryker's terms,[67] the legitimation of law through a reliance on scientific-technical rationality. The creation of RTS depoliticizes the issue of rape by shifting attention from the prevalence of violence against women to women's reaction to violence. Personalizing women's rape experiences by focusing on their post-rape reactions shifts the level of analysis away from the operation of societal stereotypes about rape and appropriate male and female behaviour to a focus on evaluating the individual women's personal reactions to rape. The reliance of syndromal evidence in court, critics argue, clouds the more important political and social issues involved and provides an easy answer to difficult jurisprudential problems. As long as RTS focuses on women's post-rape reactions and pathologizes them rather than the social environment (where violence against women is the statistical norm), its use will ultimately be distorting rather than empowering to women.[68]

Rape trauma syndrome also constructs rape as a societal aberration. The medicalization of women's reactions to male violence has explicitly supported social assumptions that such violence is aberrational, yet current statistics indicate that, every single minute in America, there are 1.3 forcible rapes of adult women. Women who have been raped are encouraged to think of the pain they suffer as their own problem, rather than to examine the social context which helps to create pain and exacerbates it. It is unclear whether the deletion of the phrase, 'outside the range of usual human experience', from the DSM-IV will solve the problem of assuming that sexual violence is an unusual experience for women because the very inclusion of RTS in PTSD evokes a definition of rape as aberrant, especially since sources of traumatic stress that are acknowledged to be common, such as the death of parents, the loss of a job, or chronic illness, are not generally regarded as causing PTSD.[69]

As recognition of the individual and collective consequences of the use of RTS testimony in court increases, legal and social science scholars are beginning to evaluate critically the use of RTS as evidence. In recent years there has been a slow move towards the use of rape myth testimony rather than RTS testimony. Rape myth testimony, offered in the form of social framework evidence,[70] allows for rape and the victim's post-rape behaviour to be placed in its larger social context without medicalizing or deviantizing the victim.

Conclusion

In an effort to illustrate the sociopolitical origins and processes which shaped, and continue to shape, the production of RTS as science and as evidence we have traced the emergence of RTS in its historical and legal context, examined the evidentiary issues surrounding the admissibility of RTS and outlined the debate in the United States over whether or not such evidence should be, and can be, considered scientific. We concluded with an examination of the functions and consequences, both anticipated and unanticipated, of the use of RTS as evidence in criminal rape trials. In so doing, we provided an example of the way legal evidence, such as RTS evidence, is socially produced through a process of evidence entrepreneurship involving the interaction between multiple claims makers and policy makers.

After examining the sociopolitical emergence and production of RTS testimony and the development of the evidence industry that surrounds that production, the question remains one of whether or not RTS testimony has a place in the court. Feminists, activists and others advocated the introduction of RTS testimony in rape trials to give voice to women, to empower them and to combat negative myths and stereotypes about women and rape. However, while RTS was introduced into the court with the best of intentions, it has not had the intended consequences. Any perceived benefits of its introduction must be weighed against its negative impact. In deciding what place RTS evidence should have in the court, we must recognize its social and political history and the social and political consequences of its use in the court. We must question the legitimacy of a type of evidence that medicalizes and pathologizes women, that removes rape from its political and social context and potentially opens the door for the revictimization of women by the legal system. Increasing the awareness on the part of decision makers and policy makers that the development of scientific evidence is a social process helps guard against the influence of interest group pressure to accept allegedly scientific evidence, or to reject novel or unpopular scientific evidence. It also cautions against the use of science to obscure larger social issues. It is, therefore, important to recognize that scientific testimony is not an objective and independent 'scientific' representation of reality, but rather a social product.

Notes

1 P. Berger and T. Luckmann, *The Social Construction of Reality* (New York, 1967); P. Conrad and J.W. Schneider, *Deviance and Medicalization: From Badness to Sickness* (Philadelphia, 1992); S. Fuller, *Philosophy of Science and its Discontents* (2nd edn, New York, 1993); S. Jasanoff, *Science at the Bar* (Cambridge, Mass., 1995); S. Jasanoff, 'What Judges Should Know About the Sociology of Science' (1993) 77(2) *Judicature* 77; M. Spector and J.I. Kitsuse, *Constructing Social Problems* (Hawthorne, NY, 1987).

2 Berger and Luckmann, *Social Construction of Reality*; Conrad and Schneider, *Deviance and Medicalization*; D. Edwards and J. Potter, *Discursive Psychology* (London, 1992); M. Foucault, *The Archaeology of Knowledge* (New York, 1972); M. Foucault, *The Birth of the Clinic: An Archaeology of Medical Perception* (New York, 1973); Fuller, *Philosophy of Science*; J.R. Gusfield, *The Culture of Public Problems: Drinking-Driving and the Symbolic Order* (Chicago, 1981); R. Harre and G. Gillett, *The Discursive Mind* (Thousand Oaks, Cal., 1994); Jasanoff, 'What Judges Should Know'; T.R. Sarbin and J.I. Kitsuse (eds), *Constructing the Social* (Thousand Oaks, Cal., 1994).

3 M. Cooney, 'Evidence as Partisanship' (1995) 28(4) *Law and Society Review* 833; S.I. Gatowski, S.A. Dobbin, J.T. Richardson and G.P. Ginsburg, 'The Globalization of Behavioral Science Evidence About Battered Women: A Theory of Production and Diffusion' (1997) 15 *Behavioral Sciences and the Law* 273; J.T. Richardson, S.I. Gatowski, and S.A. Dobbin, 'The Production of Expert Scientific Evidence: *Daubert*, Partisanship and Symbolic Justice', paper presented at the Vth International Conference on Social Justice Research, Reno, Nev., 1995; J.T. Richardson and G.P. Ginsburg, 'The Production and Diffusion of Scientific Evidence: Theoretical Issues and Hypotheses', paper presented at the annual meeting of the Law and Society Association, Glasgow, Scotland, July 1996.

4 See references in note 3.

5 See references in note 3.

6 A. Burgess and L. Holmstrom, 'Rape Trauma Syndrome' (1974) 131 *American Journal of Psychiatry* 981.

7 Ibid.
8 See, for example, B.J. Buchele and J.P. Buchele, 'Legal and Psychological Issues in the Use of Expert Testimony on Rape Trauma Syndrome' (1992) 25(3) *Washburn Law Journal* 26; S. Schnepf, 'Rape Trauma Syndrome in the Rape Trial' (1986) 8 *Criminal Justice Journal* 427; S. Stefan, 'The Protection Racket: Rape Trauma Syndrome, Psychiatric Labeling and the Law' (1994) 88(4) *Northwestern University Law Review* 1271.
9 S. Sutherland and D. Scherl (1970) 'Patterns of Responses Among Victims of Rape' (1970) 40 *American Journal of Orthopsychiatry* 503.
10 Burgess and Holmstrom, 'Rape Trauma Syndrome'.
11 Stefan, 'The Protection Racket'.
12 See, for example, L.O. Ruth and S. Chandler, 'Sexual Assault During the Acute Phase: An Exploratory Model and Multivariate Analysis' (1983) 24 *Journal of Health and Social Behavior* 174.
13 See, for example, J. Kilpatrick, L. Veronen and B. Resick, 'The Aftermath of Rape: Recent Empirical Findings' (1979) 49 *American Journal of Orthopsychiatry* 658; L.O. Ruch and J.J. Leon, 'Type of Sexual Assault Trauma: A Multidimensional Analysis of a Short-term Panel' (1983) 8 *Victimology* 237.
14 J. Gornick *et al.*, 'Structure and Activities of Rape Crisis Centers in the Early 1980's' (1985) 31 *Crime and Delinquency* 247.
15 Ibid.
16 G. Steketee and E.B. Foa, 'Rape Victims: Post Traumatic Stress Responses and Their Treatment' (1987) 1 *Journal of Anxiety Disorders* 69.
17 *Diagnostic and Statistical Manual of Mental Disorders - IV* (1997) American Psychiatric Association, 427.
18 D. McCord, 'Syndromes, Profiles and Other Mental Exotica: A New Approach to the Admissibility of Non-Traditional Psychological Evidence in Criminal Cases' (1987) 66 *Oregon Law Review* 19.
19 P.A. Tetreault, 'Rape Myth Acceptance: A Case for Providing Educational Expert Testimony in Rape Jury Trials' (1989) 7 *Behavioral Science and the Law* 242.
20 D.L. Rhode, *Justice and Gender* (Cambridge, Mass., 1989).
21 C.F. Feagan, 'Rape Trauma Syndrome Testimony as Scientific Evidence: Evolving Bèyond *State* v. *Taylor*' (1992) 61(1) *University of Missouri Kansas City Law Review* 145; Tetreault, 'Rape Myth Acceptance'.
22 A.Z. Soshnick, 'Comment: The Rape Shield Paradox: Complainant Protection Amidst Oscillating Trends of State Judicial Interpretation' (1987) 78 *Journal of Criminal Law and Criminology* 644.
23 Feagan, 'Rape Trauma Syndrome'; J.C. Marsh, *Rape and the Limits of Law Reform* (Boston, Mass., 1982); R. Tong, *Women, Sex and the Law* (Towowa, NJ, 1994).
24 Feagan, 'Rape Trauma Syndrome'.
25 M.W. Stewart, S.A. Dobbin, and S.I. Gatowski, 'Reasonableness and Gender in the Law: Beyond the Reasonable Woman and Reasonable Person Standards', *Law and Society Review* (at proof stage).
26 *People* v. *Bledsoe* 681 P.2d 291, 298 (Ca. 1984).
27 C. Barron, 'Rape Trauma Syndrome' (1984) 7(1) *Harvard Women's Law Journal* 301 (reviews cases in which the rape victim was a child and argues that RTS testimony should be allowed in such cases).
28 In *Henson* v. *State* the court ruled that the alleged victim's conduct after the fact was clearly probative of whether rape occurred; and it was abuse of discretion to bar its use by defence (*Henson* v. *State* 535 N.E.2d 1189 (Ind. 1989)); in *State* v. *Liddell* the court

rejected a claim that evidence by a doctor, a psychological counsellor and a psychiatric nurse on RTS would confuse or mislead the jury. Rather the court said that any relevant evidence that tends to support the existence or non-existence of a fact in issue can only aid the jury, not mislead or confuse it (*State* v. *Liddell* 685 P.2d 918 (Mont. 1984)); in *State* v. *Kim* the court rejected a challenge that the prejudicial effect of RTS testimony outweighed its probative value (*State* v. *Kim* 645 P.2d 1330 (Haw. 1982)).

29 In *People* v. *Bledsoe* the court noted that the syndrome is an 'umbrella' concept, reflecting the broad range of emotional trauma experienced by clients of rape counsellors, and it does not consist of a relatively narrow set of criteria or symptoms whose presence demonstrates that the client has in fact been raped (*People* v. *Bledsoe* 681 P.2d 291 (Ca. 1984)); in *State* v. *McGee* the court reversed a third degree criminal sexual conduct conviction on the grounds that the prosecution erroneously introduced RTS into evidence; the peril of prejudice and confusion resulting from the testimony was said to substantially outweigh any probative value it might possess (*State* v. *McGee* 324 N.W.2d 232 (Minn. 1982)); in *State* v. *Bowman* the court ruled that RTS evidence would mislead and confuse the jury (*State* v. *Bowman* 715 P.2d 467 (NM App. 1986)); and in *People* v. *Coleman* the court found that admission of a physician's testimony that the complaining witness's conduct and responses were consistent with RTS was in error since it was likely to mislead the jury into inferring that the witness was in fact raped (*People* v. *Coleman* 255 Cal. Rptr 813, 768 P.2d 32 (1989)).

30 In *People* v. *Reid* the expert was not allowed to testify as to whether she believed the alleged victim (*People* v. *Reid* 475 N.Y.S.2d 741 (1984)); in *State* v. *Brodniak* the court ruled that the expert's testimony with regard to malingering and statistical percentage of false accusations was an improper comment on the credibility of the rape victim (*State* v. *Brodniak* 718 P.2d 322 (Mont. 1986)).

31 *State* v. *Taylor* 663 S.W.2d 235 (Mo. 1984).

32 In *Henson* v. *State* the court found that, even though testimony did corroborate victims, and one effect of corroboration is to support or bolster credibility of witnesses, that did not amount to violation of the rule against vouching for credibility; it assists the jury in understanding some aspects of behaviour of victims and, so long as there is no comment on credibility or truthfulness of victims, it does not invade the providence of the jury (*Henson* v. *State* 535 N.E.2d 1189 (Ind. 1989)); in *People* v. *Stull* the court found that the rape counsellor did not express her opinion as to the complainant's credibility, noting that the opinion was admitted in response to an issue raised by defence as to whether a rape victim should have acted as the complainant did (*People* v. *Stull* 338 N.W.2d 403 (Mich. App. 1983)); see also *State* v. *Staples* 415 A.2d 320 (NH 1980).

33 In *State* v. *Kim* the court found a sufficient factual foundation for a paediatrician's testimony comparing behavioural characteristics and the mental condition of the teenage prosecutrix with those of others who have experienced similar trauma; the court also found that the expert's method of evaluation was not lacking in usefulness, reliability or precision (*State* v. *Kim* 645 P.2d 1330 (Haw. 1982)); in *State* v. *Marks* the court commented that the psychiatrist's opinion on RTS had been shown to be generally accepted as reliable within the expert's particular scientific field (*State* v. *Marks* 647 P.2d 1292 (Kan. 1982)); and in *People* v. *Reid* the court noted that the syndrome had been the subject of numerous scientific research efforts since 1974 (*People* v. *Reid* 475 N.Y.S.2d 741 (NY 1984)).

34 In *State* v. *Saldana* the court stated that the scientific evaluation of RTS had not reached a level of reliability that surpasses the quality of commonsense evaluation present in jury deliberations; the syndrome is not the type of scientific test that accurately and reliably determines whether a rape has occurred, for the characteristic symptoms may follow any

traumatic event (*State* v. *Saldana* 324 N.W. 2d 227 (Minn. 1982)) In *State* v. *Black* the judge ruled that the trial court erred in admitting and relying on expert testimony on RTS since it had not been generally established as a scientifically reliable means of proving the rape occurred (*State* v. *Black* 745 P.2d 12 (Wash. 1987)); in *People* v. *Pullins* the court found that RTS is not the type of scientific test that accurately and reliably indicates whether a rape occurred (*People* v. *Pullins* 378 N.W.2d 502 (Mich App. 1985)).

35 See *State* v. *Huey*, noting that the expert must be 'qualified by training and experience such as a psychiatrist or psychologist' (*State* v. *Huey* 699 P.2d 1290, 1293–94 (Ariz. 1985)); see, however *State* v. *Taylor*, in which the court acknowledged in the abstract the qualifications of the psychiatrist on RTS, but reversed the forcible rape conviction on the grounds that the psychiatrist had offered some testimony that he was not qualified to make (*State* v. *Taylor* 663 S.W.2d 235 (Mo, 1984)).

36 *People* v. *Housley* 8 Cal. Rptr. 2d 431, 434 (Ct. App. 1992); *People* v. *Taylor* 536 N.Y.S.2d 825, 828 (App. Div. 1988); *People* v. *Reid* 475 N.Y.S.2d 741, 742 (Sup. Ct. 1984); *State* v. *Teeter* 355 S.E.2d 804, 807 (N.C. Ct. App. 1987); *Rivera* v. *State* 840 P.2d 933, 938 (Wyo. 1992).

37 *State* v. *Liddell* 685 P.2d 918, 922 (Mont. 1984).

38 *People* v. *Stanley* 681 P.2d 302 (Cal. 1984).

39 *State* v. *Roles* 832 P.2d 311, 313–314 (Idaho Ct. App. 1992); *Simmons* v. *State* 504 N.E.2d 575, 578 (Ind. 1987); see, however, *State* v. *Goodwin*, in which an expert with a master's degree in social work was held unqualified when prosecutors 'failed to establish that the witness had any particularized training or expertise' related to post-traumatic stress disorder (*State* v. *Goodwin* 357 S.E.2d 639, 641 (N.C. 1987)) and *State* v. *Willis*, in which a social worker who counselled rape victims was not qualified to give expert testimony regarding RTS because RTS is a 'medical diagnosis requiring qualified psychiatrists' (*State* v. *Willis* 256 Kan 837, 888 P.2d 839 (Kan. 1995)).

40 *People* v. *Davis* 585 N.E.2d 214, 217–18 (Ill. App. Ct. 1992); *State* v. *Robinson* 431 N.W. 2d 165, 171 (Wis. 1988); see, however, *State* v. *McCoy*, in which a counsellor was qualified as an expert witness but the court cautioned that 'where, as in this case, the witness is a rape counselor, the trial court should evaluate the witness with extreme care ... A counselor is likely to sympathize with the victim and tend, consciously or subconsciously, to testify in a way that supports a finding of guilt' (*State* v. *McCoy* 366 E.2d 731, 737 (W. Va 1988)).

41 *State* v. *Roles* 832 P.2d 311, 314 (Idaho Ct. App. 1992); *Scadden* v. *State* 7332 P.2d 1036, 1044 (Wyo. 1987).

42 *Daubert* v. *Merrell Dow Pharmaceuticals, Inc.* 509 US 579 (1993).

43 D.L. Faigman, 'The Evidentiary Status of Social Science Under *Daubert*: Is it "Scientific", "Technical" or "Other" Knowledge' (1995) 1(4) *Psychology, Public Policy and Law* 960; T.S. Renaker, 'Evidentiary Legerdemain: Deciding When *Daubert* Should Apply to Social Science Evidence' (1996) 84 *California Law Review* 1657; J.T. Richardson, G.P. Ginsburg, S.I. Gatowski and S.A. Dobbin, 'The Problems of Applying *Daubert* to Psychological Syndrome Evidence' 79(1) *Judicature* 17.

44 C. Kelly and D. Squire, 'Scope of Judicial Gatekeeping: Does *Daubert* Apply to Areas Other than New Science?', in E.D. Brown (sr. ed.), *Judicial Gatekeeping*, Presidents and Fellows of Harvard College (Lenox, Mass., 2 May 1997).

45 Faigman, 'Evidentiary Status', 961.

46 I. Freckelton, 'Evidence: Battered Woman Syndrome' (1992) 17 *Alternative Law Journal*, 39; Richardson *et al.*, 'Problems of Applying *Daubert*'.

47 K. Popper, *The Open Society and Its Enemies* (Lawrenceville, NJ, 1952).

48 *Frye* v. *United States* 293 F. 1013, 1014 D.C. Cir. (1923).

49 This risk of false positives may not be as serious a concern as it appears, as it is based upon an assumption that a false claim of rape is a relatively common occurrence, an assumption that is not supported by research.
50 *People* v. *Bledsoe* 681 P.2d 291 (Ca. 1984).
51 *State* v. *Bledsoe* (1984) was pre-*Daubert* and the criteria of 'general acceptance' (*Frye* v. *United States* 293 F. 1013, 1014 D.C. Cir. (1923)) was used to determine admissibility.
52 Cooney, 'Evidence as Partisanship'.
53 H. Feild, 'Attitudes towards rape: A comparative analysis of police, rapists, crisis counsellors and citizens' 36(2) *Journal of Personality and Social Psychology*, 156; S. Feldman-Summers and G. Palmer, 'Rape: A view from judges, prosecutors and police officers' (1980) 7 *Criminal Justice and Behavior* 19; M.W. Stewart, S.A. Dobbin and S.I. Gatowski, '"Real Rapes" and "Real Victims": The Shared Reliance on Common Cultural Definitions of Rape' (1996) IV(2) *Feminist Legal Studies* 159.
54 Stewart *et al.*, '"Real Rapes" and "Real Victims"'.
55 Rhode, *Justice and Gender*.
56 C.W. Harlow, *Female Victims of Violent Crime* (Washington DC, 1991); M.P. Koss and M.R. Harvey, *The Rape Victim: Clinical and Community Interventions* (2nd edn, Newbury Park, Cal., 1991); Stefan, 'The Protection Racket'.
57 Cooney, 'Evidence as Partisanship'.
58 S.A. Dobbin and S.I. Gatowski, 'Rape Trauma Syndrome: The Medicalization of Women's Rape Experiences', paper presented as part of a panel on the construction of women's reality in the courtroom, Western Social Science Association, Reno, Nev., April 1996; Stefan, 'The Protection Racket'.
59 Feild, 'Attitudes Towards Rape'; Feldman-Summers and Palmer, 'Rape: A view'; Stewart *et al.*, '"Real Rapes" and "Real Victims"'.
60 Faigman, 'Evidentiary Status', 971.
61 See Stewart *et al.*, '"Real Rapes" and "Real Victims"', for a discussion of how rape shield laws may offer only technical rather than substantial protection to the alleged victim and are quite likely too little offered too late in the process. The authors argue that the power and range of rape myths and stereotypes are so pervasive that they mitigate the potential protective impact of rape shield laws which give judges discretion regarding the introduction of information about a victim's past sexual experience. The existence of such laws might be of little consequence in a cultural climate in which the participants at each level share the same 'taken-for-granteds' about 'real rapes' and 'real victims'.
62 Dobbin and Gatowski, 'Rape Trauma Syndrome'; Stefan, 'The Protection Racket'; J.R. Castel, 'Prosecutorial Uses of Rape Trauma Syndrome Evidence: A Critical Analysis' (1991) 7 *Journal of Law and Social Policy* 175.
63 In 1989 the Supreme Court of Indiana in *Henson* v. *State* (535 N.E. 2d 1189, 1192–1993 (Ind. 1989)) held that defence testimony regarding the fact that the victim was witnessed drinking and dancing the night after the alleged rape tended to prove that the victim's behaviour was inconsistent with someone who had suffered a traumatic rape and tended to 'make it less probable that a rape in fact occurred'. See N.R. Economou, 'Defense Expert Testimony on Rape Trauma Syndrome: Implications for the Stoic Victim' (1991) 42 *The Hastings Law Journal* 1143.
64 Stefan, 'The Protection Racket'; see also Economou, 'Defense Expert Testimony'.
65 L. Madigan and N. Gamble, *The Second Rape: Society's Continued Betrayal of the Victim* (New York, 1991).
66 L. Kelly, *Surviving Sexual Violence* (Minneapolis, Minn., 1988), p.659.
67 R. Stryker, 'Rules, Resources and Legitimacy Processes: Some Implications for Social Conflict, Order and Change' (1994) 99(4) *American Journal of Sociology*, 847.

68 Dobbin and Gatowski, 'Rape Trauma Syndrome'; Stefan, 'The Protection Racket'.
69 DSM-IV, at 427.
70 J. Monahan and L. Walker, *Social Sciences in Law: Cases and Materials* (3rd edn, Westbury, NY, 1994).

8 The Application of Patent Law Principles to Scientific Developments: The Problem with Biotechnology

Margaret Llewelyn

Introduction

Developments in biotechnology have raised serious questions about the extent to which, if at all, patent law should protect inventions involving genetic material.[1] The issue is a controversial one.[2] Should companies, which have spent billions of dollars on the production of new products and processes involving genetic material, be able to protect their inventions by a patent? Or should there be a difference in patent practice between inanimate and animate material on the basis that the latter is in some way special and not to be regarded as appropriate subject matter for a monopoly right?[3]

In attempting to assess the issues which should be considered when deciding if patent protection should be available, a number of diverse and possibly irreconcilable attitudes towards the ownership and monopolization of genetic material need to be taken into account. These include the economic consequences of permitting or denying patent protection for what are potentially very valuable commodities; the effects of patenting on access to genetic information at scientific, indigenous and social levels; environmental concerns such as the impact on biological diversity and safety risks; and, underlying all of the above, whether it is appropriate to treat living material or its constituent parts in the same way as the results of other inventive activity and permit a legal monopoly which has the effect of preventing anyone apart from the holder from using that information.

Evidence over recent years from the stock market demonstrates that biotechnology is big business.[4] The level of investment being poured into the biotechnology industry, coupled with the expectation of highly profitable end products for use in sectors and industries, agricultural, food and medicinal, has led to calls for strong legal protection, usually in the form of a patent, for the results of this highly expensive R&D.[5] These calls have for the most part been successful, at least within developed countries. International agreements such as the Uruguay Round of the General Agreement on Tariffs and Trade (GATT)[6] and the Rio Convention on Biological Diversity (the Rio Convention) have been drafted to take account of the need to provide effective and appropriate[7] legal protection for biotechnological inventions.

These intergovernmental decisions appear to signal a green light to the patenting of living material, but they have not met with universal approbation. While the need to protect the commercial interest vested in biotechnology might have been met by the provisions in both GATT and the Rio Convention, concern remains about whether it is either ethically or indeed legally correct to permit the patent system to be applied in this way. Attempts are therefore continuing around the world to try to restrict the extent to which patent protection should be available for genetic material.

Underpinning these concerns over the commodification and commercialization of genetic material is the view that living material, from base genetic material through to higher life forms, is in trust to mankind.[8] The responsibility this trust brings with it includes not tampering with nature, preserving existing biological diversity and respecting nature in all its forms. As the commercial potential of biotechnology has been recognized, there has also developed a recognition that Western countries, because of their superior economic and technological positions, have an obligation to protect less developed countries. These countries are regarded as unable, either financially or technologically, to compete equally in the biorevolution, yet they are also seen as the most likely to be affected by it, either because they are the sites of rich but untapped natural resources or because of their medical or agricultural needs. These countries need protecting from unwarranted exploitation. This was one of the main rationales behind the introduction of the Rio Convention in 1992. The Rio Convention clearly indicates that, while there is a recognition that a considerable amount of useful information is lying dormant in nature which could be effectively utilized, any commercial utilization of it must be tempered with man's non-commercial role as guardian of the world's genetic inheritance and protector of those who do not have the resources to identify, research and exploit this information.

There is one final strand to the discussions surrounding the patenting of living material which must be taken into account when assessing the validity of the arguments and that is the public reaction to the science itself. Whether based on an accurate assessment of the science itself and its potential or on an irrational fear of the unknown, real concerns are nonetheless being voiced about the consequences of manipulating genetic material. These concerns extend to questions over whether there are sufficient regulatory controls being exercised over the science and its possible effects at the human and environmental level.[9] These fears have been consistently ignored by those involved in determining whether a legal monopoly should be granted over biotechnology, with the result that this has given the impression in some quarters that commercial interests and the ability to protect a commodity in the market-place are taking precedence over any safety or ethical concerns.

Each of these diverse facets of our relationship with nature, the desire to conserve and enhance, the wish to utilize and commercially disseminate and the fear of the consequences of such research and exploitation, have had an effect on decisions taken over whether or not to protect genetic material via a patent. The concerns over the patenting of genetic material are not solely to do with the legality of permitting such a grant although, as will be discussed below, there is a concern that the language of the patent system is being inappropriately manipulated in order to achieve a particular result. They also are based on whether such material *should* be patentable.

This chapter is primarily concerned with the law as it has developed with Europe.[10] Decisions such as those of the European Patent Office in respect of the *Harvard/Onco Mouse*, *Plant Genetic Systems N.V.* and *Howard Florey/Relaxin* applications clearly show that such inventions can be patented. The more complex question of whether they should be patentable remains to be resolved. The problem facing those opposing such patents is that, as the practice of granting patents over genetic material continues, any claims that this practice is not appropriate could be regarded as becoming correspondingly weakened. The fact that patent offices are granting patents over genetic material should not, however, be used as an excuse for not addressing the question of whether it is correct to allow genetic material to be patented.

At the heart of this discussion rests the fact that a patent indirectly gives to the holder an exclusive right to decide how the information protected by the patent is to be exploited. He might choose to exploit the information himself or with others, or he might decide to grant either an exclusive or a non-exclusive licence. Whichever mode he chooses the result is that decisions relating to the dissemination and control of the information lie with the patent holder. As the cost of obtaining and maintaining a patent can be very expensive, where patent protection has been sought around the world this can reach into the hundreds of thousands of dollars,[11] the holder will invariably want to exploit or disseminate the information in a manner which will ensure the recoupment of the R&D costs. This means that, for their purposes, genetic information, like any other invention, can validly be commercialized and, if patentable, be treated as exclusive property.[12]

The Function of a Patent

The traditional rationale supporting a patent grant is the provision of a reward for innovative activity which results in a new product or process being made available.[13] As the effect of a patent grant is to enable the holder to exclude others from using the information without his authorization, it serves to give the holder an incentive to put the invention into the public domain by marketing it. The patent has the effect of giving him exclusivity over its commercial dissemination.[14] The ability to sell the invention in the absence of any direct competition in turn provides the holder with the incentive to continue to develop and market new products. The effect of this is the promotion of innovative activity and the fostering of the economy through the development and commercialization of new products. That some degree of inventive act must take place before a monopoly is granted is continually impressed upon those involved with the system and this is enshrined in European patent law which states categorically that discoveries are not patentable.[15]

The highly important economic role of the patent system cannot be ignored[16] and for these reasons the patent system is constantly held out as an important industrial tool.[17] One of the main objections raised by those opposing the extension of patent protection to genetic material is that this rationale of protecting the results of innovative activity, thereby justifying the grant of a legal monopoly for a limited period of time,[18] cannot be extended to genetic material.[19]

The protection conferred by a patent is over the invention which results from the innovative activity. That invention can take the form of either a new product or a new process and as far as the patent system is concerned, it can emanate from almost any area of technology.[20] The one thing that both forms of invention have to have in common for patent law purposes is that they are the novel result of an inventive step and have an industrial or commercial use.[21] Those who oppose the granting of patents over living material claim that genetic material cannot be patented as it is at best a discovery and not an invention; that it is not possible to demonstrate that living material, such as a gene sequence, is novel; and that the identification of the presence and function of a gene is not particularly inventive.[22] In short the argument is that genetic material cannot be regarded as an invention for patent law purposes.[23] The one thing both sides to the debate appear to agree on is that products and processes utilizing genetic material are extremely lucrative and that there is clear commercial or industrial applicability.

Underlying all the following discussion over the practice and policy of European patent law is the question whether the fact that the patent system plays an important part in the economic underpinning of many countries should be used as a reason for allowing it to protect the results of all types of innovative activity irrespective of concerns over the science involved. This is an impossible question to answer, for it begs the statement that there are some types of innovative activity which cannot be condoned and scientists engaged in research in those areas should forfeit a reward for that research. If it is accepted that there are some forms of innovative activity which should not be sanctioned or rewarded then how are these to be determined? Is it on the grounds that some inventions are not acceptable according to current standards and, if this is the arbiter, can we be sure that these standards are correct and do not in fact act as a barrier to progress?[24] The determination of acceptable and unacceptable science is an imperfect art if only because it is shrouded in shifting social perceptions.[25]

The basis upon which the issue over the patenting of living material appears to have been decided is that of pragmatism. Can inventions which involve genetic material meet the normal requirements for patentability, novelty, inventive step and industrial applicability? If they can then the patent should be granted. The fact that living material is concerned is not a primary issue.[26] It is to be treated in the same way as any other technology. While it is debatable whether this is the correct approach, there is no doubt that this is the prevalent attitude of patent-granting offices.

This chapter will look at the way the European Patent Office (EPO) has responded to the calls from industry for patent protection for biotechnological inventions through a number of controversial decisions. It will also look at the way the EU has tried to ameliorate the controversy without either jeopardizing the investment in biotechnology or avoiding the concerns of those opposed to such patents through its proposal for a directive on the legal protection of biotechnological inventions.[27]

European Patent Law and Practice: Present and Future

Current European patent law and practice is dominated by the European Patent Convention (EPC). The first and most important fact about the EPC is that it is not an instrument of the European Union. The decision to introduce a European patent was taken during the 1950s when it was recognized that differences in national patent practices could act as a barrier to the introduction, and proper functioning, of the proposed European

Community. However, as the form and constituency of that Community continued to be a matter of political debate through the 1960s, it was felt that the need to harmonize European patent practice was too important to continue to put off until the political wrangling had been resolved. It was decided therefore to introduce two patent conventions. The first, the European Patent Convention, would be independently constituted from the EEC to enable all European countries, irrespective of whether they were members of the EEC, to benefit from its harmonizing provisions. This convention would permit a patent grant made by the European Patent Office to be effective in all member states of the EPC through a single granting system. The matter of specific Community patent protection was to be dealt with in the second convention, the Community Patent Convention (CPC). The European Patent 606 Convention was introduced in 1973 and all current member states of the European Union are also members of the EPC. The CPC was signed in 1975 but it has yet to come into force owing to procedural and administrative delays.

The fact that the EPC is independent of the European Union is important. The EPC is not directly affected by any decisions made within the EU. This is crucial because, as will be discussed below, the EPO is currently developing its own jurisprudence in respect of the patenting of living material. Since the EPO is an independent legal entity, its decisions are not subject to any appeals procedures other than the internal procedures of the EPO. Considerable concern has been expressed within the European Union over some of these decisions. As a result the European Commission has stepped in to attempt to dispel these concerns through the introduction of a directive which is intended to clarify the position on the patenting of genetic material for member states of the EU. It might be thought that the introduction of a directive which clarifies the patentability of living material could only be regarded as beneficial, but the directive, as it is currently drafted, diverges from the provisions of the EPC in a number of crucial areas. The impact of these differences could be significant.[28]

As the directive emanates from the EU it will not have any direct effect on the application or interpretation of the EPC. It will, however, have a direct impact on the laws of member states of the EU. The fact that it will not affect the EPC but will affect member states of the EU could have serious consequences for those countries which are members of both. The reason for this is the dual nature of the relationship between the EPC and the patent laws of its member states. First, the EPC allows an applicant to acquire as many national patent grants for his or her invention as desired upon the submission of a single application to the EPO. Second, as the effect of a European patent grant is to give the patent holder national rights in those countries designated in the patent it is necessary for each member state of the

EPC to provide equivalent protection. The result is that each member state has had to bring its national laws into line with the provisions of the EPC and national courts have had to give effect to patents granted by the EPO.

With the adoption of the directive by the European Parliament in November 1997, all member states of the EU are required to amend their national patent laws to bring them into line with the provisions of the directive. If the provisions of the directive differ from those of the EPC, those member states of the EU which are also members of the EPC could find themselves in the position of being in violation of their obligations under the EPC if they amend their national law according to the provisions of the directive. Equally if they do not amend their national patent laws in accordance with the directive they could be held to be in violation of their obligations under the EU.

It is not surprising therefore that, where possible, the directive has followed the language and intention of the EPC.[29] This does not necessarily mean that the issue of the patenting of living material has been either correctly or appropriately resolved. It is proposed to look at the following specific areas: discoveries/inventions and inventions which are excluded on the grounds that they offend against morality.[30]

Discoveries/Inventions: the View of the EPO

Article 52(1) of the EPC states: 'European patents shall be granted for any inventions which are susceptible of industrial application, which are new and which involve an inventive step.' No further definition of an invention is given. Instead the remainder of Article 52 and Article 53 of the EPC set out material which cannot be regarded as an invention and those inventions which are excluded from patent protection. This latter group, which is contained within Article 53, will be discussed in the next section.

The second paragraph of Article 52 reads: '(2) The following in particular shall not be regarded as inventions within the meaning of paragraph 1: (a) discoveries, scientific theories and mathematical methods'. There then follow five other categories of material which are not regarded as inventions under the EPC, but these are not relevant for the purposes of this chapter. It is clear, therefore, that a distinction is made between inventions and discoveries, the former being patentable, if the requirements of novelty, inventive step and industrial application are met, and the latter not being patentable. Other than Article 52, paragraphs 1 and 2, no further guidance is given in the EPC as to the distinction between the two in practice. Yet the distinction between the two is critical in respect of certain types of biotechnological invention.

Many new products are being produced as a result of the utilization of material which has been found in nature. Every week the press heralds the 'discovery' of a new gene with the propensity for curing or alleviating a particular medical condition or which has desirable agricultural properties. The sources of these discoveries can range from plant material in Papua New Guinea to the human genome. One of the most important aspects of this research is the capacity to harness the natural information and apply it in a particular way, either through the genetic manipulation of agricultural material or through the development of a new drug. Whatever the method of utilizing the information, it will involve considerable expenditure from the moment the decision is taken to look for the information, through the identification of its properties, to the point where it is possible to apply it in a given form. The question is, should this naturally occurring material properly be regarded as appropriate subject matter for a patent? Aside from the fundamental issue of whether living material should be regarded as capable of being monopolized, the issue which has had to be addressed by the European Patent Office and the Commission is whether products or processes incorporating such material constitute discoveries or inventions.

The position taken by the European Patent Office is that inventions involving animate material have always been patentable and patent grants have been made the world over in respect of all forms of genetic material including human somatic cell lines and hybridomas.[31] There is therefore no question in the minds of those administering the office that genetic material should not be patentable.

An example of the attitude towards the patentability of living material can be seen in the attempt in the United States by Craig Venter on behalf of the National Institute of Health (NIH) to patent 2000 DNA sequences identified as a result of the continuing research into the Human Genome Project (HUGO).[32] The application ultimately failed on the grounds that no utility or function[33] had been specified for the sequences. The US Patent Office did accept that, in principle, the material itself, if a function had been identified, would have been patentable. The initial reaction in Europe was to condemn the patenting of parts of the human genome and several prominent geneticists from both sides of the Atlantic spoke out against the initiative of the NIH; these included James Watson.[34] However, once it became clear that the NIH was going ahead with its application, some of the European partners in the HUGO project decided to follow suit in order not to lose any rights they might have over their research and any commercial products which might result from it.[35] At no time did any of the patent offices involved state that this type of material would be regarded as unpatentable simply on the basis that it consisted of human gene sequences.[36]

It is the view of patent offices that, because of existing patent practice, no distinction should be drawn between a patent application in respect of a micro-organism and one involving a human gene sequence. This view does not deter those opposed to exclusive rights being granted over genetic material. Their response is that a distinction can be drawn for the following reasons:

- there is a difference between claiming a micro-organism as reproduced in a specific context and claiming a natural property such as a cell line of a particular group of people[37] or the medicinal elements of a plant;[38]
- that simply because the patent office has taken it upon itself to regard as acceptable the patenting of genetic material does not mean that this practice should be allowed to continue in light of growing public awareness;[39] and
- that a clear distinction should be drawn between those types of animate material which are to be regarded as appropriate for patent protection (micro-organisms are the most common in this group) and material which is not appropriate, for example human genetic material.[40]

The problem with pursuing this latter line of argument is that it is not always possible to draw a distinct line between what is permissible as patentable material and that which is not. This can be clearly seen in the EPO decision in *Howard Florey/Relaxin.*

Howard Florey/Relaxin[41]

In 1991 the EPO had granted a patent to the Howard Florey Institute for the process for obtaining the human protein H2-relaxin and the DNA encoding it. The protein had been identified from tissue obtained from pregnant women. In 1992 the Fraktion der Grünen of the European Parliament filed an opposition to the patent on the grounds that the subject matter (a) lacked novelty and inventive step, (b) was a discovery and was excluded under Article 52(2)(a), and (c) offended against morality and was excluded under Article 53(a). Objections (a) and (b) will be discussed here, the issue of morality will be discussed below. The opposition was heard by the Opposition Board of the EPO.

The arguments put forward by the Fraktion der Grünen that the claimed for protein was a discovery and not an invention were as follows.[42] The protein was naturally occurring within pregnant women. All that the Howard Florey Institute had done was to identify the protein. The claim for a patent over the protein was, therefore, tantamount to the US landing on the moon in 1969 and claiming it as American territory. The Opposition Board did not accept this argument, stating that the arguments put forward by the Fraktion demonstrated a lack of understanding of the patent system and ignored the long-standing practice of the EPO to grant patents over natural substances. The Board referred to the Guidelines of the EPC which state, in C-IV, 2.3, that to find 'a substance freely occurring in nature is a mere discovery and therefore unpatentable'. In this specific instance, however, the Institute had isolated the substance from its natural source, had characterized it and by so doing had produced something new in the sense that it had not existed in that form before. As a result the protein was patentable.[43] The Opposition Board went on to define an invention for their purposes:

> An invention must have a technical character, that is, should constitute an industrially applicable technical solution to a technical problem, and must be reproducibly obtainable without undue burden. A product must be furthermore novel in the sense of not having had a previously recognised existence and must in addition be inventive ... the subject-matter of the disputed patent does not represent a discovery, and is hence not excluded from patentability under Article 52(2) EPC.

It is clear from this decision that the EPO is using purely a technical assessment of whether living material should be patentable and it sees no problem in granting patents over genetic material which is naturally occurring provided that it is material which was not previously available to the public. Not surprisingly the decision has enraged those opposed to patents over living material and a second appeal against the patent has been filed.[44] This practice of the EPO is open to criticism.[45] There is an argument for saying that whilst, on a technical level, there might be a degree of inventiveness in identifying and isolating naturally occurring properties lying latent within a human, animal or plant host, and that the isolation of this material could be regarded as bringing into the public domain novel information, on a different level the genetic information per se cannot be regarded as anything other than a discovery. It existed before the intervention of the patent applicant and the applicant should not be allowed to claim as an invention material which he has merely brought to wider attention. Inherent in this argument is the concern that patent rights could be claimed over indigenous genetic material which has been traditionally used by local people because of its medicinal or agricultural properties but the actual properties of which have not been previously identified. The most famous example of this is the Neem patent. Indians had used for generations the bark of the Neem tree for a number of medical purposes. The local population were aware of the effects of using the bark, but they do not know why it has this effect. The properties of the bark were identified by the US pharmaceutical company W.R. Grace and led to a number of patents being taken out which encompass these properties. This has resulted in a considerable attack being made on the patent system by, amongst others, the Indian environmentalist Vandana Shiva on the grounds that the material covered by the patent could be regarded neither as novel nor as the result of an inventive step, since it was known and used by the Indian community.[46] This opposition has not been accepted by the patent fraternity as valid grounds for discontinuing the practice of granting patents.[47]

What is perhaps surprising about the decision in *Relaxin* is that it has attracted very little academic criticism from within intellectual property law circles. This can probably be attributed to the fact that the focus of attention in the last year or so has centred increasingly on the proposals for the EU Patent directive and away from the decisions of the EPO. The reason for this is that the directive is anticipated as setting out once and for all the precise delineation between what is patentable and what is not. Even though the decisions of the EPO will not be directly affected by the introduction of the directive, it is expected that they will be influenced by its provisions.[48]

Discoveries/Inventions: the Patent Directive

The starting point for the directive is that biological material per se should not be excluded from patent protection.[49] The Recitals make it clear that the basis for this premise is that there must be effective and harmonized protection throughout the EU which will encourage and maintain investment in biotechnology.[50] The commercial desirability of ensuring patent protection for genetic material is therefore clearly stated to be a primary motivating force. The rationale for this approach is that biotechnology research is important in combating disease and hunger. If this research is to be encouraged it needs effective and appropriate protection.[51] This protection is provided by the grant of a patent. There is also recognition of the fact that, irrespective of the fate of the directive, the EPO will not stop its practice of granting patents over biotechnological inventions.

The fact that there is considerable concern over the monopolization of genetic material is not, however, overlooked in favour of purely commercial interests. The directive does state in Recital 13 that fundamental principles which safeguard the dignity and integrity of the person must be respected and that 'the human body, at any stage in its formation or development, its elements, including germ cells, its products and the sequence or partial sequence of a human gene cannot be patented; whereas these principles are in line with the criteria of patentability proper to patent law, whereby a mere discovery cannot be patented'. This would appear to indicate that a patent claim such as that considered in *Relaxin* would not be permitted under the directive. However Recital 15 qualifies the exclusion in Recital 13, stating that 'it should be made clear that an invention based on an element isolated from the human body or otherwise produced by means of a technical process which is capable of industrial application, *is not excluded from patentability*, even where the structure of that element is identical to that of a natural element' (emphasis added). This means that, where an element has been isolated and a use identified for it, it will be regarded as patentable.

Recital 16 provides the final general statement on the issue of the patentability of naturally occurring material:

> Whereas such an element isolated from the human body or otherwise produced is not excluded from patentability as it is the result of a technical process used to identify, purify and classify it and to reproduce outside the human body, techniques which human beings alone are capable of putting into practice and which Nature is incapable of accomplishing by itself ...

Recital 16a then simply adds that such 'inventions' must meet the same criteria for patent protection as apply to all other areas of technology.

Recital 16b provides an illuminating statement as to the actual distinction between patentable and unpatentable material. It states that the difference lies in that a sequence in situ does not contain a technical teaching; that is, it does not provide any information as to its components or as to how it can be replicated. A sequence which has been isolated and applied does, however, provide information as to its constituent parts and how to reproduce it. The innovative act which is being rewarded therefore is the placing into the public domain of the information contained within the invention together with the instructions on how to reproduce it. On the above grounds it is accepted that human genetic material which is isolated and for which a function has been identified will be patentable under the terms of the directive.[52]

One of the most interesting and potentially significant differences between the amendments tabled by the European Parliament and the revised text published by the Commission in September 1997 is in respect of the need to obtain consent before a patent application can be made. Following the John Moore case[53] in the United States of America and mindful of the increasing concerns over gene piracy, and in order to indicate compliance with the Rio Convention on Biological Diversity (the Rio Convention) signed in 1992, the members of the European Parliament amended the directive to include a specific provision requiring a patent applicant to provide evidence that he has obtained consent from either the person from whom the genetic material has been isolated or from the country within which the material is indigenous. The Commission has not accepted this amendment. It is the only amendment which the Commission has not incorporated into the latest revision. This omission could place the European Union in contravention of its obligations under the Rio Convention. It should be noted that there are no equivalent statements in the directive relating to genetic information which is naturally occurring within animals and plants.

As has already been stated, the directive has been approved by the European Parliament, but this should not be taken as indicating that the text resolves all the problems thrown up by the decisions of the EPO. The directive in all its guises has been criticized as promoting an unacceptable extension of the patent system based on commercial dictates rather than on a proper application of a system of protection which is intended only to apply to inventions which, but for the work of the inventor, would not otherwise exist.[54] The debate continues.

Notwithstanding the fact that both the EPC and the directive permit patent protection over genetic material, there are some categories of inventions which will not be patentable irrespective of whether they can meet the requirements of novelty, inventive step and industrial applicability. Generally speaking the EPC and directive appear to be in agreement over the categories of excluded inventions. These are inventions which would offend against morality and those which take the form of a plant or animal variety or an essentially biological process for the production of a plant or animal.

Excluded Material under the EPC

Article 53 of the EPC states:

> European patents shall not be granted in respect of:
> (a) inventions the publication or exploitation of which would be contrary to 'ordre public' or morality, provided that the exploitation shall not be deemed to be so contrary merely because it is prohibited by law or regulation in some or all of the Contracting States;
> (b) plant or animal varieties or essentially biological processes for the production of plants or animals; this provision does not apply to microbiological processes or the products thereof.[55]

It is proposed to look only at the first of these exclusions.

Inventions Excluded on the Grounds of Morality[56]

Article 53(a) is intended to exclude inventions which could prove to be a danger or threat to society if used. This is reflected in the Guidelines C-IV,

3.1 to the EPC which state that Article 53(a) is likely to be invoked only on rare occasions and would apply to such universally abhorrent inventions as 'letter bombs'. The Guidelines go on to state: 'A fair test to apply would be whether it is probable that the public in general would regard the invention as so abhorrent that the grant of patent rights would be inconceivable.' The prescient nature of the statement in the Guidelines that the use of Article 53(a) will be 'rare' can be appreciated by the fact that it was invoked for the first time in the 1990s. The reason for its invocation was a European patent application filed by Harvard University in respect of a mouse[57] which had been genetically engineered to develop cancerous tumours.

Harvard/Onco Mouse[58] The so-called '*Harvard/Onco Mouse*' had already been successfully patented in the United States of America. In 1989 the original European patent application had been refused by the examiners of the EPO on the basis that, as the application concerned an animal, it was excluded under Article 53(b). The applicant filed an appeal which was heard by the Technical Board of Appeal in 1990. The Technical Board of Appeal used Article 53(a) as the primary basis for its finding that the refusal of the patent application had been incorrect and that the grant should go ahead.

There were two matters which the Technical Board had to address. First, was the EPO a suitable forum for deciding on issues relating to morality? Second, if the answer to the first question was yes, then on what basis should the concept be applied? In respect of the former, there was considerable doubt expressed from both within the EPO and from those opposed to the patent grant as to whether a patent-granting office was the appropriate forum to decide upon such an abstract concept as morality.[59] However the view was taken that, as Article 53(a) was a properly constituted part of the European Patent Convention, decisions over its application were properly a matter for determination by the EPO.[60]

The specific issue which the Technical Board had to consider was whether the exploitation of an animal which had been genetically engineered to develop carcinogenic tumours would be contrary to morality. In making its decision the EPO chose to apply a utilitarian approach: did the benefits to mankind of being able to conduct research on genetically engineered mice outweigh any disbenefits to the mice caused by being so genetically engineered? The answer was a resounding 'yes' and the patent was granted.[61] An appeal was immediately lodged by opposition groups and a final decision on the *Harvard/Onco Mouse* patent is still being awaited.[62] The appeal is on the grounds that 'balancing morality against usefulness is not a fit basis for patenting animals'.[63]

Since *Harvard/Onco Mouse*, Article 53(a) has been increasingly cited as grounds for opposition to patent grants over biotechnological inventions. In particular the question was addressed in two key cases. One was the *Relaxin* case, but that case followed in the wake of the decision in *Plant Genetic Systems*.

Plant Genetic Systems[64] In 1990 the EPO granted a patent to Plant Genetic Systems N.V. (PGS) over products and processes relating to the herbicide 'Basta'. The patent claims included plant cells which had been genetically engineered according to the process described in the patent and to any seeds or plants which incorporated those cells.

In 1992 Greenpeace filed an opposition on the grounds that the patent violated both parts of Article 53. The opposition was heard by the Opposition Division of the EPO in 1993 and it upheld the patent. Greenpeace immediately lodged an appeal against this decision which was heard by the Technical Board of Appeal in 1994. The decision of the Technical Board of Appeal was given in February 1995. Greenpeace's opposition to the patent was based on two grounds. The first was that the use of the genetically engineered plant material could cause harm to the environment. This was contrary to morality and therefore the patent should fall on the basis of Article 53(a). The second ground for the appeal was that any plants which resulted from seeds containing the genetically engineered cells constituted a variety and these were excluded from patent protection on the basis of Article 53(b).[65]

Greenpeace submitted that the patent offended against morality on three grounds. The first was that plant material should be regarded as the 'common heritage' of mankind. As such it should be freely available and not subject to monopolization by any one company or individual. In particular Greenpeace drew attention to the fact that free access to genetic material is regarded as vital to the plant-breeding industry. It would be undesirable, and indeed immoral, to permit extensive monopoly rights, such as is conferred by the grant of a patent, over plant material.[66] Contained within this argument was the contention that an effect of patenting plant material would be to encourage plant breeders and plant bioindustries only to commercialize those plants which are patented. This course of action would be economically sound as it would ensure that the cost of applying for and maintaining the patent would be met. However a consequence of pursuing such a strategy would be that those plants which cannot be patented would not be used on the basis that they were not economically viable and this would result in a depletion of biological diversity. This, Greenpeace argued, would be contrary to the principle of moral responsibility. This argument was supported by a 1988 survey which had been conducted amongst farmers within Sweden, one of the countries designated in the patent, in which 82 per cent said that they felt it was right to prohibit the grant of a patent for those reasons outlined by Greenpeace.

The second ground of appeal was that the Opposition Board had failed to apply properly the standard of morality laid down in *Harvard/Onco Mouse*. Greenpeace argued that the benefit/detriment analysis used by the Technical Board of Appeal in the earlier case set a binding precedent which the Opposition Board was bound to follow. On this basis the Opposition Board should have addressed the question of whether the benefits to be gained from the use of the herbicide-resistant material would outweigh any detriment which might result from this use. This detriment was stated to be the likelihood of harm to the environment either through the plants becoming uncontrolled and turning into pests or weeds, or through the transmission of the modified genetic material to naturally occurring plants, or that, through being non-naturally occurring, the plants could disrupt the ecostructure of the planet. The third ground was that it was immoral to treat living material in the same way as inaminate material.

The Technical Board of Appeal dismissed each of these objections. The primary basis for the dismissal was that Greenpeace had not provided sufficient evidence in support of its claims. The Board took as its starting point EPC Working Party Document IV/2767/61-E which states that there is no single European definition of morality. Because of this the Technical Board felt that any attempts to provide a definition of morality should be left to European institutions. It accepted that it was one of these institutions, but commented that it stood at the crossroads between science and policy and neither of these could be regarded as standing alone. Instead all relevant institutions had to take account of the diverse and increasingly numerous regulatory frameworks which are being implemented to deal with complex issues such as the effects on the environment of the release of genetically engineered plants. In respect of the part that the EPO has to play in determining the morality of permitting the exploitation of genetically engineered plants, it had to take as its primary consideration the actual risk posed by the invention rather than any presumed risk which must result from its exploitation. The Board said that, unless an actual risk can be demonstrated at the time when the patent is being prosecuted, it is not the function of the EPO to make a speculative evaluation of possible risk. In other words the presumption will be in favour of the patentee rather than the opponent in such cases.

The Board then looked at the specific question of morality in respect of the PGS patent. It noted that the evidence provided by Greenpeace was heavily dependent on the results of the survey undertaken in Sweden and also on an opinion poll conducted in Switzerland which stated that the patenting of living material should be regarded as immoral. The Board held that neither of these was conclusive of attitudes within the member states of the EPC: surveys and opinion polls are not reflective of society; results can fluctuate and the statistical evidence is open to diverse and numerous interpretations. The Board also said that surveys and polls which specifically set out to ask slanted questions about the morality of a particular activity have to be treated with extreme caution.

The next matter for consideration was whether the ownership of living material could be regarded as immoral. The Board held that it was not, and cited the example of the plant variety rights system which is commonly cited as being of benefit to the plant-breeding community rather than an immoral impediment.[67] The only way in which the Board would have accepted Greenpeace's arguments was if they had been able to show that the engineered plants would be used for 'destructive purposes'.[68] As the patent did not appear to relate to an invention which could be used in a destructive manner, and Greenpeace had not provided the Board with any concrete evidence that it did have an actual destructive use, the opposition was rejected.

On the question of whether the plant material could pose a threat to the environment, the Board took the view that this more properly came under the heading 'ordre public' rather than morality. In making this assessment the Board asked whether the material would, through its exploitation, constitute a serious risk to the environment. The burden of proof lay with Greenpeace to demonstrate that it did. The evidence that serious prejudice to the environment would result from the exploitation had to be 'sufficiently substantiated at the time the decision to revoke the patent is taken'.[69] In contending that such a risk was likely, Greenpeace had relied upon a number of academic writings, but they did not have any actual proof that harm would result from the use of the patented material. The Board concluded therefore that it would not be appropriate to deny the patent on the basis of the possibility of risk.

In response to the argument that the Opposition Division had not applied the test set down in *Harvard/Onco Mouse*, the Board simply said that the balancing exercise was 'not the only way of assessing patentability with regard to Article 53(a), but just one possible way'.[70]

The effect of the decision in *Plant Genetic Systems* was to make it clear that the EPO would interpret the exclusions contained in Article 53 narrowly. From the perspective of the specific case, it is questionable now as to what exactly will constitute an exploitation which would be contrary to morality. The basis still appears to be one of whether it is abhorrent or not. It is difficult, however, to understand just how Greenpeace could have provided the necessary evidence to support its argument that the use of the patented material would be harmful, for to do this would have meant doing the one thing which Greenpeace was trying to avoid, namely using the material and seeing what the effect was. Equally the release of such material into the environment might not have an immediate serious effect. It could take several years for the full consequences to manifest themselves and this possibility should be recognized instead of avoided for reasons which could be deemed expedient and disingenuous. As Hubbard and Wald state:

> Scientist-entrepreneurs argue that they should be able to take out patents on genetically modified organisms because these are inventions which do not occur naturally. Yet when environmental groups try to prevent the release of genetically modified organisms into the environment because such releases might have unanticipated, harmful consequences, the same scientists argue that it is foolish to be concerned because these are natural organisms and tweaking a gene here or there does not change them in any fundamental way.[71]

The most recent case where the EPO discussed the issue of morality was *Relaxin.*

Relaxin The Fraktion der Grünen gave three reasons why the patent over the human protein H-2 Relaxin violated Article 53(a). These were: (a) that the taking of tissue from a pregnant women constituted an offence against human dignity; (b) that the patenting of human genes amounts to slavery; and (c) that it amounted to the patenting of human life.[72] In comparison with the statements on morality given by the Technical Board of Appeal in *PGS*, the Opposition Division handed down a relatively short decision.

The Division began by stating that Article 53(a) should only be invoked in respect of inventions which would be 'universally regarded as outrageous'.[73] An example of such an outrageous invention would be the letter bomb example given in the Guidelines to the EPC. The Division then went on to reiterate the statement that the criterion to be used in assessing whether an invention fell within Article 53(a) is whether the public would find the granting of patent over the invention 'abhorrent'. It was the view of the Division that none of the grounds raised by the Fraktion could be regarded as relating to an abhorrent invention and so it 'emphatically'[74] rejected the arguments, for the following reasons.

1 The women from whom the tissue had been obtained had consented to its being taken. There was no question therefore that it could be regarded as being contrary to human dignity. In addition, it is common practice to use human tissue for the development of new drugs and treatments (the Division used the example of blood clotting factors) and to decide that this is now unacceptable would run contrary to acceptable medical practice.[75]

2 The contention that the practice was tantamount to slavery demonstrated a misunderstanding of the patent system. A patent simply confers a right over the material as isolated and described in the patent. It does not and cannot extend to proteins created freely by pregnant women.[76]

3 It was not correct to claim that the patent had the effect of patenting life. The protein was a chemical substance, it was not 'life' and the patenting of a human protein or human gene 'has nothing to do with the patenting of human life'.[77]

The opponent had also tried to argue that the EPO should place itself under a self-imposed moratorium on the patenting of living material until the EU had made its final decision about the proposed patent directive. This was also rejected by the Division.[78]

These decisions of the EPO demonstrate that it has adopted a restrictive approach in respect of Article 53(a). There are obvious questions which result from this decision, the most crucial being when, if at all, Article 53(a) will be deemed an appropriate ground for revoking a patent grant. The ambiguous status of Article 53(a), it remaining in theory an important consideration but appearing to have in practice only a limited application, has proved to be a key issue in the decisions being taken over the EU directive, with views ranging from the omission of any equivalent provision to the detailed drafting of those activities which will always be regarded as contrary to morality.

Morality and the Patent Directive

As might be expected, the relationship between morality and a patent directive, which explicitly permits the patenting of genetic material, has proved extremely controversial.[79] It is important to remember that the directive, insofar as it is possible without failing to achieve its aim of harmonizing national laws and eradicating any discrepancies in trade practice, is intended to stand alongside the EPC and not contradict it. The function of the directive in relation to the EPC is to clarify any remaining areas of uncertainty.

The starting point for the draftsmen of the directive was that, as morality is referred to in the EPC, it should naturally be present within the directive. This has not been the universal view. It has been suggested in some quarters that, since morality has proved so problematic in respect of its interpretation within the EPO, it should be omitted from the directive.[80] Indeed the European Commission's Committee on Legal Affairs and Citizen's Rights recommended that the provision be removed when it submitted its report on the 1995 proposal.[81] This view was emphatically rejected by the members of the European Parliament in July 1997.

The current presence of morality in the directive is not simply due to the existence of Article 53(a) EPC. In addition to the fact that the issue of the moral basis for granting a monopoly right over genetic material has proved to be politically very sensitive and that therefore MEPs have been placed under considerable pressure to retain a concept of morality within the patent law,[82] the governing convention on intellectual property rights and international trade, TRIPs, also makes provision for the exclusion of inventions from patent protection if their exploitation would be contrary to morality.[83]

Following the acceptance by the Commission of the majority of the amendments tabled by the members of the European Parliament,[84] the position of the concept within patent law is firmly established. There remain, however, questions about the form the concept should take, which have not been resolved despite the 12 years of debate which have followed the initial decision to introduce a directive specifically directed at the patenting of living material. Looking at the current drafting of the provision, there is clear evidence of the shift in attitudes towards biotechnology and those areas regarded as being of most moral concern. The current version of the directive restates quite explicitly the principle that inventions must be excluded from patentability if their commercial exploitation would offend against public policy or morality.[85] In this the directive restates, almost word for word, Article 53(a) EPC.[86] However the fact that there has proved to be difficulty in interpreting and applying Article 53(a) has not gone unnoticed, and therefore the directive sets down a number of categories of invention which will always be regarded as morally unacceptable for patent law purposes. This list is intended to be illustrative and non-exhaustive.[87] Those activities which are to be regarded as immutable are procedures for human reproductive cloning, processes for modifying the germ line genetic identity of human beings, methods which use human embryos and procedures for modifying the genetic identity of animals which causes them proportionately greater suffering than any benefits which might accrue from the research (this latter exclusion is a straight reiteration of the decision in *Harvard/Onco Mouse*). This is encapsulated within Article 6.

The standard to be adopted in applying this provision is determined according to those ethical and moral principles generally observed within member states or in scientific and professional circles. These standards are intended to supplement existing legal concepts of morality and are not intended to prejudice or deviate from those moral norms already set down in such conventions as the European Convention on Human Rights and Fundamental Freedoms 1950 or the Convention on Human Rights and

Biomedicine 1996.[88] Overseeing all this will be the Commission's Group of Advisers on Ethical Implications of Biotechnology.[89]

It is too early to evaluate fully the significance of the most recent text of the directive, but one thing is apparent and that is that the focus of attention has moved away from environmental concerns, such as those expressed in the *PGS* case, and indeed has shifted from many of the underlying concerns over animal experimentation which have been argued in, for example, *Harvard/Onco Mouse*. The focus of moral attention is now firmly on the ethics of human genetic manipulation. According to the current text, the only other specific moral issue which needs to be considered is that of the costs/benefits of the genetic manipulation of animals and, as has already been discussed, this view as set down in *Harvard/Onco Mouse* has not met with universal approval. Those moral questions which have been raised over the environmental impact of the genetic manipulation of plant material are apparently ignored. Also absent is any reference to the morality of removing from one country indigenous plant material, or indeed any other genetic material, which is then patented in another. This is despite the express provisions of the Rio Convention which the European Parliament attempted to introduce in its amendments. These concerns are identified as legitimate in Article 27(3) of TRIPs and it is disappointing that the directive has not followed suit. Oppositions over patents which encourage what is regarded as 'gene piracy' will continue to be raised under the general heading of inventions the exploitation of which would be contrary to morality, but it is debatable as to the extent to which they will be successful given the precedents set by the EPO. Equally doubtful must be the case of the extent to which national patent offices will deviate from the example set by the EPO given that they, like it, are patent-*granting* offices. The matter will therefore become one for the national courts and they will be acting in the absence of any guidance from within the directive. This probable continuation of the status quo is unlikely to provide the necessary reassurance for those who fear that the attitude towards the monopolization of living material is being driven by economic considerations rather than by any concerns for the material itself and the varying forms in which it manifests itself.

Conclusion

The issue of how to protect the results of biotechnological research and development is an extremely complex one. For those involved in developing policy and practice a fine line has to be drawn between the provision of effective and appropriate protection, on the one hand, and the concerns that science and the law are reducing living material to the status of a commodity, on the other.

The European Union has had a unique opportunity to reconcile these differences. The 12 years which have elapsed since the initiative was taken to introduce the directive should have enabled the Commission to produce a text which would temper the extremes of patent protection so feared by those who oppose its use. Instead the result has been an acquiescence to the demands of industry and through this an implicit acknowledgment that genetic material is nothing more than a commodity to be gathered, manipulated, bought and sold as any other type of material. For many involved in the science itself, this recognition of the value of the work they are doing and of the inherent ordinariness of the subject-matter, in that it can be equated with other traditionally patentable material, is welcome and long overdue. For others, the reduction of life to a series of chemical compounds over which property rights can be sought, fought over and bought signifies the beginning of the end of respect for life itself. The lasting impression is that everything and anything for which a use can be found can now be legitimately monopolized and that there is little left which will remain as the common property of us all, untainted by the trappings of commerce.

Notes

1 See, for example, W. Lesser *Equitable Patent Protection in the Developing World* (Eubios Ethics Institute, 1991) L. Busch, W. Lacy, J. Burkhardt and L. Lacy, *Plants, Power and Profit* (Cambridge, Mass., 1991) chs. 1, 7 and 8; National Academy of Sciences, *Global Dimensions of Intellectual Property Rights in Science and Technology* (Washington DC, 1993); R. Cook-Deegan, *The Gene Wars: Science, Politics and the Human Genome* (New York, 1994) ch. 19; Swanson, *Intellectual Property Rights and Biodiversity Conservation* (Cambridge University Press, 1995); R. Hubbard and E. Wald, *Exploding the Gene Myth* (Boston, Mass., 1997) ch. 9 and Afterword; S. Sterckx, *Biotechnology, Patents and Morality* (Aldershot, 1997).

2 It would be impossible to cite all the publications which discuss the controversial issue of the patenting of biotechnological inventions. The range of diverse publications include *The Times*, *The Independent* and *The Guardian* newspapers; science journals, *Science*, *Nature*, *Bio/Technology* and *New Scientist*; intellectual property law journals, the *European Intellectual Property Review* (*EIPR*), *International Review of Industrial Property and Copyright* (*IIC*) and *Patent World;* law journals, *BioScience Law Review* (*BSLR*) and *Modern Law Review*, and journals concerned with ethical and environmental aspects of patenting biotechnology, *Eubios*, *The Bulletin of the Working Group on Traditional Resource Rights* and *GenEthics News*. There have also been numerous conferences, workshops and meetings, for example Biotechnology, Patents and Morality: Towards a Consensus, University of Ghent, January 1996; The Legal Protection of Biotechnological Material, SIBLE/ESC London, June 1996; Patenting Biotechnology, Global 2000/European Parliament Brussels, October 1996 and Legal Claims to Biogenetic Resources, University of Berne, June 1997.

3 Questions have been raised about the possibility of protecting genetic material via copyright, although apparently only in a semi-serious vein, see H. Laddie, P. Prescott and M. Vitoria, *The Modern Law of Copyright* (2nd edn, London, 1995); H. Speck, 'Genetic Copyright' (1995) 4 *EIPR* 171; G. Karnell, 'Protection of Genetic Research by Copyright or Design Rights?' (1995) 8 *EIPR* 355; M. Llewelyn, *Utility Models/Second Tier Protection* (London, 1996).

4 *The Sunday Times* on 21 September 1997, for example, listed the top 100 British companies. The top five were Shell, Glaxo-Wellcome, Smith Kline Beecham, British Petroleum and Zeneca, each of which is engaged in biotechnological research of one kind or another. The same article stated that those sectors with the most market value were integrated oil, drugs and food manufacturing. One specific example of the lucrative nature of biotechnology is British Biotechnology, which made £1.2 billion for its shareholders in the last financial year.

5 In 1994 it was estimated that 1300 biotechnology companies had the combined annual turnover of $8.1 billion, with an estimated $40 billion by the year 2000. See C. Roberts, 'The Prospects of Success of the National Institute of Health's Human Genome Application' (1994) 1 *EIPR* 30.

6 In respect of GATT, it was decided early on in the negotiations for the Uruguay Round that intellectual property rights played a significant part in international trade. The decision was taken to introduce special provisions ensuring comparability of protection in all member states, the Trade Related Aspects of Intellectual Property Rights Agreement (TRIPs), the Recitals to which state that it is intended to: 'reduce distortions and impediments to international trade ... taking into account the need to promote effective and adequate protection of intellectual property rights, and to ensure that measures and procedures to enforce intellectual property rights do not themselves become barriers to legitimate trade'; see M. Blakeney, *Trade Related Aspects of Intellectual Property Rights: A Concise Guide to the TRIPs Agreement* (London, 1996); F-K. Beier and G. Schricker, 'From GATT to TRIPs – The Agreement on Trade Related Aspects of Intellectual Property Rights' (Munich, 1996) 18 *IIC Studies*. In order to ensure that member states did not exclude biotechnological inventions from their patent systems, as was the case in many Third World countries, Article 27(1) of TRIPs states that 'patents shall be available for *any* inventions ... in *all* fields of technology' (emphasis added). In recognition of the concerns over genetic material, two optional exclusions were included in the TRIPS Agreement permitting member states to exclude from patent protection inventions which would offend against morality and plants and animals. In respect of plant varieties, however, member states must provide either a patent or an effective *sui generis* right. This latter provision is to be reviewed in 1999. With regard to the Rio Convention, the original draft text referred to genetic material as being 'the common heritage of mankind', the inference being that it could not be monopolized. However, in recognition of the fact that the genetic resources would be commercialized irrespective of views to the contrary, the text was amended to ensure that member states could retain some control over indigenous material and claim at least an initial right over it. Article 1 now reads: 'The objectives of this Convention ... are the conservation of biological diversity, the sustainable use of its components and *the fair and equitable sharing of the benefits arising out of the utilization of genetic resources*' (emphasis added). Article 3 gives to states 'the sovereign right to exploit their own resources'.

7 The issue of appropriate protection will not be discussed here, but it should be noted that there is a school of thought that intellectual property protection, and in particular patent protection, is not the most suitable form of protection for living material. Instead there is being put forward the argument that a right more akin to a traditional resource right

which is not as monopolistic or as Westernized as the patent system would be more appropriate. See *Agrobiodiversity and Farmers' Rights: Proceedings of a Technical Consultation on an Implementation Framework for Farmers' Rights* (M.S. Swaminathan Research Foundation 1996); Kothari, *Conserving Life: Implications of the Biodiversity Convention for India* (Kalpavriksh, 1996); Baumann, Bell, Koechlin and Pimbert, *The Life Industry: Biodiversity, People and Profits* (1996); Rothschild, *Protecting What is Ours: Indigenous Peoples and Biodiversity* (1995).

8 See note 6 above and A. Wells, 'Patenting New Life Forms: An Ecological Perspective' (1994) 3 *EIPR* 111; R. Moufang, 'Patenting of Human Genes, Cells and Parts of the Body? – The Ethical Dimensions of Patent Law' (1994) 25(4) *IIC* 287; J. Robertson and D. Calhoun, 'Treaty on Biological Diversity: Ownership and Access to Genetic Materials in New Zealand' (1995) 5 *EIPR* 219; S. Verma, 'TRIPs and Plant Variety Protection in Developing Countries' (1995) 6 *EIPR* 281; M. McGrath, 'The Patent Provisions in TRIPs: Protecting Reasonable Remuneration for Services Rendered – Or the Latest Development in Western Colonialism?' (1996) 7 *EIPR* 398; M. Blakeney, 'Bioprospecting and the Protection of Medical Knowledge of Indigenous Peoples: An Australian Perspective' (1997) 6 *EIPR* 298.

9 The reaction to the cloning of Dolly the sheep is a case in point. While the possibility of successfully cloning an animal from an adult cell had been known to the scientific community for a considerable period of time, the reality of the project caused great excitement. The public reaction was a mixture of horror at the ability of scientists to manipulate living material to such an extent, repugnance at the dispassionate manner in which the scientists were viewing the results and wild speculation over the extension of the technology to humans. These reactions can possibly be explained by the rather extreme reporting of Dolly by the media. The level of international concern were sufficient, however, to move President Clinton to comment publicly on the event and led him to endorse a recommendation from the US National Bioethics Advisory Committee to ban research on human cloning for a period of five years. This action has not met with the support of the scientific community. Eminent scientists such as Richard Dawkins and Francis Crick, who see the move as based primarily on emotive reasoning rather than on scientific understanding, have strongly opposed the ban. It will be interesting to note whether the five-year ban holds when looking at the precedent set down in respect of the patenting of living material in the mid-1980s. In 1987 the US Congress issued a two-year moratorium on the patenting of living material following an extensive round of public hearings. The moratorium did not make it to its first birthday.

10 At present the relevant legislation is the European Patent Convention, but it is expected that the European Parliament will have adopted a Community directive on the Legal Protection of Biotechnological Inventions dealing specifically with the issue of the patentability of living material. (COM(95) 661 as revised by the European Commission in September 1997 COM(97) 446 final.)

11 The creators of valuable new inventions will not simply wish to exploit their inventions on a localized basis, they will also want to trade in international markets. It is not possible to obtain a world patent as such. In order to ensure protection in the global market place the inventor will have to apply for a national patent in each country. This application will be subject to a fee covering examination and grant. Subsequently the holder will have to renew his patent at an annual rate which is assessed according to how long the patent has been in force. The longer the protection sought, the more onerous the fee; this is intended to act as a counter to the monopoly position given to the holder by virtue of the patent grant. Where an important invention is concerned or where a highly competitive market is involved, the patent holder will also have to bear the cost of

litigation against unauthorized use and oppositions based on claims of invalidity.

12 P. Drahos, *A Philosophy of Intellectual Property* (Aldershot, 1996), p.78, refers to Hegel's vision of the mind being able to place almost anything into the category of thing. If living material and life forms are regarded as things then they are capable of being appropriated.

13 W. Cornish *Intellectual Property* (3rd edn, London, 1996), pp.108–16.

14 The protection conferred by a patent is primarily commercial in nature. Activities involving the invention which are not commercial will usually not be regarded as infringing. For example, section 60 of the UK Patents Act 1977 states that use of a protected invention for research purposes will not infringe a patent over that invention.

15 Article 52(2)(a) EPC.

16 See F. Machlup, *An Economic Review of the Patent System* (Study No 15 of the Subcommittee on the Judiciary) (US Senate, 85th Congress, 1958); C.T. Taylor and A. Silberson, *The Economic Impact of the Patent System* (Cambridge, 1973); Drahos, *A Philosophy*, p.5 and ch. 6.

17 Drahos, *A Philosophy*, questions whether it is the only method of fostering research and development and cites China as an example of a society which has managed to thrive in science and technology without, until the advent of GATT/TRIPs, intellectual property rights.

18 Article 33 of the TRIPs Agreement now requires member states to make protection available for a period of up to 20 years.

19 See M. Llewelyn, *GenEthics News* (January/March 1997), 6.

20 Article 53(b) EPC excludes two areas of technology, those involving plant and animal varieties unless they result from the use of a microbiological process. There is a further exclusion contained in Article 53(a) of inventions which would be contrary to morality, but this is not a technology-specific exclusion.

21 Articles 54, 56 and 57, respectively, of the European Patent Convention.

22 Eeach of these criticisms will be dealt with in more detail later.

23 See, for example, Sterckx, *Biotechnology*, Part Five.

24 A famous British example of inability to recognize the value of a new invention is that of the initial refusal to grant a patent over the jet engine to Frank Whittle. The Patent Office could not see a use for it! The Patent Office later revised its opinion.

25 One only has to look at the controversy over in vitro fertilization during the 1970s and early 1980s to see evidence of public concern over scientific developments, yet today, post-Warnock, these techniques are sufficiently commonplace for the BBC to run a series of highly popular 'fly on the wall' documentaries about the trials and tribulations of undergoing such treatment, *Making Babies*; more specifically the *UK National Consensus Conference on Plant Biotechnology Final Report* (Science Museum, 1994) showed a representative sample of the very diverse views held by the general public. These ranged from ambivalence through to outright opposition and selective support. It is interesting to note that the views of the panel, which was drawn from the general public, shifted during the Conference from hesitant opposition at the beginning to qualified support by the end.

26 Increasingly, however, the EPO is recognizing that, where a patent application involves living material, particular caution has to be exercised in making the initial decision over whether it meets the patent-granting criteria. See the chapters by Gruszow and Schatz on the practice of the EPO in S. Sterckx, *Biotechnology*.

27 The present directive was first published in December 1995. It has subsequently undergone a number of revisions, the latest being that published on 1 September 1997 by the Commission based on the 64 amendments tabled by the European Parliament in July

1997 when voting to adopt the directive. It is this latest text which is referred to here (COM(97) 446 final).

28 M. Llewelyn, 'The Legal Protection of Biotechnological Inventions: An Alternative Approach' (1997) 3 *EIPR* 115.

29 There is an argument that, in taking the provisions of the EPC as its starting point, the directive is not actually resolving many of the problems which have resulted from the application of the EPC; see Llewelyn, 'An Alternative Approach'.

30 There are other issues which could equally have been addressed, such as the exclusion of plant and animal varieties from patent protection and, in particular, the problems which have been encountered in defining what constitutes a plant or animal variety (this in turn has raised questions about the relationship between the patent system and plant variety rights), the issue of extending protection to the progeny of protected material and the thorny issue of farmers' privilege; see Llewelyn, 'An Alternative Approach'.

31 For example, Pasteur obtained a patent over yeast in 1973; equally there have been patent grants made over inventions which reproduce naturally occurring products such as vitamin B12 and human tissue plasmogen activator. See Moufang, 'Patenting of Human Genes', 487.

32 For a fuller discussion of this case, see M. Llewelyn, 'Industrial Applicability/Utility and Genetic Engineering: Current Practices in Europe and the United States' (1994) 11 *EIPR* 475; R. Moufang, 'Patenting of Human Genes', 492; Roberts, 'Prospects of Success'.

33 This is the US equivalent to the European concept of industrial application; the two are not identical but comparable.

34 See Roberts, 'Gene Patents - Scientists Voice Their Opposition' (1992) 256 *Science*, 1273; *The Sunday Times Magazine* (26 July 1992), 16; *New Scientist* (18 January 1993), 12; M. Davis, 'Patents and the Human Genome Project' (1993) 11 *Bio/Technology*, (June) 736; *Nature* (4 November 1993) 6.

35 In the UK, for example, the Medical Research Council filed a patent for 1000 gene fragments. This application was withdrawn when the NIH application failed.

36 The only doubts raised in the UK were over whether the isolation of the gene fragments would be sufficient to meet the inventive step requirement.

37 For example, in 1995 the US government took out a patent, US Patent 5397696, on the cell line of a Papua New Guinean tribe which had proved to be immune to the HTL.V virus which causes leukaemia.

38 In 1993 US Patent 540104 was granted to the University of Mississippi Medical Center in 1993 giving protection over 'Method of promoting healing of a wound by administering turmeric to a patient afflicted with the wound'.

39 See Sterckx, *Biotechnology*, ch. 1; Wells, 'Patenting New Life Forms'; Bruce, 'Patenting human genes - a Christian view' (January 1997) *Bulletin of Medical Ethics* 18.

40 S. Sterckx, *Biotechnology*, Part Five; M. Reiss, 'Is it right to patent DNA?' (January 1997) *Bulletin of Medical Ethics* 21.

41 [1995] European Patent Office Reports 541; see also V. Vossius, 'Patenting Inventions in the Fields of Biology and Chemistry: Case Law' (1997) 1 *BioScience Law Review* 11.

42 At paras 4.1-5.5.

43 Para 5.1.

44 See Gruszow, Sterckx, *Biotechnology*, ch. 13.

45 At an EU Advanced Workshop on Biotechnology Ethics and Public Perceptions of Biotechnology in Oxford in September 1997, considerable disagreement was expressed by the participants, who came from a variety of backgrounds including science, philosophy, law and government, over this practice of holding naturally occurring material, once isolated, to be an invention.

46 See V. Shiva and R. Hollar-Bhar, 'Intellectual Piracy and the Neem Tree' (1993) 23(6) *The Ecologist*; Wells, 'Patenting New Life Forms'; Robertson and Calhoun, 'Treaty on Biological Diversity'; and Blakeney, 'Bioprospecting'.

47 S. Crespi, 'Biotechnology Patenting: The Wicked Animal Must Defend Itself' (1995) 9 *EIPR*, 437.

48 See Llewelyn, in Sterckx, *Biotechnology*, p.21.

49 Article 1. It is perhaps not surprising that this premise has been continually challenged by organizations such as Greenpeace and Global 2000, as well as by animal rights groups and some patients' groups. When the European Parliament voted to adopt the directive in July 1997 this was met with a barrage of criticism including articles and letters in the British press: see *The Guardian*, 'The Theft of Our Souls' (11 July 1997); *The Guardian*, 'Letters to the Editor' (14 July 1997); *The Guardian*, 'Europe to allow firms to patent genes' (16 July 1997); *The Independent*, 'Europe gives green light to gene law' (17 July); *The Independent*, 'Letters to the Editor' (23 July 1997).

50 Recital 3.

51 Recital 9b.

52 Articles 2 and 3.

53 The University of California obtained a patent, US patent 4,438,032, over a cell line developed from cells taken from John Moore's cancerous spleen. John Moore challenged their right to obtain a patent over his genetic material. The Californian Supreme Court held that he did not have any property rights in his tissue and that the university was perfectly within its rights to obtain a patent over the results of their research work. See *Moore* v. *Regents of the University of California* 793 P. 2d 479 (1990).

54 See *GenEthics News*, 'MEPs Approve EU Patent Directive' (June/July 1997), 1.

55 For a more detailed discussion of the exclusion of plant and animal varieties, see M. Llewelyn, 'Future Prospects for Plant Breeders' Rights Within the European Community' (1989) 9 *EIPR* 303; B. Greengrass, 'The 1991 Act of the UPOV Convention' (1991) 12 *EIPR* 466; R. Nott, 'Plants and Animals: Why they should be protected by patents and plant variety rights' (July/August 1993) *Patent World*, 45; J. Ardley and C. Hoptroff, 'Protecting plant "invention": the role of plant-variety rights and patents' (March 1996) 14 *TIBTECH*, 67; Llewelyn, 'An Alternative Approach'; N. Peace and A. Christie, 'Intellectual Property Protection for the Products of Animal Breeding' (1996) 4 *EIPR* 213.

56 The morality of the science itself will not be discussed here, although as will be seen this has crept into some of the arguments levelled against the grant of a patent over biotechnological material; for an example of the types of discussions which have focused on the ethical aspects of biotechnology, see D. Suzuki and P. Knudtson, *Genethics: The Ethics of Engineering Life* (London, 1988); A. Dyson and J. Harris (eds), *Ethics and Biotechnology* (London, 1994).

57 The patent does not in fact specify mice but rather refers to any non-human mammal animal exhibiting the particular genetically engineered characteristic.

58 T19/90; [1990] *EPOR* 501.

59 For a flavour of these discussions, see V. Di Cerbo, 'The Patentability of Animals' (1993) 24(6) *IIC* 788; D. Beyleveld and R. Brownsword, *Mice, Morality and Patents* (Common Law Institute of Intellectual Property, 1993); Armitage and Davis, *Patents and Morality in Perspective* (Common Law Institute of Intellectual Property, 1994).

60 See Gruszow, in Sterckx, *Biotechnology*, p.150.

61 For a discussion of this decision, see Llewelyn, 'Industrial Applicability'.

62 The hearings for the opposition took place in November 1995. It is speculated that the reason is that the EPO is awaiting the outcome of the decision in the EU over the patent

directive.

63 *New Scientist* (16 January 1993), 7; see also Llewelyn, 'Industrial Applicability', 477.

64 T356/93; [1995] European Patent Office Reports, at 357. For a fuller discussion of this case, see Jaenichen and A. Schrell, 'The European Patent Office's Recent Decisions on Patenting Plants' (1993) 12 *EIPR* 468; M. Llewelyn, 'Article 53 Revisited: Greenpeace v. Plant Genetic Systems N.V.' (1995) 10 *EIPR*, 506; A. Schrell, 'Are Plants (Still) Patentable? Plant Genetic Systems (EPO Decision T356/93)' (1996) 4 *EIPR* 242; T. Roberts, 'Patenting Plants Around the World' (1996) 10 *EIPR* 534.

65 As previously noted, the opposition based on Article 53(b), that the claimed for plants constituted plant varieties and were excluded from patent protection, succeeded; for a discussion of this aspect of the case, see M. Llewelyn, 'Article 53 Revisited'.

66 While it was not discussed as such, implicit in Greenpeace's argument was that a form of monopoly right could be appropriate if it did not restrict breeders from using the protected material for the purpose of research and the development of new plant varieties. Such a system of protection does exist in the form of the plant variety rights system.

67 See Llewelyn, 'Future Prospects'; Greengrass, 'The 1991 Act'; Nott, 'Plants and Animals'; Ardley and Hoptroff, 'Protecting plant "invention"'.

68 Note 56 at paragraph 17.1.

69 Paragraph 18.5.

70 Paragraph 18.8.

71 R. Hubbard and E. Wald, *Gene Myth*, p.174.

72 [1995] EPOR 541, at paragraph 6.1.

73 Paragraph 6.2.1.

74 Paragraph 6.3.

75 Paragraph 6.3.1.

76 Paragraph 6.3.3.

77 Paragraph 6.3.4.

78 Paragraph 6.4.

79 N. Scott-Ram, 'Ethics and the directive for the legal protection of biotechnological inventions' (January 1997) *Bulletin of Medical Ethics*, 25.

80 R. Nott, 'The Biotechnology Directive: Does Europe Need a New Draft?' (1997) 1 *BSLR* 24.

81 *Report on the proposal for a European Parliament and Council Directive on the Legal Protection of Biotechnological Invention* (COM(95)0661 - C4-0063/96 - 95360 (COD)); for a discussion of all the recommendations made by the Committee, see the 'Opinion' of the Sheffield Institute of Biotechnology Law and Ethics, SIBLE, March 1997.

82 See, for example, the proceedings of the meeting convened by MEPs and held in Brussels on 29 October 1996, which addressed amongst other issues the place of morality within the patent law.

83 Article 27(2) states: 'Members may exclude from patentability inventions, the prevention within their territory of the commercial exploitation of which is necessary to protect ordre public or morality, including to protect human, animal or plant life or health or to avoid serious prejudice to the environment, provided that such exclusion is not made merely because the exploitation is prohibited by their laws.' For a variant of this concept in the context of another system of intellectual property protection, see Article 13(8) European Council Regulation on Community Plant Variety Rights.

84 Commission Press Release IP/97/767, 1 September 1997.

85 Recital 19c.

86 There is one obvious difference between the two provisions in that the term 'public

policy' is substituted for 'ordre public' in the directive. The reason for this has not been made clear by the Commission. It is not proposed to discuss the difference in meaning here.

87 Recital 22.

88 Recitals 23-25.

89 Article 7.

9 Using Law to Define Uncertain Science in Environmental Policy

Lynda M. Warren

Science and Environmental Policy

Yearley[1] has pointed out that the influence of science on the process of formulating environmental policy has increased in recent years. Scientific justification is regarded as a means of giving credibility to green thinking, changing it from a 'hippie' attribute to a mainstream respectable stance worthy of inclusion in the political agenda. Environmentalists, governmental and non-governmental, use scientific arguments to support their campaigns and politicians justify their actions (or inactions) with 'hard' scientific fact. Yearley made the observation in support of his call for social scientists to pay more attention to environmental policy. This chapter uses similar arguments to explain why there is an urgent need for those involved in drafting, implementing and enforcing environmental legislation (mostly non-scientists) to understand the scientific foundations for environmental policy.

The issue of legal interpretation of science is not a new one. Much has been written on the use of scientific evidence in court (see, for example, Alldridge[2] and Bernstein[3]) and, in some jurisdictions, the courts have attempted to formulate rules for handling scientific evidence.[4] Two main types of case have attracted attention – those in the areas of criminal law and toxic torts. The emphasis in analyses of these types of cases has tended to be the ability of juries to understand the evidence put before them. In Britain, however, there are few occasions for a jury to be faced with environmental issues requiring an understanding of science which, as Bernstein[5] acknowledges, may account for the lack of rules. This does not mean, however, that there is no need for the courts to address the understanding of science. The fact that the judiciary may take the place of the jury in deciding the issue may explain why there are no express rules for admissibility of scientific evidence, but it does not mean that there is any less need for the decision makers to be able to assess the evidence put before them.

The evaluation of scientific evidence establishing the facts of a case raises some general questions concerning the legal profession's understanding of science and the need for clear communication between expert witness and court. While it is abundantly clear that this communication is not as lucid as it might be,[6] the reasons are not connected with the environmental issues but rather with the general differences between law and science. These points, which centre on the need to allocate blame, have been considered elsewhere, especially in the context of expert evidence,[7] and are not developed further in this chapter. There is another situation in which the courts may be expected to deal with scientific concepts, however; that is, where the courts have to interpret an environmental statute or environmental policy. Environmental legislation has become far more technical in recent years, probably because of the European imperative, but little thought has been given to ensuring that the courts can cope with the scientific terminology.

Despite Yearley's assertion as to the increased importance of science, and scientists, in the development of environmental policy, it is important to remember that the law is made by politicians and that, for the most part, these are not scientists. It follows that the scientists, whether they are environmentalists lobbying for statutory change or scientific civil servants charged with advising the government on the formulation of environmental policy and, ultimately, draft legislation, must communicate the key scientific points in a manner that is intelligible to these people.

The relationship between scientist and policy maker is, therefore, crucial for the development of good environmental law. Indeed, according to Jasanoff,[8] it is the single most important factor. It is clear that, in the view of the environmentalists at least, the relationship is not as good as it might be. Nevertheless there is a closer understanding now than existed even 20 years ago. The fact that Margaret Thatcher, the first prime minister to have a degree in science, happened to be in office at the time when environmental issues were first gaining credence on the global stage undoubtedly did much to raise the profile of science within the policy-making machinery. It remains the case, however, that scientific need is not the only, or even the prominent, factor determining the shape of environmental policy and law. The underlying purpose behind the law may be to deal with a problem expressed in scientific terms but, from then on, social, economic, political and other pressures shape the outcome.

It is the purpose of this chapter to consider whether the apparent enhanced scientific nature of environmental law will, in practice, lead to more effective measures. This involves looking at the use of science to fix legal issues.

Because of the mismatch between scientific and legal epistemologies,[9] there is a danger of compounding two errors – the fallacy that science will provide a certain answer (the 'hard facts notion') and society's misapprehension that law will always provide an answer. These errors are symptomatic of our failure to integrate thinking across disciplines: we often believe that 'simple' questions outside our area of expertise can be answered with simple answers by some other appropriate expert. The chapter looks at the interpretation of science against the background of non-scientific assumptions about science and uses case studies to illustrate potential areas of difficulty.

Scientific Uncertainty

The hard facts notion is one of the most entrenched misunderstandings of science. Because scientific experimentation is designed to reveal factual answers to support or refute hypotheses, it is assumed that there will be a 'right' answer to every question. The government's chief scientific advisor, Sir Robert May, explained the problem succinctly when he stated that there is a 'common misapprehension that science gives definite answers'.[10] Instead, of course, as he goes on to say, it is much more about the process of asking the right questions: in other words, of handling uncertainty. An open debate, in which disagreements are fully aired, is a positive aspect of scientific deliberations because it is more likely to lead to an understanding of the 'truth' and give the certainty that politicians crave to provide them with some fixed points on which they can hang their policies. Unfortunately politicians and the public alike regard such debate as a sign of weakness. Roberts and Willmore,[11] commenting on the fact that forensic science evidence is not as objective as popular representation suggests, note that all science is subject to inherent uncertainty, but observe that, when problems arise, the tendency is to blame individuals with no consideration for the system itself.

O'Riordan and Cameron[12] describe three aspects of scientific uncertainty, each of which is of relevance for informing the environmental debate: (a) uncertainty as lack of data, (b) uncertainty as variability of scientific process, and (c) uncertainty as indeterminacy. Predictive models form an important part of the advice that is given to legislators. The reliability of such models is, in part, a feature of the degree and nature of the inherent uncertainty. Lack of data is an important consideration in environmental policy because of the long timescale of environmental change. There are many occasions, for example, where there are no baseline data against which to measure the effect of an environmental impact. Similarly a data set may extend over too short a period of time to enable a reliable model to be drawn up. Faced with uncertainty of this type, the scientist has to extrapolate back from more recent data, making presumptions about the environmental conditions in the past.

Data can also be uncertain because of variability in the scientific process. We simply do not know enough about the way biological processes work. If we are trying to solve a complex problem, such as a prediction of the impact of global warming, we are faced with a whole suite of processes each with their own, largely unknown, variability. In some cases it is likely that we would not be able to put a figure on the degree of likely variability even if we had the time and resources to carry out the appropriate investigations, which we do not. Politicians certainly cannot afford to wait anyway. It follows that the scientific advice given to the policy maker is based on 'integrate[d] guess work'.[13]

Finally it may prove impossible to model a future scenario because the phenomenon in question is indeterminable. We now know that some systems do not operate according to 'the rules', in other words they are chaotic, operating in a manner that is totally unpredictable. As a result, even the most reliable predictive model may be subject to the proviso that it could be rendered inaccurate by an open-ended event.

The recognition that uncertainty is an integral part of scientific thinking puts a different complexion on the view that science is about trying to tell the truth. It admits that truth is not absolute but is subject to change if and when more data become available. The next section looks at two examples of science and law, the first founded on the idea of scientific certainty and the second on scientific uncertainty.

Scientific Uncertainty in Law

The Dangerous Dogs Act 1991

The Dangerous Dogs Act 1991 was rushed through Parliament by a government eager to be seen to be doing something in response to public demand. It followed a spate of attacks by dogs on children, some of them leading to fatalities. Media attention focused on particular breeds of dogs bred for fighting purposes and urged the government to take immediate action. Section 1(1) of the Act states that the restrictions imposed by the Act apply to (a) any dog of the type known as the pit bull terrier, (b) any dog of the type known as the Japanese tosa, and (c) any dog of any type designated by an order of the secretary of state, being a type appearing to him to be bred for fighting or to have the characteristics of a type bred for that purpose.

On the face of it, this section is clear and unambiguous. It refers specifically to the types of dog for which there is particular concern and gives the secretary of state powers to extend the measures to other types if necessary. In practice, however, the Act has been a disaster because of disputes over whether or not an individual dog is, or is not, a member of one of the named types. Parliament failed to appreciate the fact that science does not recognize dog types and that there is no definition of any given type of dog. Even a dog breed is not a fixed identity like a species. While a pedigree is evidence that an individual dog belongs to a given breed, there is no simple way to establish that a dog that is *not* registered with the Kennel Club is *not* a member of a given breed. Furthermore the characteristics for which the legislation was introduced might also occur in a cross-breed. In scientific terms, a dog breed, let alone a type, does not have a certain, determinable genotype[14] or an exclusive phenotype.[15] The penalty for being in possession of a pit bull terrier under certain circumstances was the death of the dog. Not surprisingly, this legislation has given rise to litigation on the part of aggrieved owners seeking to save the lives of their pets. The issue was considered in *R* v. *Crown Court at Knightsbridge ex parte Dunne*,[16] which held that 'type' was not synonymous with 'breed' and that any dog having a substantial number of or most of the physical characteristics of a pit bull terrier came within the remit of section 1(1). Whether this was the case was a matter of fact. In reaching this decision the court relied on the Scottish case of *Parker* v. *Annan*,[17] in which Lord Hope stated that the Act was deliberately allowing a broad and practical approach to the problem of identifying types of dog because of the absence of precise characteristics for the positive identification of a pit bull terrier. *Dunne* was unsuccessfully challenged in *Britton* v. *Lambourne*,[18] which concerned a cross-bred dog. The defendant argued that the wording of section 1(1) excluded cross-breeds because of its use of the definite article before both 'type' and 'pit': that is, *the* type known as *the* pit bull terrier. The appeal was dismissed on the basis that the Act could clearly apply to cross breeds.[19] Although the Act has recently been amended,[20] the scientific incongruity remains.

The Precautionary Principle

The precautionary principle is a concept introduced with the purpose of addressing the failure of science to provide a certain answer in every case. The idea is highly laudable and it presents a turning point in our attempt to deal with scientific concepts in a legislative and policy framework. Unfortunately the concept itself has suffered from a lack of certainty. Much has been written about the concept, trying to explain what it means, what it should mean and whether or not it is a legal concept. For the purposes of this chapter, the most important feature of the precautionary principle is that it provides a non-scientific approach to dealing with scientific uncertainty. It alerts the policy maker and legislator to the fact that a failure to establish a cause and effect does not mean that one does not exist and invites him to consider whether the possibility of such a connection is sufficient to warrant action on his part. In criminal and civil law a failure to prove a case against a defendant results in that defendant being cleared of liability. Adopting a similar approach in matters of environmental policy could lead to serious, unacceptable environmental degradation that could be avoided.[21] The precautionary principle simply allows for this option. It is, in effect, a form of risk management.

The main criticism of the concept is that it does not explain what is meant by 'scientific uncertainty'. As noted above, there are different types of scientific uncertainty. The government's definition of the precautionary principle is as follows: 'Where there are significant risks of damage to the environment, the Government will be prepared to take precautionary action to limit [pollution], even where the scientific knowledge is not conclusive, if the balance of likely costs and benefits justifies it.'[22] It could be said that this definition merely replaces the problem of establishing scientific significance with the comparable one of establishing significant risk. There is no indication of what constitutes a significant risk of damage to the environment or even whether the degree of significance is dependent upon the magnitude of the potential damage. What is clear is that the measure of significance of risk is not scientific.

The phrase 'where the scientific knowledge is not conclusive' is also open to more than one interpretation.[23] One understanding of this phrase is that it is referring to data sets where the inherent variability is so great that it is impracticable to obtain sufficient results to determine scientific relationships that are of statistical significance. It could also refer to situations in which there is no available scientific information because no one has conducted the necessary experiments. This interpretation has given rise to polarized views on the burden of proof. The extreme view, favoured by some environmentalists, is that a proper application of the precautionary principle means that it is up to the person wishing to carry out a novel activity to demonstrate that it will not cause environmental damage. Without some limits to the scope of potential damage, this is an open-ended task that cannot be completed. From the perspective of environmental protection, however, it is easy to see that it is more attractive than the standard situation in which it is up to the objector to prove that damage will occur because it defeats the argument that an activity is safe until the contrary is proved.

It is over 20 years since the precautionary principle first arose in international environmental policy. It is just beginning to acquire a veneer of legal and political respectability.[24] There is a recognition that a politician needs to consider all implications of a proposed policy or law before proceeding; in other words, there is an unarticulated acceptance of the uncertainty of science and the limitations of scientific justifications. Adopting the precautionary principle is not a scientific approach but a procedural change.

Sophisticated Scientific Concepts

The two examples outlined above demonstrate the pitfalls of trying to use science and quasi-scientific principles to fashion law. The Dangerous Dogs Act 1991 suffered from the need to introduce legislation without due reflection and consultation and was unlike most environmental legislation in this respect. In this section, two far more sophisticated legal formulations of science will be considered, namely the second sulphur protocol of the UN ECE Transboundary Air Pollution Convention and the EC Habitats Directive. In each case, the scientific content of the legislation is fundamental to its purpose and implementation. It is axiomatic, therefore, that this scientific foundation is correct, relevant and understandable.

Second Sulphur Protocol

The Transboundary Air Pollution Convention[25] is a framework agreement under which contracting parties agree to take measures to reduce emissions that might contribute to transboundary air pollution. The first sulphur protocol,[26] agreed in 1985, committed parties to reduce their emissions of sulphur dioxide by at least 30 per cent against 1980 levels.[27] The degree of reduction was agreed during negotiations on the basis of political and economic acceptability; there was no attempt to relate the extent of emission control to the amount of damage being caused. The advantage of this approach is its simplicity; the disadvantage, the inability to know whether the reduction has achieved any material improvement in the environment.

The second sulphur protocol[28] was negotiated with these limitations in mind. In this case, the emission controls were firmly linked to the environmental impact of the sulphur across Europe and, in particular, the critical load concept. Article 2(1) states:

> Parties shall control and reduce their sulphur emissions in order to protect human health and the environment from adverse effect ... and to ensure, as far as possible, without entailing excessive costs, that depositions of oxidised sulphur compounds in the long term do not exceed critical loads for sulphur given, in Annex I, as critical sulphur depositions, in accordance with present scientific knowledge.

The term 'critical load' is defined as a quantifiable threshold level of exposure below which there is no significant deleterious effect.[29] The critical load of any given area of land will depend on the nature of the soil and its ecology but is, in theory, predictable for the full range of types. Once the critical load is known, the next stage is to determine what volume of emissions from a given chimney will give rise to a critical load. This is no simple task. It means assessing the amount and pattern of rain, the prevailing wind directions, the quality of the fuel burned and so on. In other words, the determination of acceptable emission levels on a critical load basis is dependent on the integration of a whole variety of scientifically determinable parameters. Predictive models have been developed to do just this and have played an important part in the determination of emission levels.[30] The second sulphur protocol is, therefore, based on scientifically based models adjusted to take account of political realities.

The strength of the critical loads approach is that it attempts to shape policy according to scientific need. The main disadvantage is that it could lead to a sense of false security. The final model is built up from a number of simpler models each of them with its own inherent uncertainties. In turn, this model is used as a basis for negotiations on the emissions limits for each contracting party. The need for feedback to test the efficacy of the models is obvious but, in practice, hard to obtain. Although the protocol includes requirements for monitoring and reporting,[31] it will be difficult to relate the results back to the models. This is because the emission limits are not determined purely on scientific grounds. Socioeconomic and political factors are also taken into account.

Habitats Directive

The aim of the EC Habitats Directive[32] is to conserve biodiversity within the European territory of the member states. There are two main approaches to achieving this aim: measures aimed at habitats and measures aimed at species. In both cases the level of protection to be aimed at is one that maintains the protected feature at a 'favourable conservation status'. According to Article 1(e), the conservation status of a natural habitat will be taken as favourable when:

- its natural range and areas it covers within that range are stable or increasing,
- the species structure and functions which are necessary for its long-term maintenance exist and are likely to continue to exist for the foreseeable future, and
- the conservation status of its typical species is favourable.

The conservation status of a species is, in turn, defined in Article 1(i) as 'the sum of the influences acting on the species concerned that may affect the long-term distribution and abundance of its populations' within EC territory. The conservation status of a species will be taken as favourable when:

- population dynamics data on the species concerned indicate that it is maintaining itself on a long-term basis as a viable component of its natural habitats,
- the natural range of the species is neither being reduced nor likely to be reduced for the foreseeable future, and
- there is, and will probably continue to be, a sufficiently large habitat to maintain its populations on a long-term basis.

Despite the precise wording in these definitions, it could be argued that favourable conservation status is really a social objective. It implies a presumption that a habitat or species that is holding its own is in a satisfactory state. Even if this is scientifically true in theory, favourable conservation status is difficult to work with in practice. The problem is that it implies a degree of scientific understanding that simply is not there. For the majority of species, we have very little information on population dynamics and cannot predict future population sizes or ranges with any degree of accuracy.

Annex I to the directive, which lists the habitats for protection, also reflects patchy scientific knowledge. Those categories of habitat based on terrestrial plant communities are defined in detail and, in some cases, subdivided into more precise categories.[33] Marine habitats, however, are defined in far more general terms. Is a lagoon, which is listed as one of six categories of 'open sea and tidal areas', really the habitat equivalent of, say, an active raised bog, which is listed as one of five categories of 'sphagnum acid bogs'? The danger in inconsistencies of this type is that site selection, which is to be based on the habitats in the Annex, will result in an overrepresentation of the better described habitats. Similarly the lack of knowledge about population dynamics and species status is proportionately worse for some groups than others. In general birds and mammals are much better understood than other vertebrates and most invertebrates are poorly understood. Those responsible for implementing the directive must, therefore, devote considerable resources to building up a knowledge base or else accept that implementation will be patchy and may fail vulnerable species and habitats if they are not well known.

Here, then, we have a scientifically based directive whose implementation has generated a considerable expansion of research and scientific bureaucracy but which has not, as yet, demonstrated any real conservation benefit. This is not to say that the directive is a failure but it is, perhaps, rather overoptimistic in its scientific obligations. The main impact of the directive, to date, has been to generate activity to address the problem of scientific uncertainty rather than to improve the conservation status of any natural habitat. The situation is reminiscent of what Hiscock[34] has described as 'scientific displacement activity'.

Conclusions

The cases discussed above are evidence that science is playing an important role in the formulation of environmental law. The criticisms raised relate to the overreliance on the science rather than to its inclusion: it is surely desirable for environmental policy development to be informed by scientific knowledge. The process would be improved, however, if the policy was translated into law by people who understand the limitations of science and do not place too much reliance on it to provide the answers. The scientific community can assist this process by ensuring that policies include adequate proposals for monitoring so that the scientific basis can be refined in the light of experience.

There is also a need for further development of concepts such as the precautionary principle which use risk-based criteria to combine measures of scientific uncertainties with estimates of public acceptance of possible impacts. This would need further research into the social scientific aspects of science and, in particular, the public's perception of the consequences of scientific predictions.

Perhaps most importantly, however, there is a colossal need to improve the scientific education of politicians and others involved in the formulation of environmental policy and its enactment in law. Evidence suggests that there has been an improvement over the last 20 years, but there is still much more needed.[35] We have made considerable progress since the age of the scientific aristocracy of the 1960s, when there was a general deference to science and its leading intelligentsia, an attitude caused by the alien nature to most politicians of scientific method. In 1967, the government sought the advice of the Royal Society to assist it in deciding how to deal with the *Torrey Canyon* oil spill. Compare this with the government's response to the spill from the *Sea Empress* in 1996. Even in the mid-1970s, however, the petroleum revenue tax, introduced as an early incarnation of the windfall tax to cream off the profit from the Forties Oil Field, was subject to almost no scrutiny in Parliament, presumably because of the lack of scientific understanding on the part of MPs. There was a strong belief in the power of science to solve any problem. Things were gradually improving, however, and, by the time Margaret Thatcher appointed herself to the post of minister for science, the foundations for a closer interrelationship between law and science had been laid. The Intergovernmental Panel on Climate Change, set up by the UN Environment Programme and the World Meteorological Organisation is, arguably, the most advanced manifestation of this deepening arrangement. It is a panel that is as much part of government as it is scientific. In other words, it breaks the mould of a scientific advisory committee on the outside of policy development and replaces it with an integrated system with scientists as an integral part of the policy development. The next stage will come when the level of scientific education is raised sufficiently to ensure that policy is made by people who can work with the scientific information in the knowledge that they understand the philosophy behind it.

Notes

1 S. Yearley, 'The Environmental Challenge to Science Studies', in S. Jasanoff, G.E. Markle, J.C. Petersen and T. Pinch (eds), *Handbook of Science and Technology* (Thousand Oaks, 1995), p.457.

2 P. Alldridge, 'Recognising novel scientific techniques: DNA as a test case' [1992] *Criminal Law Review* 687.

3 David E. Bernstein, 'Junk Science in the United States and the Commonwealth' (1996) 21 *Yale Journal of International Law* 123.

4 The most notable case in this respect is *Frye* v. *United States* 293 F. 1013 (D.C. Cir. 1923) at 1014, which laid down the rule that evidence was only admissible if it was sufficiently established to have gained general acceptance in the relevant field.

5 Bernstein, 'Junk Science', 180.

6 L.M. Warren, 'The Precautionary Principle: Use with Caution!', in K. Milton (ed.), *Environmentalism. The View from Anthropology* (London, 1993), p.97, conducted empirical research into the understanding of basic scientific terms by lawyers and administrators and found that there was misunderstanding over the meaning of some of these. In particular, there was little understanding of the nature of scientific reasoning or of the presentation of scientific results in a probabilistic format.

7 Bernstein, 'Junk Science', presents a full overview of cases where the science has been questioned by the court.

8 Point raised in discussion at the Law and Science Colloquium, University College London, 30 June 1997.

9 C. Oddie, *Science and the Administration of Justice*, Report of a Committee set up by Justice and the Council for Science and Society (London, 1991), puts the differences quite succinctly. Thus, while scientists are taught to be sceptical, law courts do not question facts where there is agreement between the parties: they will not go behind an admitted fact. This is because a scientific hypothesis can never be final, whereas law seeks finality. As Alldridge, 'DNA', 687 states, a conclusion reached by a scientist is just as much a matter of human judgment as any other forming of a view.

10 Statement made in *Whitehall and the Boffins* Part II, BBC Radio 4, 25 September 1997.

11 P. Roberts and C. Willmore, *The Role of Forensic Science Evidence in Criminal*

Proceedings, The Royal Commission on Criminal Justice. Research Study No 11 (London, 1993), p.135.

12 T. O'Riordan and J. Cameron, 'Editorial Introduction' to section on 'Implications for Science', in T. O'Riordan and J. Cameron (eds), *Interpreting the Precautionary Principle* (London, 1994) pp.62 ff.

13 O'Riordan and Cameron, *Precautionary Principle*, p.64.

14 The genetic make-up of an organism.

15 Characteristics manifested by an organism.

16 [1993] 4 All ER 491.

17 1993 SCCR 185 HC.

18 1993 QBD CO/1545/93.

19 See also *DDP* v. *Williams* 1993 QBD CO/780/93, which concerns the need for expert evidence. The Act makes a presumption that a dog described as a pit bull terrier is, in fact, a pit bull terrier, placing the onus on the defendant to adduce expert evidence to prove otherwise. In this case, a police officer conceded in his evidence to the court that the eyes, legs and tail of the dog in question were also characteristic of a Staffordshire bull terrier. The magistrates concluded that this amounted to a rebuttal of the presumption, a decision that was overruled in the higher court.

20 The Dangerous Dogs (Amendment) Act 1997 amends the 1991 Act to enable owners of certain dangerous dogs which are not yet registered under the scheme provided for in the original Act to register their dogs.

21 Not only could, but has. The British government's refusal to admit that there might be a link between emissions from British power stations and the impact of acid rain in Scandinavia is a powerful example.

22 *This Common Inheritance*, Cm. 1200, 1990, p.11, para. 1.18.

23 For an example of the debate over the meaning of the term, see J.S. Gray, 'Statistics and the Precautionary Principle' (1990) 21(4) *Marine Pollution Bulletin* 174–6 and R.C. Earll, 'Commonsense and the Precautionary Principle – an Environmentalist's Perspective' (1992) 24(4) *Marine Pollution Bulletin* 182–6.

24 Paul Stein refers to a number of cases coming before the Land and Environment Court of New South Wales, Australia in which the precautionary principle was an issue (P. Stein, 'Specialist Environmental Courts – the Land and Environment Court of New South Wales, Australia', unpublished paper presented at the Conference on Environmental Justice: New Directions in Environmental Dispute Resolution, Aberystwyth, 31 October 1997). For an example of a discussion of the principle in an English court, see *R* v. *Secretary of State for the Environment ex parte Duddridge* [1995] Env LR 151.

25 UN Treaty Series vol. 1302, at 217.

26 Protocol on the Reduction of Sulphur Emissions or their Transboundary Fluxes by at least Thirty Per Cent (1988) 27 ILM 707.

27 Article 2.

28 Protocol on Further Reductions of Sulphur Emissions (1994) 33 ILM 1540.

29 Article 1(8). The definition is qualified by the addition of the phrase 'according to present knowledge'.

30 For further details, see R.R. Churchill, G. Kütting and L.M. Warren, 'The 1994 UN ECE Sulphur Protocol' (1995) 7(2) *Journal of Environmental Law* 169.

31 Articles 4(2) and 6 and Annex IV, Part VI.

32 Council Directive on the Conservation of Natural Habitats and of Wild Fauna and Flora (92/43/EEC).

33 These habitats are characterized according to the hierarchical classification of habitats

produced by the Corine programme undertaken under Council Decision 85/338/EEC of 27 June 1985 (OJ L176/14 6.7.1985).

34 K. Hiscock, 'Use Available Data' (1997) 34(2) *Marine Pollution Bulletin*, 74–7.

35 The examples that follow are taken from *Whitehall and the Boffins* a two-part investigation into the changing relationship between scientists and politicians since World War II, BBC Radio 4, 18 and 25 September 1997.

10 Some Challenges for Science in the Environmental Regulation of Industry

Patricia Park

Introduction

The essence of this chapter is to look at the way in which science is a part of environmental regulation. That is essentially the regulation of industry in the environmental field. It builds on McEldowney's article which examined the historical perspective[1] and looks at the *current* regulation of industry and the control of emissions which may damage either humans or the ecosystem. The chapter also addresses the way in which science is used in the negotiating of the licence issued by the regulatory bodies for a particular plant to operate and carry out a particular process within a specific industrial sector. This is a very British and pragmatic way of determining levels of emissions and is unlike the system which operates, for example, in Germany. Finally it looks to the future. Regulation in most fields is changing with the policy of deregulation and the move towards self-regulation at both European and UK state level. This movement again poses challenges for the scientific community as the demands of industry and monitoring certain processes change. Most of the countries in the developed world are experimenting with the use of market mechanisms to replace the old 'command and control' method of regulation of industry. Where does science fit into this and what challenges does it present?

Science as a Part of Environmental Regulation

The reality of the regulatory relationship in industry is more complex than the structure of rules by which it is formally defined. As well as formal rules, there appear to exist sets of informal rules. An example of this is a regulated company agreeing to do something, possibly under threat of regulatory action if it does not, but in the absence of the regulator possessing any powers of enforcement. In addition a number of informal rules, which are not at all tightly specified, have operated, such as assumptions that levels of emissions should generally improve over time and certainly that there should be no sustained declines in any individual dimensions of environmental protection. Accordingly it is possible to identify a 'hierarchy' of regulatory instruments, in ascending order of the degree of difficulty involved in their amendment, but all of which have a scientific input:

- the provisions of legislation,
- licence/authorization/conditions,
- contract obligations,
- informal rules.

There is an assumption that the environment is different and the traditional rules just do not apply. This is highlighted by the imprecision of the relevant regulations which makes it difficult to define what constitutes a criminal offence. For instance, a high degree of discretion is conferred on the regulators to determine the requisite degree of what, for instance is 'detrimental to health or a nuisance' under the Environmental Protection Act 1990.

A Miscellany of Principles for Environmental Protection

The precautionary principle was introduced by the Treaty of Rome as amended, which states that it is the basis for environmental protection in the EC and also in the UK.[2] The essence of the principle is that, in the absence of firm scientific evidence as to the effect of a particular substance or activity, the protection of the environment should be the first concern. There is no need to wait for conclusive scientific proof before preventive action is taken. In other words, the environment should be given the benefit of the doubt.

The White Paper, 'Sustainable Development: The UK Strategy',[3] repeats this, and in addition takes from the Rio Declaration of 1992[4] the principle that, 'where there are threats of serious or irreversible damage, lack of full scientific certainty shall not be used as a reason for postponing cost-effective measures to prevent environmental degradation'. The fundamental issue here is the phrase, 'cost-effective'. The regulation of industry is generally based on 'risk assessment'. The problem which this highlights for the scientific community is the fact that technical and scientific (that is dispassionate and objective) views of risk differ dramatically from lay views. How is this conflict to be managed and resolved? It lies at the heart of issues of accountability, regulatory objectives and institutional design.

Scientists tend to reduce risk to 'one dimension', a single variable, expressed in terms of expected mortality and morbidity ('expected' referring to the probabilistic nature of risk). In contrast to this 'one-dimensional' nature of the technical approach, experimental studies by cognitive psychologists[5] show that lay people tend to take an 'n-dimensional' view of the matter. In other words, they emphasize the holistic rather than the particular.

It is easy for views on the merits or otherwise of policies and processes to become polarized where there is conflicting data as to the consequences of a particular activity. Predictions of the consequences of a particular process may have a strong element of subjectivity in them. There may be initial disagreement regarding the test parameters used in the collection of data and of the final evaluation of that data.

If the results show a degree of danger as a result of a particular activity, it may be felt necessary to build a further margin of safety into the regulation or applicable standard. This is a further evaluative step which moves the final result away from strict scientific criteria, but could be argued to be the application of the precautionary principle. In the *Duddridge* case,[6] the issue was whether the secretary of state should take precautionary action to prevent risks of childhood leukaemia arising from exposure to electromagnetic fields generated by power cables. Smith J pointed out that there is 'no comprehensive and authoritative definition of the precautionary principle' but rejected arguments that precautionary action is needed where there is evidence 'of a possible risk even though the scientific evidence is presently unclear and does not prove the causal connection', notwithstanding the exhortation that 'where the mere possibility exists of a risk to the environment or to human health' the precautionary principle should prevail. On the contrary, Smith J considered that the government was perfectly entitled to formulate the much more restricted view of precautionary action found in *This Common Inheritance*, which makes the threshold for taking action the perception of *significant* risk of harm, but again it is unclear as to whose subjective/objective perception is being referred to.

Another challenge for science in the regulation of industry is the charge that the limits of science drives the regulation. This was the theme of the 'Garner Lecture' by Sir Hugh Rossi to the UK Environmental Law Association in 1994.[7] Science from the earliest days has been an expanding frontier. As we learn more about the world around us, we also learn that there is more that we do not know. In law, as in life in general, we have to make decisions all the time based on that which we know and that which is unknown. Again uncertainty raises some difficult questions.

First of all, how do we decide? Eventually we agreed that gravity only goes one way, but that was not always obvious. What happens in the interim period, when there is a theory over which there is no scientific consensus? For example, there is growing concern about electromagnetic fields (EMFs) and their effects on human health. The theory that EMFs can trigger cancer has been tested in the courts both in the United States, when the mother of a five-year-old girl brought a case against San Diego Gas & Electric in 1993[8] and, the following year, in the UK when the *Duddridge* case[9] was brought on behalf of three children who lived in London. The decision in both of these cases went against the plaintiffs for lack of scientific evidence, but there is now an Electromagnetic Radiation Case Evaluation team working in the United States and the *Duddridge* case has gone to the European Court for a determination of the 'precautionary principle' under European law.[10]

Concerns of Industry

On the other hand, industry complains that advances in analytical science and technology have moved the standards and norms of substances permitted in emissions to a level which is not necessarily detrimental to health but is merely that which technology can produce instrumentation to measure, matching the advances in analytical science. A good example of this challenge for science is brought into sharp relief on consideration of the Draft Statutory Guidance on Contaminated Land.

Defining Contaminated Land

For land to be classed as contaminated, there must be substances on, in or under the land which cause or threaten serious harm or pollution of controlled waters.[11] In terms of the threats of harm, there must be a significant possibility of significant harm being caused. In making such determinations, local authorities must follow guidance as to what constitutes unacceptable risks in the context of the current use of 'suitable for use' criteria. However it is clear that an environmental risk will be present only if there exists a 'source' (a pollutant), a 'receptor' (a target which can be harmed) and a 'pathway' (a means of exposing the target to the pollutant).

For land to be contaminated the 'pollution linkage' (potential harm to a receptor by a source through a pathway) must exist. However it is also necessary for all other requirements of the guidance to be met in relation to the harm or water pollution in question. In particular it is necessary to have regard to risk in terms of the probability or frequency of occurrence and the magnitude of any adverse consequences. Whether and how the harm is to be considered 'significant' is a matter for guidance.[12] The draft guidance chooses greatly to limit the types of harm which will be regarded as significant. In order for harm to be significant, it would have to have the following effect in regard to humans: 'serious injury, death, disease, genetic mutation, birth defects, cancer or impairment of reproductive functions in humans (only)'. This creates an almost insurmountable evidential burden for a damaged plaintiff since the defence merely has to raise the possibility of another cause of the harm.

In the case of harm other than to human receptors, the test is whether, taking into account 'relevant, appropriate, authoritative and scientifically based information', this is more likely than not to be caused by the pollution linkage.[13] For human receptors a distinction is drawn between exposure risks and other risks (such as explosion or fire). For exposure, scientific information on the toxicological properties of the contaminant should form the basis of an assessment as to whether the intake of, or exposure to, the receptors over all or part of their lifetimes would be 'unacceptable'. This unacceptability test applies also to sudden incidents such as explosion or fire - assessing the risk against levels of risk judged unacceptable in other contexts. The possibility of significant harm being sufficient to require intervention depends upon the possibility of itself being 'significant' (significant possibility of significant harm being caused).

As for pollution of controlled waters, the test is the same as for the primary offences under the Water Resources Act 1991; that is, the mere entry into water of poisonous, noxious or polluting matters, or solid waste matter.[14] *There is, therefore, no parity in this legislation in respect of harm.* The likelihood of pollution of controlled waters merely requires the pollutant to be present on the land with a potential pathway to the controlled waters. This then constitutes the designation of 'contaminated land'. Alternatively, if the receptor of the harm is a human being, the extent of harm must be 'death, serious injury, cancer or other birth defects or the impairment of reproductive functions'. This reflects the problems for science to establish a direct causal link. All an effective lawyer has to do to defend an action is to show that there are other equally possible causes of the harm. Therefore, as a direct effect of the ability of analytical science to measure polluting matter in water, that water enjoys greater protection under the 'contaminated land' provisions than do humans.

Science and Current Regulation of Industry in the Environmental Field

Environmental control is not the preserve of any one institution or department of state. Responsibility for environmental control is shared between central and local government. The main central government departments of state with which this chapter is concerned are the (a) the Department of the Environment which has, *inter alia*, responsibility for environmental protection and related policy issues, and (b) the Department of Trade and Industry, which is concerned with the developmental technologies, particularly with regard to pollution prediction and control.

The regulatory bodies were distinct and separate until 1 April 1995, when the Environment Agency was created and became fully operational as from 1 April 1996. It subsumes the work of Her Majesty's Inspectorate of Pollution, The National Rivers Authority and the Waste Regulation Authorities. Thus there is now one agency dealing with emissions to all the receiving media and which may therefore operate a true policy of 'integrated pollution control'. Under section 1(1) of the Environment Act 1995 the Agency is a non-departmental public body, that is, a body corporate separate from government, and is not a servant of the Crown.

As part of its duties and powers the Environment Agency not only grants authorizations to operate but is required to set standards. Pollution poses problems for standard setting which are significantly more complex than those experienced in other areas. First, valuing the benefits of environmental protection is highly speculative, particularly when they comprise amenities as well as health, and when account must be taken of the preferences of future generations. The fact that some forms of pollution transcend national boundaries exacerbates the problem. Second, there is still much uncertainty regarding the impact of some pollutants and, since abatement costs are often high, it is difficult to reach a consensus on the appropriate trade-off between protection and industrial production. Third, even if agreement can be reached on desirable levels of protection, translating those goals into standards applicable to individual firms is rendered more difficult by several factors. There may be significant variations between the environmental characteristics of different regions. Within one watershed, the standard imposed on one firm may depend, to a greater or lesser extent, on the polluting activities of other firms. Finally, there is the question of whether account should be taken of the age of the industrial plant, given that the retrofitting of existing plant often requires a proportionately much higher level of capital expenditure than the fitting of new plants.

The problem of choosing an appropriate standard is compounded where there is no consensus on the desirability of regulation. Generally speaking, to be successful an environmental measure needs an agreed perception of a hazard, a body of supportive scientific evidence detailing the issues, an available corrective technology and a convergence of interest between the public and the pollution. The creation of a legal standard will depend on three rationalities: the scientific, the economic and the social.

The scientific rationality, which is what we are concerned with here, tends to be precise, analytical and observational - observing facts and coming to conclusions on those facts. Scientific rationality may conclude that, for example, the introduction of a particular pollutant into an environmental medium will cause harm and may thus demand an end to the release of that substance. *Economic rationality* is more evaluative and subjective than scientific rationality but still attempts to create principles by which particular activities can be measured and their costs and benefits analysed. *Social rationality* is even more evaluative and takes into account various moral and ethical positions.

Legal control is an end product of the interaction of all three rationalities, with that interaction varying from time to time.

The Current Law

In 1990 the previous legislation was largely consolidated and codified by the provisions of the Environmental Protection Act, which came into force on various dates. The 1990 Act is not the only recent legislation relevant to polluting emissions, although it is the principal enactment under which the UK meets its international and EU legal obligations. Additionally under section 2(2) of the European Communities Act 1972 the Air Quality Standards Regulations[15] were made to implement Directives 80/779 and 85/203 on sulphur dioxide and smoke and nitrogen oxide respectively, setting air quality limit values (AQLVs) and requiring air quality monitoring, and to ensure that the specified pollutants are reduced below the specified level. The regulations may establish quality objectives or standards for environmental media in relation to any substance which may be released from any process. National plans are made to bring about progressive reduction of environmental pollution: for example, the National Plan on Implementing the Large Combustion Plants Directive to reduce sulphur dioxide and nitrogen oxide emissions between 1990 and 2003 from power stations, refineries and 'other' industries.

Central to understanding the system is realization that there are two lists, 'A' and 'B', of prescribed matters. The 'A' list is subject to integrated pollution control (IPC) and is within the jurisdiction of the Environment Agency and comprises processes which use the most persistent and polluting substances such as fuel production and combustion, metal production, chemical industries and so on, all of which must be above certain specified production levels; the 'B' list is subject to local authority regulation with regard to atmospheric pollution only. This includes the smaller-scale processes such as combustion processes which burn any fuel in a boiler or furnace for energy production where the plant has a net rated thermal input of not less than 20MW but less than 50MW.

Because of the existence of complex processes made up of many component parts not always immediately recognizable as either 'A' or 'B', and because of the existence of complex sites with more than one process in situ, the regulations have been amended on the advice of the scientific community. Application must be made by the operator for an authorization to operate which must include details of proposed releases and an assessment of environmental consequences, proposals for monitoring releases and indications of how the best available techniques not entailing excessive costs (BATNEEC) obligation will be achieved. The implementation of the BATNEEC requirement has reflected attempts to pursue UK environmental policy which is based on the principles of stewardship and sustainable development. The IPC system is, therefore, operated with a holistic approach. In practice this may not simply lead to the regulation of processes but can be a contributory factor to their entire replacement, as is visible from the switch in electricity production from coal to gas-fired power stations because the cost of cleaning up emissions from coal-fired stations is too great.

The UK approach to the implementation of BATNEEC is that, although operators conceive, design, build and operate their plants so as to meet legal requirements, these are not all legally preset. There is, however, a dialogue with operators as to how best the objective of environmental protection can be achieved. This results in a concentration of effort on individual processes and a consideration of each process's effect on the environment as a whole, which further entails identification and qualification of releases from the plant in question, and a determination of which are significant and what are the environmentally acceptable outcomes. This is clearly a very evaluative process which demands the active cooperation of process operators if it is to succeed.

Future Trends in Regulating Industry

The future thrust of reform in the area of regulating industry – at least under the previous Conservative government – has been a move toward deregulation and self-regulation. The Deregulation and Contracting Out Act 1994, together with the evolution towards a Single European Market and its impact on regulatory policy within the European Union, have led to the general concept of the withdrawal of public authorities from detailed substantive regulation. However self-regulation implies a closer attention to monitoring than does the command and control style of substantive rules, because the real level of regulatory protection can only be determined by examination of actual standards and practice in their enforcement. Additionally the seminal work of David Pearce *et al.* in 1989[16] focused the attention of the Conservative government on the use of market mechanisms to achieve environmental objectives. This movement was then taken up by the European Commission in its Fifth Environment Action Programme in a Resolution of the Council, 93/C 138/01. Two examples of market mechanisms follow.

Environmental Taxes

In October 1996 the Landfill Tax came into force and this has served to concentrate the minds of industry on achieving a waste-free route to certain processes. As an example, Albright & Wilson paid a six-figure sum in landfill tax for a mixture of gypsum and calcium hydroxipatite waste which is formed when metal bearing residues from a phosphoric acid plant are reacted with lime. Currently the use of sewage sludge as a source of phosphate is being investigated because its metal content is at least two orders of magnitude less than that of phosphate rock. Once this has been perfected there will be a double environmental benefit.

Tradeable Emission Reduction Credits (Tradeable Permits)

Although the Conservative government decided not to implement a tradeable permit scheme for sulphur dioxide after much research, the programme in Southern California under the Clean Air Act Amendments 1990 does highlight a challenge for industry. The implementation of such a scheme involves several steps. First, a target level of environmental quality must be established. This level of environmental quality is then defined in terms of total allowable emissions. Permits, which are recognized as limited property rights, are then allocated to a firm. Each permit gives the owner the right to emit a specified amount of a certain type of pollution. If the polluter reduces his emissions below that which his permit allows, the difference then becomes an emission reduction credit (ECR) and can be traded with another polluter whose emissions are higher than his permits allow.[17] In the UK the introduction of such a scheme would necessitate a shift in the type of science used inasmuch as tradeable credits require that the quantities of emissions are measured as opposed to merely the concentration of pollutants in the emissions.

The success or failure of any regulatory programme largely rests with the monitoring and enforcement of the rules provided under that programme. A satisfactory system of registering credits and the monitoring and enforcement of emission permits is essential for the proper operation of such a system. If polluters believe that violators of the system will not be caught at all or that, if they are, sanctions are insufficient, the market will fail, as polluters will see no reason to buy credits. In a market system it is also important to define precisely the tradeable commodity and to guarantee its integrity. An imprecise quantification of emissions may devalue permits and thus undermine the market itself. In contrast the current command and control system operates adequately on less precise quantification.

Conclusion

This chapter has not only demonstrated the fundamental nature of the interaction of science and environmental regulation but has highlighted a number of challenges for the scientific community:

1 What role should science play in the interpretation of imprecise rules?
2 What type of 'risk assessment' should be used to determine acceptable levels and standards? Scientific or lay views? This really goes to the heart of issues of accountability and regulatory objectives.
3 Improvements in analytical science should not drive regulations beyond what is appropriate, as would appear to be the case in the Draft Guidance on Contaminated Land.
4 The move towards self-regulation and market mechanisms presents further challenges for measurement and monitoring of emissions.

In offering an answer to the first two challenges one may conclude that there are at least four basic reasons to give the public a right to participate in risk assessments, despite their largely scientific character. The first and most basic is logical. Numerous uncertainties underlie all of risk assessment; how to behave in situations of scientific uncertainty is not a scientific, but a policy issue, one in which the public ought to have a say. If there were no scientific uncertainties in risk assessment, grounds for public participation would be weaker. Uncertainty causes the invocation of value-based judgments.

A second reason is ethical. Because assessments have consequences not only for knowledge but also for public welfare, the public has a right to participate. If my ox is in danger of being gored, I have the right to help determine how to protect it, even if I may be wrong.

A third reason for public participation is ontological. Because risks do not affect merely current health and safety, but also human autonomy, consent, distributive equity, equal opportunity, future generations, civil liberties, social stability and so on, scientific experts ought not to be the sole assessors. Assessments of multi-attribute risks should be the products of social, ethical, cultural and legal rationality and not merely the projects of a bounded scientific rationality.

Fourth, because the applied science used in risk assessment presupposes democratically determined goals, it can never be value-neutral.[18] If the standard view of risk assessment disallows public participation, it errs in reducing democratic and procedural values to technocratic and scientific ones. The applied nature of risk assessment requires both democratic and scientific control.

Notes

1 See H. Reece (ed.), *Law and Science* (Oxford, 1998).
2 *This Common Inheritance*, Cm 1200, 1990, paras 1.16–1.17.
3 Cmnd 2426.
4 The Rio Declaration on Environment and Development, UN Doc A/CONF 15/5/Rev.1, 13 June 1992; 31 ILM (1992), p.876.
5 Kristin Shrader-Frechette, *Science Policy, Ethics and Economic Methodology* (New York, 1995).
6 *R* v. *Secretary of State for Trade and Industry, ex p. Duddridge* (1995) 7 *Journal of Environmental Law* 224. On 6 October 1995 the Court of Appeal in a short judgment upheld the Divisional Court decision.
7 Sir Hugh Rossi, 'Paying for our Past - Will We?', (1995) 7(1) *Journal of Environmental Law* 1.
8 Shrader-Frechette, *Science Policy*.
9 See note 6.
10 This case is discussed in more detail by Jane Holder in H. Reece (ed.), *Law and Science*.
11 For the precise wording, see section 78A of the Environment Act 1995.
12 By virtue of section 78A(5) of the Act.
13 See Chapter II, Table B, of the Guidance.
14 See Water Resources Act 1991.
15 SI 1989/317.
16 D. Pearce, S. Markandya and P. Barbier, *Blueprint for a Green Economy* (London, 1989).
17 Patricia Park, 'The Marketable Permit Programme in California' (1996) 8(1) *Environmental Law Materials* 26.
18 Nicholas Ashford, 'Science and Values in the Regulatory Process' (1988) 3 *Statistical Science* 377.

Index

For Product Safety Concerns and Information please contact our EU representative GPSR@taylorandfrancis.com Taylor & Francis Verlag GmbH, Kaufingerstraße 24, 80331 München, Germany

Batch number: 10725991

Printed by Printforce, the Netherlands